AMERICAN ASSOCIATION OF MUSEUMS

Covering Your Assets

Facilities and Risk Management in Museums

Edited by Elizabeth E. Merritt

American Association of Museums
1575 Eye St. N.W., Suite 400
Washington, DC 20005

D1597137

Cover: Peter Paul Rubens and Studio, Flemish, 1577-1640. *The Triumph of Divine Love* (detail), circa 1625. Oil on canvas, 152 x 204 inches, SN977.
Museum purchase, Collection of The John and Mable Ringling Museum of Art, the State Art Museum of Florida.

Design: Polly Franchini Publication Services

Library of Congress Cataloging-in-Publication Data

Covering Your Assets: Facilities and Risk Management in Museums / edited by Elizabeth E. Merritt.
    p. cm.
  Includes bibliographical references and index.
  ISBN 1-933253-01-0
  1. Museums--United States--Management. 2. Museums--United States--Planning. 3. Museums--United States--Statistics. 4. Facility management--United States. 5. Risk management--United States. 6. Emergency management--United States--Planning. 7. Museums--Space utilization--United States. 8. Buildings--Utilization--United States. I. Title: 2004 facilities and risk management survey. II. Merritt, Elizabeth E. III. American Association of Museums.

  AM121.A16 2005
  069'.068--dc22
                          2004030183

Contents

Acknowledgements 5

Introduction 6

Survey Methodology and Data Interpretation 7

The Survey 7
    Results 7
    How Many Museums Are in the United States? 7
    Are the Respondents a Random Sub-sample of Museums in the United States? 7

Interpreting the Survey Data 8
    Sample Size and Significance 8
    Presentation of Data: Percentiles 9
    Interpreting Percentiles: An Example 9
    Significant Figures (number of decimal places included) 10
    Why these Percentages Often Do Not Add Up to 100 Percent 10
    Glossary 10
    Using these Data 10
    Finding Information on Museums Like Yours 11
    What Else Is New in this Survey? 11
    Where Can You Get More Information? 12

Snapshot of Responding Museums 12
    What Is a "Typical" Museum Represented in this Survey? 12
    Demographics 12

Respondent Profile 13
    Discipline Type 13
    Institution Size: Operating Expenses 15
    Financial Size: Operating Expenses 15
    Physical Size: Total Interior Square Footage 17
    Governance 19
    Staffing 22

Facilities and Risk Management 24

Introduction to Facilities and Risk Management 24

    Space 25
    Space Allocation 25

Facilities Management 29
    "When Do We Wax the Floor?"
        The Facilities Team, Senator John Heinz Pittsburgh Regional History Center 29
    "A Burning Issue"
        Susan Robertson, Gore Place 32
    Integrated Pest Management 33

"I've Got Bugs in My Pockets and I Don't Know What to Do with Them"
Tom Strang, Canadian Conservation Institute 33
Space Rentals 35
"Room for Rent"
Janet Van Delft, Robie House 39

Emergency Preparedness/Safety and Security/Risk Management 42
Who Is Responsible for Risk Management? 42
"Avoid, Transfer, Assume, or Insure?"
J. W. Croft, Field Museum, and Alexander Sherman, Ulanov Partnership 44
Assessing Risk 46
"Know Thine Enemy: Be It Fire, Pestilence, Rot, or Other"
Robert Waller, Canadian Museum of Nature 46
Emergency Preparedness and Training 48
"It's All in the Planning Not the Plan"
Courtney B. Wilson, Baltimore & Ohio Railroad Museum 49
Health/Safety/Emergency Training 51
Insurance 52
"What Part Does Insurance Play in Overall Risk Management?"
Eric S. Fischer, Willis Fine Art, Jewelry & Specie 52
"Just D&O It!"
Margo Dundon, Museum of Science and History, Jacksonville, Fla. 55
"Knowing Your Collections Are Insured . . . Priceless"
Elizabeth Merritt, AAM Museum Advancement & Excellence 57
"Museums Share in Health Benefits Cost Squeeze. But Who Pays?"
Richard O'Sullivan and Lester Salamon, Johns Hopkins Center for Civil Society Studies 61
Policies, Plans, and Other Documents 62
"Why? Because We Said So! A Guide to the Development, Implementation, and Enforcement of Museum Policies"
Elise V. LeCompte, Florida Museum of Natural History 68

Specialized Breakouts 71
Museums by Discipline 71
Museums with Municipal or County Governance 137
Museums with State Governance 143
Museums that Have a Museum Parent Organization or Are Part of a Museum System 149
Museums with a University Parent 156
Museums with Other Nongovernmental Parent Organizations 162
Museums with Operating Expenses over $6 million 169

Glossary 176

Resources 178

Appendices 181
I. List of Responding Institutions 181
II. Copy of the Survey Instrument 193
III. List of Figures 200

Index 201

American Association of Museums

Acknowledgements

Thank you to the numerous people in the museum field who contributed to the creation of the Facilities and Risk Management Survey, particularly the advisory committee members:

Charlene Akers, Director, Scurry County Museum, Snyder, Tex.

C. Douglas Alves, Jr., Director, Calvert Marine Museum, Lusby, Md.

Gwen Bitz, Head of Registration Department, Walker Art Center, Minneapolis

Rebecca A. Buck, Chief Registrar, The Newark Museum, Newark, N.J.

Zahava D. Doering, Senior Social Scientist, Policy & Analysis Smithsonian Institution, Washington, D.C.

William Dupont, Architect, National Trust For Historic Preservation, Washington, D.C.

Becky Duval Reese, Director, El Paso Museum of Art, El Paso, Tex.

David W. Freece, Director, Cowlitz County Historical Museum, Kelso, Wash.

Tracie Kowalczyk, Event Services Manager, Indianapolis Museum of Art

Elise V. LeCompte, Registrar, Florida Museum of Natural History, University of Florida, Gainesville

Roger W. Lidman, Director, Pueblo Grande Museum, Phoenix

Kathryn Longstreth-Brown, former Director, Collection Services & Access, Colorado Historical Society, Denver

Allyn Lord, Assistant Director, Rogers Historical Museum, Rogers, Ark.

Harry P. Lynch, President & CEO, Stan Hywet Hall & Gardens, Akron, Ohio

James C. McNutt, former President and Executive Director, Witte Museum, San Antonio, Tex.

Claudia M. Oakes, COO, Cradle of Aviation Museum, Garden City, N.Y.

Craig R. Olson, former COO, Kelmscott Rare Breeds Foundation, Islesboro, Maine

Patricia J. Whitesides, Registrar, Toledo Museum of Art, Toledo, Ohio

Vivian F. Zoë, Executive Director, Noah Webster House, West Hartford, Conn.

By representing the great variety of types and sizes of museums, the advisory committee members helped ensure that the completed survey gathered useful information for the field. They contributed many excellent ideas to the creation of the survey and the interpretation of the survey data. AAM staff take responsibility for any deficiencies in how these ideas were executed.

Thank you to all museum staff who took the time to answer the survey—your assistance is much appreciated. By giving your time you help advance museums as a field, and help your colleagues make better decision about their own operations. A list of survey respondents is included in appendix I.

Thank you to Megan Galaida, information specialist in the AAM Information Center, for being my "test reader." She helped ensure that the explanations of the data make sense and the data tables are readable and also contributed to the Resources section.

Special thanks to Tony Casilio of AWP Research, Herndon, Va., who helped design the survey and collected and analyzed the data. As always, his experience with museum research helped us frame our questions in a way most likely to elicit useful answers.

And heartfelt thanks to the Trustee's Philanthropy Fund of the *Fidelity* Charitable Gift Fund[SM], which made this survey possible through its generous support.

Introduction

When we radically reshaped AAM's Museum Financial Information Survey in 2002—published a year later as 2003 *Museum Financial Information*—we eliminated many of the non-financial questions in the interest of brevity and sharper focus. However, that left us with no venue for many of the non-financial questions to which the field seeks answers. For this reason, we initiated what is for us a new kind of survey, one on museum operations. In contrast to a financial survey, which primarily looks at what museums spend and earn, an operational survey examines how museums behave—their policies, procedures, and practices.

We gather such data so it can be used by:
- •AAM, to advocate for museums at the national level
- •museums, to compare their operations to those of their peers
- •the press, to shape its coverage of museums
- •funders, to inform their decisions about grant programs and awards

There are many, many surveys conducted on the museum field (as some museum staff tell us, perhaps too many). These are conducted by national, state, and regional museums associations; nonprofit sector think-tanks; museums themselves; and students in museum studies programs. AAM does not seek to add unnecessarily to this burden of information gathering, so we approached the idea of operational surveys very cautiously. To decide whether and which surveys to conduct we looked at:
- •existing sources of information (published surveys, books, articles, Web resources)
- •the need for information, as indicated by inquiries AAM receives from member museums, the press, and policy makers and by areas in which museums have persistent problems, as indicated by data from the Museum Assessment and Accreditation programs
- •the feasibility of gathering useful representative data in various topic areas

After much discussion, we identified several areas in which museums seek information about their peer's practices and for which a good, representative, national source of data does not exist. From this list, we identified facilities and risk management as an important area, much needed by the field, that is relatively simple to survey. Under this heading, we included the following topics:
- •insurance (who carries what kinds of coverage, how much it costs, what sort of support museums receive from parent organizations)
- •facilities management (policies and procedures about use of space, and provision of amenities such as catering and parking)
- •space usage (how is it allocated, whether that is changing)
- •emergency preparedness/risk management (planning, training, implementation, assignment of responsibility)

These issues have a big impact on how a museum uses its resources (time, money, space) to serve the public. Clearly this is a huge area to explore, and the advisory committee helped AAM shape the survey by identifying the specific items that they, as museum staff, would most like to know. There were some items that did not fit into a manageable survey and others were not appropriate for the survey format. We intend to supplement the data gathered here by conducting smaller follow-up surveys on targeted issues (use of offsite facilities, renovations and expansions), distributing sample policies and procedures to AAM member museums through the AAM Information Center, and exploring topics through annual meeting sessions and articles in *Museum News*.

Survey Methodology and Data Interpretation

The Survey

AAM staff conducted the survey with the assistance of AWP Research, Herndon, Va. We asked the survey advisory committee members (see page 5) to list what they most want to know regarding facilities and risk management and selected a manageable set of questions from that list. The draft survey was filled out by a number of committee members as a road test and then edited based on their comments.

In late March 2004, AAM mailed the 2004 Museum Facilities and Risk Management Survey to:

2,136 AAM institutional member museums

4,000 non-member museums

743 AAM-accredited museums (member and non-member)

A total of 6,879 museums were surveyed. Non-member museums were selected from the AAM database and, for the most part, were museums that had had some dealings with AAM— through participating in the Museum Assessment Program, purchasing a publication, or attending a seminar or annual meeting.

We offered survey recipients an AAM Bookstore coupon as an incentive, good for 10 percent off any bookstore order of $50 or more. We also promised them that the results would be reported in the aggregate and asked if they wanted to be listed as a survey respondent. Those museums that did not opt out or did not say "no" are listed in appendix I.

AAM staff provided assistance to several dozen museums that asked for help in completing the survey. However, submitted surveys were not validated or checked for accuracy or consistency. Eight museums that did not identify their discipline type were coded by staff, based on our knowledge of the museums and their missions. Otherwise missing data were not pursued. Extreme or improbable values were excluded from the analysis when it seemed appropriate.

Results

We received 1,210 responses by the survey deadline of May 21, an overall return rate of 17.6 percent. To assess whether this response as a whole accurately reflects the museums of the United States, we need to know:

a) how many museums are in the United States, and

b) whether the sample is "unbiased", i.e., is it a truly random sample of these museums?

How Many Museums Are in the United States?

The only published survey we know of that attempts to count all the museums in the United States is "Compilation of the Survey Results from the National Conference of State Museum Associations 1998" by Ellen Riske and Roger Lidman, published in April 1999 by the Museum Association of Arizona. This report presents the results of a survey funded by the Institute of Museum and Library Services and conducted for the National Conference of State Museum Associations. The survey asked each state museum association for the estimated total number of museums in its state. The responses totaled 15,848 museums (see page 29 of that report). It cannot be overemphasized that this number is extremely approximate. Some state associations reported the number of their own museum members; others provided an estimate of the total museums in their state.

Within the last few years, the Institute of Museum and Library Services has compiled a database of U.S. museums from lists of grant applicants, association members, and other sources, vetted for duplicates, valid addresses, etc. IMLS's estimate of the number of U.S. museums falls between 16,000 and 18,000. This uncertainty factors in non-identical duplicates, non-museums included in source lists, and other hard-to-resolve issues. It is reassuring that this independent estimate is in the same ballpark as the Riske and Lidman figure.

These sources suggest the total number of museums can be conservatively estimated to be about 16,000. This is exact enough for our purposes, since statistically speaking any population over 10,000 is essentially infinite. The inexactness of this count does not affect our ability to calculate the statistical significance of the responses we received. With this population size, our response rate gives us a confidence level of 95 percent with a confidence interval of 2.7 percent (see Interpreting the Survey Data, below).

Are the Respondents a Random Sub-sample of Museums in the United States?

No.

Sixty-four percent of respondents are either AAM institutional member museums, accredited, or both, and we know that neither of these groups is perfectly representative of the museum field. For example, large museums and art museums are more likely to be AAM members and to be accredited than small museums or historic houses. Thirty-six percent of respondents were non-members, but even these represent museums that chose to have some contact with AAM, and are probably larger on average than museums that do not have such contact. For these reasons, the pooled survey data is not perfectly reflective of the museum field as a whole. However, this pool of survey respondents includes more non-members and more small museums than did 2003 *Museum Financial Information*. For this reason, it is probably more representative of the field. (We suspect this improved coverage is due to the fact that this survey asked relatively few questions involving financial numbers, which are the hardest questions for people to answer.)

Interpreting the Survey Data

Sample Size and Significance

When interpreting the data in this publication, look at the number of responses (n) listed for each set of figures. For the overall data (all respondents combined) this number is 1,210. Assuming a population of 16,000 museums in the United States, this gives the overall data a confidence level of 95 percent and a confidence interval of 2.7 percent.

Confidence level tells you how sure you can be about the accuracy of the data. It tells you how likely it is that the "real" answer lies within the confidence interval.

Confidence interval is a plus-or-minus figure that gives you the range within which the "real" answer lies.

For this data, when all 1,210 respondents answer a question, you can be 95 percent sure that the real figure is within plus or minus 2.7 percent of the figure listed. For example,

•21 percent of respondents say they are art museums. If you picked a different 1,210 museums out of the 6,879 museums surveyed, 95 times out of 100 the percent of art museums responding would be between 18.3 percent (2.7 percent less than 21 percent) and 23.7 percent (2.7 percent more than 21 percent).
•The median interior size of museum buildings for all respondents is 20,000 square feet. If you picked a

different 1,210 museums out of the 6,879 surveyed, 95 times out of 100 the median interior square footage for all responses would be between 19,460 square feet (2.7 percent less than 20,000) and 20,540 square feet (2.7 percent more than 20,000).

However, this confidence interval of +/- 2.7 is for all 1,210 responses. The number of responses for any given question usually is lower than 1,210 surveys returned (since most respondents skipped some questions), and the confidence interval correspondingly larger (e.g., we are less certain about what the real value is). We have taken this into account when commenting on the data.

The number of responses within a given data segment (discipline type, region, governance) is much smaller than 1,210—sometimes lower than 20. Strictly speaking, the confidence interval for each of these segments can be calculated by comparing the sample size of that segment to the total number of museums in that segment (for example, number of responding art museums relative to all art museums in the country). However, there are few good numbers for the total number of museums in any of these segments. (See page 14 of this publication for some estimates of these numbers.) In any case, these segment sample sizes are usually too small to detect differences between segments with any real meaning—the confidence interval for small samples is too big (sometimes as big as plus or minus 23 percent). Why did we include them then? For one thing, for many of these segments, there is no better data out there. Data for these segments can give you a feeling, though highly approximate, for the behavior of different museum types. Also, you can consult the list of responding museums (see appendix I) to get a feeling for which museums in that segment are answering the survey and therefore have a context in which to understand and interpret their answers.

Presentation of Data: Percentiles

The data in many of the tables in this publication are reported in the form of **percentiles**. Percentiles are a way of presenting data so that the reader can tell how many museums fall above or below that point in their responses. For example, the 90th percentile is the value that is greater or equal to at least 90 percent of the data from all responding museums: Ninety percent of responses fall at or below this point, 10 percent fall above. The **median** is the 50th percentile, i.e., half of all responses fall at or below this point, half fall above it.

Interpreting Percentiles: An Example

The following data look at the relative space museums allocate for exhibits. We arrive at this by dividing the square feet each museum devotes to exhibits by its overall interior square footage.

Space devoted to exhibits as a percent of total space

Overall (all responding museums)		
	10th percentile	12%
	25th percentile	24%
	50th percentile	38%
	75th percentile	56%
	90th percentile	75%
	Number of responses	793

In this case the "10th percentile" row shows that only 10 percent of responding museums devote 12 percent or less of their interior space to exhibits, and 90 percent devote more. The 50th percentile is the **median**—half of respondents devote more than 38 percent and half devote that much or less. The 90th percentile row shows that 90 percent of respondents devote 75 percent or less of their interior space to exhibits, 10 percent devote more.

Significant Figures (number of decimal places included)

In this publication's data tables, when reporting dollar figures under $100, we report to the second decimal place (e.g., $23.31). When reporting dollar figures over $100, we round off to the nearest dollar (e.g., $7,320.13 becomes $7,320). Percentages are reported with one decimal place (e.g., 48.1%) for the whole survey pool, but the smaller segments of the data are rounded off (e.g., 48%) due to the wide confidence interval of the segments. In the narrative that accompanies the tables we round figures off to the nearest appropriate number for the comparison being made (e.g., 24.2% may be referred to as "nearly 25%", or $20.59 as "about $21").

Why these Percentages Often Do Not Add Up to 100 Percent

Often the percentages given in the following tables do not add to 100 percent because these calculations almost always use the medians, not the means, of the data, and the data set is not perfectly "normal" in a mathematical sense. Trust us. Also, there may be a rounding-off error (see above for a summary of how we are rounding off the data).

Glossary

Throughout the text words that appear in the glossary (page 176) are marked in **bold**.

Using these Data

This survey examines issues that museum staff struggle with everyday. There are so many important decisions to be made, so many tradeoffs to weigh. Consider allocation of resources to risk management: is it better to spend your money on additional insurance or on better disaster preparedness training? Does space rental generate enough money and enough good will to offset the increased risks to collections and wear and tear on the facilities?

In talking with members of the survey committee, it was clear that there were several motivations for their suggestions about what data to collect. For example, museums want information for:

•benchmarking—a desire to compare their operations to their peers and find out how they measure up. This can be used to exert leverage with board members or funders, among others, to help the museum get the basic resources it needs.

•validation—the desire to prove what we already (intuitively) know to be true or right but must be able to point to in black-and-white for some audiences. For example: More than 95 percent of museums don't allow food or drink in their collections storage areas, and we shouldn't either.

But there are limits to this approach, because this survey strives to represent what a wide range of museums actually do, not just how the best behave. The fact that only 66 percent of respondents have disaster preparedness plans does not mean it's okay not to have one. A disaster preparedness plan is clearly an important part of risk management. The survey may be telling us that the field needs to provide more funding, training, and support for disaster preparedness, but it does not validate sloppy practices. To help put the survey in context, we have interspersed short essays on key topics among the data. We hope these essays, which were written by various authorities from the field, will help guide your museum's decision-making.

Finding Information on Museums Like Yours
The section titled "Facilities and Risk Management" presents data for respondents overall and, when there are interesting comparisons to be made between groups within the data, may include breakouts by discipline, governance, operating expenses, and physical size. The chapter titled "Specialized Breakouts" presents survey data for some of these groups, including:
- museums with university parent
- museums with a museums/museum system parent
- museums with other non-governmental parents
- state museums
- municipal/county museums
- museums by discipline (arboreta, art, etc.)
- museums with operating expenses over $6 million

If you don't see a breakout by group for a particular piece of data in this section, check "Specialized Breakouts."

What Else Is New in this Survey?
We experimented with a different way of asking museums about their governance and **parent organizations**. In every previous survey and other forms of data collection, we have asked museums to identify their governance from the following choices:
- municipal
- county
- state
- federal
- tribal
- college/university
- private nonprofit
- for-profit
- other

We found, however, that this combined apples (governance) with oranges (parent organizations), obscuring the true diversity of museums' organizational structures and forcing museums to make arbitrary choices. For example, a museum that is part of a state university might identify itself either as a state-governed museum or as a university museum. We also realized that these categories did not encompass museums with joint governance: a county museum that is operated by a nonprofit organization, for example, or a municipal museum with a private nonprofit friends group that pays some of the staff and participates in institutional planning.

So in this survey we provided recipients with a different set of choices. First, we asked them to identify whether they have a parent organization and, if yes, what kind (college/university, museum/museum system, or other). Then they identified the nature of their **governing authority**:
- county
- state
- federal
- tribal

- private nonprofit
- for-profit
- dual-governance (any two of the others)

Even this is a simplification, as some museums turn out to have not two, but three or four entities collaborating to govern them. Still, at least we can now provide more nuanced data about how museums are organized and governed. See page 19 for a discussion of these results.

Where Can You Get More Information?

We present selected data from the survey in this publication—choosing the information we anticipate will be used most often. However, as you might imagine, there are many ways to parse the data. We requested some data (about renovations, off-site storage, completion of the RC-AAM *Standard Facilities Report*) only for the purpose of identifying museums who might participate in specialized surveys on these topics in the future; these data are not reported here.

More tables from the survey data are available to AAM-member museums through the AAM Information Center as part of our personalized reference services. Contact the Information Center staff at infocenter@aam-us.org, give your institutional member ID number (or ask staff to look it up), and tell them what you are looking for. If it is analysis we have not yet run, we might charge a small fee to cover our costs; otherwise the data will be provided free as a benefit of your museum's AAM membership.

Snapshot of Responding Museums

What Is a "Typical" Museum Represented in this Survey?

Based on the median responses, a "typical" museum responding to this survey is likely to have:
- a budget (e.g., annual operating expenses) of $390,000
- four full-time and three part-time paid staff
- a building of 20,000 square feet
- almost 23,000 visitors per year

But there is a huge range of variation—from museums with annual operating expenses of more than $100 million and over 500 staff to all-volunteer organizations operating on a few hundred dollars a year.

Demographics

Governance: Twenty-four percent of these museums are governmental (municipal, county, state, federal, or tribal), 71 percent are private nonprofits, and 4 percent have **dual governance** (two separate legal entities sharing governance of the museum). Thirty-nine percent are organized inside a larger parent organization. One quarter of these parents are colleges or universities, one quarter are museums or museum systems. A little over a quarter are various other types of organizations (corporations, foundations, churches, hospitals, service organizations, school systems) and the remainder are government entities.

Geography: about 20 percent each are in the Southeastern and Midwest regions, 17 percent in the Mid Atlantic, about 15 percent each in Western and Mountain-Plains areas, and almost 10 percent in New England.

Size: about one quarter of the responding museums had annual operating expenses under $125,000, one quarter between $125,000-$400,000, one quarter between $400,000-$1.75 million, and one quarter over $1.75 million.

Respondent Profile

Survey respondents—other than the 47 museums that asked not to be credited by name—are listed in appendix I. Sixty-one percent of respondents are AAM member museums; 24 percent are accredited.

Discipline Type

As in past surveys, history museums responded to the survey in the greatest numbers (29 percent) followed by art museums (21 percent).

General museums are defined as addressing two or more disciplines to a significant extent, such as both art and history, or history and science. **Specialized museums** are defined as museums that do not fall into or combine any of the other discipline areas. Museums identifying themselves as "specialized" in this survey include transportation, ethnic-specific, maritime, religious, sport, and object-specific museums (e.g., textiles, clocks, quilts).

1.1 Discipline Type

	% of sample	Number of responses
Aquarium	0.3%	4
Arboretum/botanic garden	1.8%	22
Art museum	20.7%	250
Children's/youth museum	2.3%	28
General museum	9.8%	118
Historic home/site	12.2%	148
History museum/historical society	29.1%	352
Natural history/anthropology museum	3.8%	46
Nature center	1.4%	17
Science/technology center/museum	3.3%	40
Specialized museum	12.9%	156
Zoo	2.0%	24
Other	0.4%	5

Pay particular attention to the number of responses (n) for each discipline type. This can give you a feeling for how representative the survey data are when broken out by discipline type. (In some tables we have not listed n because of space constraints—in these cases n is close to the numbers given in the segment totals in the respondent profile section.) The significance of the data for each discipline depends on the number of responses from that type of museum relative to the total number of museums of that type. Unfortunately, there are no accurate counts of how many U.S. museums exist in each of these disciplines. However, to estimate the significance of these discipline type samples, we have prepared the table below, which approximates the total number of museums of each type in two ways:

a. by assuming that the percentage of museums of this type responding to this survey is their actual percentage in the United States, and multiplying this by our estimate of 16,000 U.S. museums to arrive at a total for this discipline

b. by contacting the relevant discipline-specific museum associations and requesting their best estimate of the number of museums in their disciplines

1.2 Estimated Number of Museums by Discipline

Discipline	a. Estimate by %	b. Estimate by professional association	Number of survey responses (n)
Aquarium (see zoos, below)	—	—	—
Arboretum/botanic garden	288	500[1]	22
Art museum	3,313	—[2]	250
Children's/youth museum	368	300[3]	28
General museum	1,568	—[4]	118
Historic home/site	1,952	5,000[5]	148
History museum/historical society	4,656	6,000[6]	352
Natural history/anthropology museum	608	—[7]	46
Nature center	224	—[8]	17
Science/technology center/museum	528	216[9]	40
Specialized museum	2,064	—[10]	156
Zoos and aquaria[11]	368	212	28
Other	—	—	0

1. From the American Association of Botanical Gardens and Arboreta—the number of AABGA members. (AABGA currently has no formal membership criteria.) Some members of AABGA are also members of AZA.

2. No association we can find has prepared an independent estimate of the number of art museums in the U.S. AAM contacted the Association of Art Museum Directors (AAMD) and Americans for the Arts (AFA).

3. Informal estimate by the staff of the Association of Children's Museums (ACM). ACM has approximately 219 member museums, and they are aware of 85 in various stages of planning.

4. There is no professional association specifically for "general" museums, which we define as museums that "address two or more disciplines to a significant extent."

5 Estimate provided by the American Association of State and Local History of the number of historic house/sites in the country. There are 2,000 house museums listed the AALSH Directory of Historic House Museums in the U.S. (published in 2000).

6. Estimate provided by the American Association of State and Local History—midpoint of its estimate of 5,000 to 7,000, based on the AALSH 2002 Directory of Historical Organizations in the U.S. and Canada, with assumptions regarding what percentage of these listings represent history museums and allowing for up to a 50-percent undercount.

7. Informal estimate by the staff of the Natural Science Collections Alliance (NSCA). However, NSCA serves primarily academic/research collections, which both includes academic collections that may not be inside museums, and excludes many natural history museums that do not have research collections.

8. We are unaware of any professional association serving primarily nature centers.

9. Estimate provided by the Association of Science-Technology Centers—this represents the 52 percent of their members who categorize themselves as science/technology centers.

10. Because "specialized museum" encompasses many different types of museums, there is not one discipline-specific association representing them. While there are many, many associations for various kinds of specialized museums (e.g., the Association of Railroad Museums) we have not attempted to gather membership numbers from all of them.

11. Estimate from the American Zoo and Aquarium Association (AZA). Because AZA represents both zoos and aquaria, these discipline types have been combined for this table. AZA's figure of 214 represents the number of members of their association. Institutions need to be accredited by AZA to be AZA members. Some members of AZA are also members of AABGA.

The confidence interval on these discipline-specific segments of the data are all pretty big, ranging from +/- 5 percent for the history museum segment, to +/- 23 percent for the arboretum/botanic gardens. Since most of these segment samples are too small to be statistically significant, it may be particularly helpful to examine the list in appendix I that shows what museums in each category responded to the survey. You can judge for yourself how well they represent museums of their type.

Institution Size: Operating Expenses

We partitioned the survey data by institution size (**operating expenses**) using the following quartiles. Quartiles are percentages that break the data into four sections of equal size—quarters, in fact.

2.1 Operating Expenses Categories (FY2003)

	Percentage of sample	Number of responses
Under $125,000	22.2%	269
$125,000–$400,000	22.2%	269
$400,001–$1,750,000	21.5%	260
$1,750,001+	22.0%	266
No response	12.1%	146

These are not the same size categories used in 2003 *Museum Financial Information*. While that survey also was analyzed by quartiles, its respondents included fewer museums with small operating expenses. We suspect that is because small museums, which have fewer staff members on hand, had less time to answer the complex document. This survey, which consists mainly of yes/no multiple choice questions, takes less time to complete, and so small museums responded in larger numbers.

Because so many small museums are represented in the survey, the largest quartile combines all museums with operating expenses over $1,750,000. We realize that a museum with $1.75 million in expenses is very different from one with multi-million dollar expenses, so we also have created a table (see page 169) presenting just the data for museums with operating expenses over $6 million (roughly the largest 10 percent of respondents).

Financial Size: Operating Expenses

Zoos are the largest institutions in the survey, with median operating expenses over $6 million, and history museums/historical societies the smallest, with median operating expenses of just under $168,000.

2.2 Operating Expenses

	10th percentile	25th percentile	50th percentile	75th percentile	90th percentile	Number of responses
Overall	**$38,987**	**$123,593**	**$393,076**	**$1,755,594**	**$6,291,120**	**1,064**
Arboretum/botanic garden	$150,696	$720,856	$1,200,000	$4,299,328	$22,423,889	21
Art museum	$93,700	$359,250	$1,321,310	$3,751,335	$9,902,995	232
Children's/youth museum	$343,300	$412,960	$1,307,643	$2,134,077	$6,325,172	25
General museum	$40,060	$101,250	$769,500	$1,991,670	$8,120,545	100
Historic house/site	$30,000	$102,224	$219,756	$532,897	$1,566,687	125
History museum/ historical society	$23,893	$64,312	$167,592	$457,750	$1,710,000	298
Natural history/ anthropology museum	$90,000	$137,250	$937,300	$4,430,000	$13,500,000	44
Nature center	$72,360	$167,672	$336,000	$716,292	$1,172,068	15
Science/technology center/museum	$150,000	$593,588	$1,214,604	$6,000,000	$20,500,000	39
Specialized museum	$21,746	$90,000	$265,000	$904,417	$2,915,694	135
Zoo/aquarium	$638,194	$2,257,476	$6,085,085	$16,559,889	$24,053,394	26
Government	$40,316	$148,938	$394,696	$1,859,670	$6,473,360	232
Private nonprofit	$38,530	$118,783	$387,175	$1,639,655	$6,157,651	782
Dual	$33,098	$124,000	$567,205	$3,488,025	$8,099,700	42
Under $125,000	$9,245	$26,500	$51,476	$86,391	$109,000	269
$125-$400,000	$142,000	$162,698	$211,000	$289,500	$351,032	269
$400,001-$1,750,000	$475,500	$570,384	$842,500	$1,124,445	$1,425,963	260
$1,750,001+	$1,997,984	$2,500,000	$4,427,241	$9,761,951	$18,724,587	266
Under 8,000 sq. ft.	$16,960	$38,665	$102,224	$200,000	$295,411	214
8,000-20,000 sq. ft.	$49,405	$109,715	$225,000	$500,000	$999,983	243
20,001-55,000 sq. ft.	$123,954	$283,000	$800,000	$1,539,951	$2,319,773	233
55,001+ sq. ft.	$747,800	$1,869,093	$4,384,929	$9,564,162	$18,339,690	238

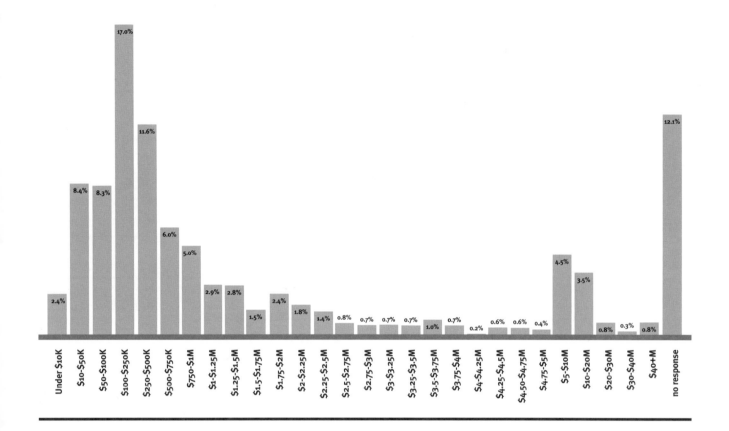

Physical Size: Total Interior Square Footage

We partitioned the survey data by physical size (**interior square feet**) using the following quartiles.

3.1 Physical Size Categories (interior square feet)

	Percentage of sample	Number of responses
Under 8000 sq. ft.	20.6%	249
8,001–20,000 sq. ft.	21.8%	264
20,001–55,000 sq. ft.	20.5%	248
55,001+ sq. ft.	20.7%	250
No response	16.5%	199

The median interior square footage for all respondents is 20,000 square feet. The largest museum answering the survey, Colonial Williamsburg, has more than 3 million square feet; the smallest has only 200 square feet. Note that in this survey of facilities management, we looked only at buildings, leaving the issue of grounds management for another day. Many of institutions, particularly arboreta, botanic gardens, and zoos, have extensive grounds that house key portions, if not the majority, of their functions.

3.2 Total Interior Square Footage

	10th percentile	25th percentile	50th percentile	75th percentile	90th percentile	Number of responses
Overall	**3,810**	**8,000**	**20,000**	**55,000**	**150,000**	**1,011**
Arboretum/botanic garden	4,160	15,782	23,000	119,322	422,105	17
Art museum	5,000	13,680	33,000	82,883	168,147	234
Children's/youth museum	5,490	17,626	26,460	44,250	93,150	26
General museum	5,900	13,500	30,000	77,500	172,857	95
Historic house/site	3,400	6,016	12,000	25,699	61,000	109
History museum/ historical society	3,454	6,092	14,000	31,000	78,000	283
Natural history/ anthropology museum	3,518	8,500	45,705	150,000	222,647	39
Nature center	2,250	4,681	6,300	15,750	29,315	14
Science/technology center/museum	5,327	13,050	49,500	155,000	377,296	38
Specialized museum	2,500	5,000	16,000	43,000	112,180	135
Zoo/aquarium	15,000	38,000	113,302	278,621	500,000	19
Government	4,040	10,000	23,000	62,000	171,115	231
Private nonprofit	4,000	7,925	19,944	52,000	141,332	726
Dual	2,600	6,000	20,000	115,000	357,800	43
Under $125,000	2,309	3,758	6,500	13,847	24,122	216
$125–$400,000	3,989	6,216	12,000	20,000	40,000	238
$400,001–$1,750,000	8,720	16,000	30,000	44,467	71,800	231
$1,750,001+	30,397	55,000	108,076	195,881	378,000	243
Under 8,000 sq. ft.	1,800	3,000	4,450	5,905	6,800	249
8,000–20,000 sq. ft.	8,800	10,000	13,366	16,500	18,925	264
20,001–55,000 sq. ft.	22,990	26,499	31,980	40,000	50,000	248
55,001+ sq. ft.	65,000	80,000	119,000	200,000	399,796	250

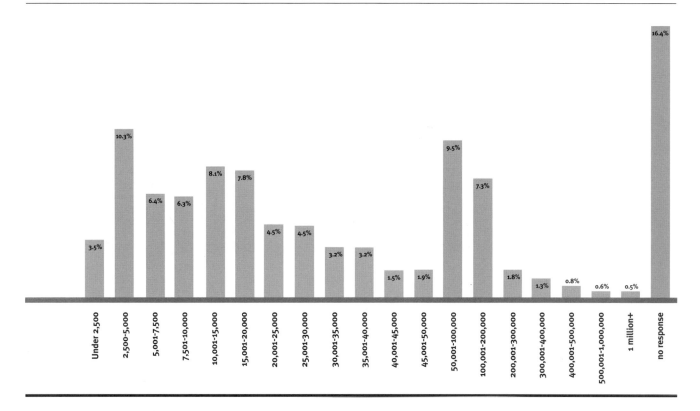

Governance

In a departure from our previous surveys, this time we looked at institutions' **parent organizations** separately from their type of governance (see page 11 for a discussion of this change in categorization). Our premise, borne out by the data, is that being part of a larger parent organization has considerable effect on a museum's resources for facilities and risk management. A parent often supplies resources that are not captured in the museum's budget. Governance is also a key variable—a museum with municipal/county governance has different constraints in resource allocation and setting policy than, for example, a private nonprofit. For this reason, we parse the data in the rest of the analysis by parent type and major governance groupings (government, nonprofit, dual) and also present the data separately for museums with university parent, a museums/museum system parent, or other non-governmental parent; state museums; and municipal/county museums.

Almost 39 percent of respondents report having a parent organization.

Twenty-eight percent have governmental parents—city, county, regional, state, federal, tribal—which include park departments, government or state agencies, and the U.S. Army. Twenty-seven percent have college or university parents, 24 percent are part of a larger museum or museum system, and 20 percent have parents of some other type, including historical societies, foundations, corporations, the Junior League, and (in one instance) a society of former nuns.

4.1 Have a Parent Organization

	Have parent	Do not have parent
Overall	38.8%	61.2%
Arboretum/botanic garden	18%	82%
Art museum	44%	56%
Children's/youth museum	4%	96%
General museum	42%	58%
Historic house/site	49%	51%
History museum/historical society	32%	68%
Natural history/anthropology museum	65%	35%
Nature center	35%	65%
Science/technology center/museum	28%	73%
Specialized museum	40%	60%
Zoo/aquarium	36%	64%
Government	83%	17%
Private nonprofit	22%	78%
Dual	69%	31%
Under $125,000	41%	59%
$125,000–$400,000	39%	61%
$400,001–$1,750,000	33%	67%
$1,750,001+	31%	69%
Under 8,000 sq. ft.	43%	57%
8,000–20,000 sq. ft.	41%	59%
20,001–55,000 sq. ft.	36%	64%
55,001+ sq. ft.	34%	66%

4.2 Type of Parent Organization

	Government parent	College/ university	Museum/ museum system	Other non-government parent	No response
Overall	**27.9%**	**26.6%**	**24.0%**	**20.4%**	**1.1%**
Arboretum/botanic garden	75%	25%	0%	0%	0%
Art museum	9%	67%	8%	15%	1%
Children's/youth museum	0%	0%	100%	0%	0%
General museum	44%	16%	26%	14%	0%
Historic house/site	33%	3%	32%	30%	3%
History museum/ historical society	35%	5%	37%	23%	1%
Natural history/ anthropology museum	20%	53%	20%	3%	3%
Nature center	67%	0%	17%	17%	0%
Science/technology center/museum	27%	36%	9%	27%	0%
Specialized museum	21%	24%	25%	30%	0%
Zoo/aquarium	70%	0%	20%	10%	0%
Government	47%	28%	21%	3%	1%
Private nonprofit	2%	27%	27%	43%	1%
Dual	38%	18%	32%	12%	0%
Under $125,000	20%	24%	28%	27%	1%
$125–$400,000	27%	27%	23%	21%	2%
$400,001–$1,750,000	29%	33%	22%	15%	0%
$1,750,001+	27%	27%	28%	17%	1%
Under 8,000 sq. ft.	24%	32%	20%	25%	0%
8,000–20,000 sq. ft.	25%	29%	24%	20%	2%
20,001–55,000 sq. ft.	33%	27%	23%	17%	1%
55,001+ sq. ft.	26%	23%	35%	16%	1%

The majority of museums (71 percent) are private nonprofits, and most of the rest are governed by municipal, county, state, federal, or tribal government. For the purposes of data analysis, we will refer to these as "government."

5.1 Governing Authority

	% of sample	Number of responses
Municipal	6.7%	81
County	3.6%	43
State	10.4%	126
Federal	3.1%	37
Tribal	0.4%	5
Private nonprofit	70.7%	856
For-profit	1.1%	13
Dual	4.1%	49

We also, for the first time, gave museums the chance to indicate they have dual governance—a governance structure in which two separate legal entities share governance of the museum. This can involve dividing or sharing basic governance responsibilities such as determining mission and purpose; hiring, supporting, and evaluating the director; strategic planning; obtaining and managing resources; and monitoring the organization's programs and services. (See *Ten Basic Responsibilities of the Nonprofit Board* by Richard Ingram, The National Center for Nonprofit Boards, 2003.) We made this change based on our observation that many museums have such arrangements, for example a museum jointly governed by a city government, which owns the collections and the building and hires the staff, and a private nonprofit, which determines policy and operates the institution. Slightly more than 4 percent of respondents classified themselves as having dual governance. Almost all of these are private nonprofit/government partnerships, with the government partner most often being municipal, county, or state government.

Clearly we are still snapping an artificially simple picture of museum governance. Since this project started we have gathered examples of museums with as many as five organizations sharing governance responsibility. (We suspect this is rare, but will try to accommodate this possibility in future surveys.) It also is clear that how a museum views its relationships to parent and governing structure is somewhat subjective. For example, only 83 percent of museums that are government-governed say they have a parent. Perhaps a museum chartered by a state, for example, governed by a board of trustees, does not think of the state as a parent exerting direct control over policy or finances.

Staffing

Staff are a key resource in facilities and risk management as well as the major driver of overall museum expenses. Generally (a very rough rule of thumb) museums have one full-time staff for every $100,000 in operating expenses. This does not always apply to museums with budgets under $200,000 or to very large museums, but in the middle range it works pretty well.

6.1 Paid Full-time Staff

	10th percentile	25th percentile	50th percentile	75th percentile	90th percentile	Number of responses
Overall	**0**	**1**	**4**	**15**	**54**	**1194**
Government	1	1	4	15	65	288
Private nonprofit	0	1	3	15	53	845
Dual	0	1	4.5	31	109	48
Under $125,000	0	0	0	1	2	267
$125–$400,000	1	1	2	4	5	269
$400,001–$1,750,000	4	5	8	12	17	259
$1,750,001+	18	25	44	91.5	200	260
Under 8,000 sq. ft.	0	0	1	2	3.4	245
8,000–20,000 sq. ft.	0	1	2	5.8	10	264
20,001–55,000 sq. ft.	1	3	7	15	27	245
55,001+ sq. ft.	5	18	41	89	197.6	247

6.2 Paid Part-time Staff

	10th percentile	25th percentile	50th percentile	75th percentile	90th percentile	Number of responses
Overall	**0**	**1**	**3**	**10**	**30**	**1,185**
Government	0	1	3	9	24.3	286
Private nonprofit	0	1	4	11	35	839
Dual	0	1	6	10	31	47
Under $125,000	0	0	1	2	4	263
$125,000–$400,000	0	1	3	6	10	269
$400,001–$1,750,000	1	3	5	11	20	259
$1,750,001+	5	10	22.5	48.5	104.4	256
Under 8,000 sq. ft.	0	1	2	3	7	243
8,000–20,000 sq. ft.	0	1	3	6	11	264
20,001–55,000 sq. ft.	1	2	5	10.5	20.4	245
55,001+ sq. ft.	2.4	7	20	47	101.8	243

Facilities and Risk Management

Introduction to Facilities and Risk Management

We all want clean, pest-free facilities that accommodate without conflict exhibits, programs, and diverse public functions such as receptions, galas, weddings, and birthday parties. If we have collections, we want to keep them safe while making them accessible. We want to avoid flood, fire, and overcrowding, and the slow incremental wear and tear that makes facilities shabby. If the worst does happen, we want to respond quickly and gallantly, saving the day through our awesome preparation and training.

This isn't easy to achieve.

For one thing, it involves the intersection of many complex processes in the museum: how we allocate space to different functions; what we allow to happen in those spaces; how our staff work together to integrate competing demands for time and space. It involves envisioning the worst that can happen, analyzing what we can do to reduce the risk of that occurrence, and then being prepared to pick up the pieces when it happens anyway. Courtney Wilson, director of the B&O Railroad Museum in Baltimore, writes persuasively on the need for such preparation (see page 49).

It also involves allocating scarce resources (time and money) away from the things that we want to do—exhibits, programs, collections development—and toward things that may not be as fun—cleaning, trapping bugs, practicing CPR, purchasing insurance). (Though with any luck you have staff who enjoy cleaning, trapping bugs, practicing CPR, and purchasing insurance; they are called registrars.) Jim Croft, vice president, finance and administration at the Field Museum, and his colleague Alexander Sherman write about on how to integrate facilities and risk management into your financial planning to ensure you have the resources you need (see page 44).

This book attempts to make this process a little easier by providing information on how your colleagues deal with these issues. We juxtapose data on what other museums actually do (which you may or may not want to emulate) with essays on best practices by leading figures in the field. In other words—folks like you doing their best to run a good museum. Occasionally, we pull in a ringer in the form of a specialist from a related field.

The most important thing to take away from this book is an awareness of the myriad issues involved, an understanding of how they all interrelate, and the realization that you have to consider all of them to come up with a rational approach to managing your facilities and reducing your risks. Why pay for more insurance before you buy UV filters for the lights in collections storage? Why commit to a building addition to relieve overcrowding before you calculate what it will add to your yearly operating expenses? Why ban live plants in your building while leaving huge voids around the incoming plumbing that serve as perfect rat highways? (See the essay about **integrated pest management** by Tom Strang of the Canadian Conservation Institute on page 33.)

Thus we encourage you to identify all the people in your museum, staff or volunteer, who are involved in the issues discussed in this book and get them to work together as they make decisions about policies, procedures, and plans. They may hold competing positions ("No food in the galleries!" "We need food at the gala!") but they share the interest of running the museum smoothly, safely, on a financially sound basis, and fulfilling the mission. On page 29 the facilities team of the Senator John Heinz Pittsburgh Regional History Center describes how such an approach helps them manage the many activities that take place in their facilities.

Take a big picture approach to managing risk. Think carefully about all the dangers that your museum faces, their likelihood, and the magnitude of their effects should they occur. Are you in an earthquake zone? A flood zone? Hurricane Alley? Or is your greatest risk the special events that are held in the exhibit galleries most evenings and every weekend? How reliable is the power supply in your area, and what would an outage do to your ability to maintain basic services? Then assess what you would need to do to take to take the edge off this risk and what that would cost in time and money. This will help you make sound decisions about putting your resources where they will do the most good. On page 46, Robert Waller of the Canadian Museum of Nature describes how such a quantified approach to risk assessment helps to control risks to collections—an approach that can be applied in a broader way to the whole museum.

Space

Many of the things we studied in this survey—costs, staffing, insurance—vary with space. It costs more to take care of a large building than a small one. Multiple buildings may require more staffing than a single building with the same total square footage as well as separate security systems. On the other hand, multiple buildings may partition risk—if collections are divided between different buildings, loss from one catastrophic event likely will be smaller than if all the eggs were in one basket.

7.1 Number of Buildings

	10th percentile	25th percentile	Median	75th percentile	90th percentile	Number of responses
Number of buildings per institution*	1.0	1.0	2.0	4.0	6.0	1,059
Building date**	1852	1900	1950	1986	1999	2,929

* = the number of buildings per institution was capped at 16 due to database space limitations.

** = the building date is based upon an aggregate of all dates provided by all respondents for all buildings tracked in the survey

Looking at how museums with space similar to yours allocate resources (money, staff, parking) and what they "earn" (money, attendance) may help you assess your operations. (See the tables 7.2 and 7.3 on page 26.)

Space Allocation

Space is arguably the most contested resource in a museum, even more so than money. Money, after all, is easily shifted to meet changing needs—don't buy that copier, repair the furnace instead. Swapping space around—e.g., converting offices to collections storage or exhibit space to a store—takes money and time. While for most museums money is chronically short, budgets are relatively flexible; they can expand or contract year to year to meet needs. Museums can apply for grant funding to cover special expenditures or choose to incur a deficit in one year to invest in infrastructure that will help them grow in future years. Building new space is a large commitment that not only takes money up front but adds to the museum's ongoing operating expenses each year thereafter. Since space is a commodity that is relatively expensive to expand or repurpose, space allocation becomes a major decision. (See tables 7.4 and 7.5 on page 27.)

7.2 Interior Space (Quartiles)

Space and Related Measures (All numbers except percentages are medians)	Under 8,000 ft²	8,000 – 20,000 ft²	20,001- 55,000 ft²	55,001 and up
Operating income	$94,678	$220,000	$740,000	$4,395,383
Operating expenses	$102,224	$225,000	$800,000	$4,384,929
Full-time staff	1	2	7	41
Part-time staff	2	3	5	20
Attendance	6,500	13,404	37,634	150,000
Parking				
Have on-site	64%	67%	73%	79%
No. on-site spaces	20	30	60	170
Have off-site	9%	16%	11%	12%
No. off-site spaces	25	30	90	150
Charge fee	5%	5%	9%	25%
Fee, auto	$4.25	$3	$3	$5
Fee, bus	—	—	$10	$10
Revenue from parking	—	—	$17,080	$92,427

7.3 Space

Present/Absent	Present in Institution			Median Square Feet	N for Median
	Yes	No	No response		
Exhibitions	89.4%	1.7%	8.9%	7,334	861
Collections storage	82.8%	6.7%	10.5%	2,000	783
Non-collections storage	76.9%	7.7%	15.5%	1,000	703
Offices	87.7%	2.6%	9.8%	1,200	820
Education (classrooms)	46.4%	31.7%	21.9%	1,500	444
Library/research	64.1%	19.7%	16.2%	597	580
Museum store	72.2%	13.3%	14.5%	500	687
Public space/ public functions	62.3%	18.4%	19.3%	2,500	541
Food service	31.1%	46.9%	22.1%	912	296
Auditorium/theaters	34.6%	42.7%	22.6%	2,200	312
Maintenance	60.3%	19.8%	19.8%	740	543
Conservation/ collections prep	49.2%	28.1%	22.7%	785	448

7.4 Space Allocation (as a % of total interior square feet)

	10th percentile	25th percentile	50th percentile	75th percentile	90th percentile	Number of responses
Exhibitions	11.7%	24.1%	37.5%	55.5%	75.0%	793
Collections storage	2.3%	5.0%	10.4%	20.0%	33.3%	731
Non-collections storage	1.1%	2.2%	4.3%	8.7%	15.8%	668
Offices	1.8%	3.6%	6.7%	11.2%	18.8%	768
Education (classrooms)	1.0%	1.9%	4.3%	8.9%	16.5%	421
Library/research	0.5%	1.1%	2.2%	4.7%	9.2%	547
Museum store	0.5%	1.0%	1.9%	3.4%	6.2%	646
Public space/ public functions	2.0%	4.0%	8.3%	17.2%	32.0%	498
Food service	0.5%	1.0%	1.7%	3.1%	5.1%	281
Auditorium/theaters	1.0%	2.0%	4.0%	8.0%	15.1%	299
Maintenance	0.4%	1.0%	2.5%	5.7%	13.1%	511
Conservation/ collections prep	0.5%	1.0%	2.3%	4.8%	8.2%	422

7.5 Space Allocation (in square feet)

	10th percentile	25th percentile	50th percentile	75th percentile	90th percentile	Number of responses
Exhibitions	1,200	3,000	7,334	20,550	50,000	861
Collections storage	274	800	2,000	6,000	17,800	783
Non-collections storage	117	364	1,000	3,000	7,976	703
Offices	200	500	1,200	4,292	12,613	820
Education (classrooms)	400	750	1,500	3,600	8,489	444
Library/research	100	245	597	1,800	4,964	580
Museum store	100	200	500	1,296	2,973	687
Public space/ public functions	400	1,000	2,500	8,069	20,600	536
Food service	100	250	912	2,775	7,150	296
Auditorium/ theaters	500	1,000	2,200	5,000	10,000	312
Maintenance	87	200	740	3,500	12,892	543
Conservation/ collections prep	120	308	785	2,095	6,000	448

We asked respondents how they allocate space in their buildings to major functions (collections, exhibits, offices, food service). As might be expected, the largest amount of space usually is devoted to exhibitions (median of 38 percent), followed by collections storage (median of 10 percent), with all else trailing far behind. See "Specialized Breakouts" for more detailed information by discipline and by selected governance/parent type.

We also asked how the space allocated to these functions has changed, as a percent of total space, in the last five years. The intent was to evaluate the tradeoffs museums are making as they allocate this precious resource. Is the need for earned income driving stores and food service to "win" the space battle over collections storage and exhibits? Does the data uphold our informal perception that many recent museum additions have added unprogrammed public space, in the form of entryways, reception halls, and interior courtyards?

Unfortunately, we suspect that respondents focused on the "has the size of this space changed" part of the question and missed the part about "as a percentage of total institutional space." As you can see below, almost all the areas show increases, and very few museums report decreases for any area. This leads us to conclude that people reported absolute rather than relative increases in size. Otherwise, where is the space coming from?

Forty-two percent of respondents have expanded their building in the last three years. This is consistent with 2003 *Museum Financial Information*, in which 44 percent of respondents reported expansion or renovation in the past three years. Regardless of how the question was interpreted by respondents, the data shows exhibits and collections space are those most likely to be increased by the museum, followed in descending order by office space, non-collections storage, and the museum store.

7.6 Space Increase/Decrease (changes in last five years)

	Increase	Decrease
Exhibitions	27.3%	3.6%
Collections storage	24.5%	2.7%
Non-collections storage	16.4%	5.8%
Offices	21.5%	2.7%
Education (classrooms)	12.6%	1.2%
Library/research	13.6%	1.8%
Museum store	15.6%	4.5%
Public space/ public functions	13.6%	1.9%
Food service	6.9%	0.3%
Auditorium/ theaters	5.5%	0.6%
Maintenance	9.0%	2.6%
Conservation/ collections prep	12.0%	1.7%

Facilities Management

We lumped issues of facilities management and risk management into one survey because they are two sides of the same coin. Any conservator will tell you that the safest way to preserve an object is to lock it in the proverbial "black box," with no light, no bugs, perfect temperature and humidity, preferably an inert atmosphere, and, most of all, no people to break, steal, or lose it. However, it does no one any earthly good in that black box. While we may choose methods of preservation almost this draconian for some iconic and irreplaceable objects, for the most part, museum collections are preserved so that people may benefit from them through some kind of access.

The same is true of our buildings. If we could lock the doors and keep everyone out, it would be much easier to keep them clean, and reduce the risk of fire, being sued should someone slip next to the water-play area, or having something stolen or vandalized. But then there would be no reason to have these buildings. So the tension begins—between preservation and access, between managing risk and realizing the utility of an object or building; and sometimes between the departments responsible for these functions. Are there debates at your museum between the events staff ("people booking weddings want flowers!") and the conservator ("flowers can bring in bugs!")? Perhaps there are tensions about scheduling ("We need to rent this hall for a special function!" "But we need that area for staging exhibit installation!").

These data are not going to settle these arguments. But they may give staff an objective basis for discussion and encourage thoughtful decisions that balance preservation with access, use, and risk.

This essay by the Facilities Team of the Senator John Heinz Pittsburgh Regional History Center presents a model for how museums can make decisions on facilities and risk management as they relate to the day-to-day operations of the museum.

When Do We Wax the Floor?

By The Facilities Team, Senator John Heinz Pittsburgh Regional History Center

Weekend family festival, exhibit load-in, wedding, or waxing the floor? All of these activities are vital to the effective management of a museum facility that relies on attracting and serving a diverse audience through public programs, exhibitions, facility rentals, and best-foot-forward customer service. Communication is the key to providing all these services and reaping the rewards of admissions and event rental dollars. At the Senator John Heinz Pittsburgh Regional History Center, we've found a way to accomplish these activities smoothly: a weekly Facilities Team meeting. The team is lead by our senior vice president and regular attendees include the director of operations and security, assistant director of operations and security, events manager, exhibits assistant, and director of education and visitor services. Team members represent key activity areas in our organization—security, physical plant operations, exhibits, admissions, events, public programs, educational services, and financial management.

At our weekly Wednesday afternoon meetings we cover three key areas: communications (what do we need to know about the past week and the next week); coordinating activities (how do we manage all our activities with the greatest efficiency); and competing interests (what's the best way to serve our customers with the materials and staff resources we have on hand).

Communicating such an understanding of the whole operation is a vital aspect of the Facilities Team's success because it connects the areas we represent to each other and to the whole museum operation. The weekly meeting begins with a review of the past week—what went well and what didn't. We have the opportunity to "vent" with one another in a safe environment, away from the public eye. We discuss timing, such as the fact that the tables weren't set up soon enough for the caterer to get the linens on them in time, and how we can make it easier on ourselves during the next event. For example, we might determine that the weekend family festivals need to end at 3 p.m. rather than 4 p.m. and take place in the Great Hall (our first floor entry area and program/event space). This kind of discussion usually yields a compromise—such as the weekend programming ending at 3:30 p.m. and having the program staff use the same tables used by the caterer, which reduces the set-up time and gives the operations staff an additional half hour for clean-up. This dialogue fosters ongoing open communications throughout the week so that any changes can be managed easily and any conflicts resolved.

Facilities Team meetings also look ahead to the next couple of weeks, particularly toward potentially challenging events and programs. Those are the ones that have a large expected attendance, take place right after another program or event, or require extensive media or computer equipment. A 10- to 15-minute discussion at the Facilities Team meeting about these challenges usually eliminates the need for problem-solving by the events manager or museum educator during the actual event or public program

Coordinating activities goes hand-in-hand with resolving competing interests. At Facilities Team meetings, these are issues such as, When do we wax the floor in the Great Hall? After the school groups leave on Friday at noon? Before the Saturday evening wedding rental? How will we accommodate the Saturday family festival programming? And how will we ensure that the Great Hall is ready to receive the exhibit crates from storage first thing on Monday morning?

This coordination of competing yet vital activities is a regular feature of Facilities Team meetings. Since our success depends on "all of the above," a team approach to problem-solving works for us. The meeting represents a free-form exchange of ideas. We toss out suggestions without fear of criticism, and often it's the "out-of-the-box" suggestion that works best. For example, one recent situation involved covering Earth 2 U crates with black drape for a wedding.

On the surface this kind of coordination may seem simple—why would a museum staff need a weekly meeting to figure this out? In fact, we operated without a Facilities Team meeting for several years with moderate success. But there always seemed

to be one or two departments that felt neglected. Some staff felt that their concerns hadn't been heard or that their work was regarded as less important. For example, School Programs would feel less valued if the museum rented the Multipurpose Room—where visiting students eat their bag lunches—to an outside group without making accommodation for the students' meals. The root of this discord was irregular communication and a lack of understanding of each other's contributions, concerns, and objectives. Our senior vice president initiated the Facilities Team meeting to give all concerned a voice at the table. Other museum staff join the meeting's regular attendees when they are responsible for a particular event, program, or activity—for example, a development staff member planning a fund-raising dinner or a marketing staff member organizing a press preview or photo-shoot. Coordination of potentially competing activities takes minutes to resolve and avoids hours of rancor among staff, each of whom views her activity as a priority. Participating on the Facilities Team encourages each of us to understand our roles and compromise for the overall gain of the organization.

There's a fourth key item to Facilities Team meetings—humor. A "no apologies needed" attitude of constructive criticism injects humor into the weekly meetings. This is maintained and fostered through the team leader, who has a positive and practical approach to problem-solving that allows us to make light of our situations in a way that makes us a team. It also provides us the opportunity to see the History Center as a whole operation—exhibits, programs, collections, security, public safety, and earned income.

The History Center Facilities Team:
Betty Arenth, Senior Vice President
Craig Britcher, Exhibits Assistant
Brad Burmeister, Assistant Director of Operations & Security
Ann Fortescue, Director of Education & Visitor Services
Devon McSorley, Events Manager

■

The process of making decisions regarding facilities and risk management starts with the policies that the museum establishes regarding use of space.

8.1 What Is Allowed in Building by Policy (overall responses)

	Collection areas	Exhibit areas	Staff offices	Public spaces	Grounds
Open flames	1.3%	3.4%	2.4%	9.5%	21.3%
Food	5.3%	20.6%	71.8%	64.9%	71.7%
Beverages (other than water)	5.0%	20.2%	75.9%	65.4%	71.4%
Live plants	8.4%	22.9%	57.2%	50.1%	65.2%
Fresh flowers	8.6%	27.0%	64.5%	59.8%	59.3%
Dried plant material	12.6%	29.9%	43.0%	42.6%	41.2%
Personal artwork	6.7%	13.1%	60.9%	14.6%	12.7%
Filming	25.7%	59.8%	35.8%	65.5%	68.2%
Photography	30.5%	64.5%	43.0%	69.5%	73.7%

For some issues, there is a strong consensus—few museums allow open flames, food, and beverages other than water in the collections area. Beyond that, it becomes more variable, as one would expect, depending on a museum's circumstances. In "Specialized Breakouts," you will see other areas of consensus by discipline. To see an example of the diversity of policy decisions, look at the following table on what is allowed in exhibit areas.

8.2 What Is Allowed in Exhibit Areas

	Food	Beverages other than H2O	Live Plants	Fresh flowers	Dried plants
Overall	20.6%	20.2%	22.9%	27.0%	29.9%
Arboretum/botanic garden	23%	18%	91%	64%	68%
Art museum	22%	23%	20%	33%	20%
Children's/youth museum	25%	18%	36%	21%	29%
General museum	24%	20%	22%	29%	40%
Historic house/site	16%	14%	23%	32%	40%
History museum/ historical society	14%	15%	13%	16%	24%
Natural history/ anthropology museum	24%	22%	28%	28%	37%
Nature center	24%	24%	65%	47%	53%
Science/technology center/museum	35%	35%	45%	33%	45%
Specialized museum	23%	25%	17%	20%	21%
Zoo/aquarium	54%	39%	79%	64%	79%

It is hard to make blanket pronouncements about what should and should not be allowed in a building, because each museum has to make these decisions in light of its mission and circumstances. Here Susan Robertson, executive director of the AAM-accredited Gore Place Society, Waltham, Mass., writes of the museum's decision to allow open flames in its historic building.

A Burning Issue

By Susan Robertson, Executive Director, Gore Place

This book presents information about how museums, in the aggregate, operate. But every museum makes individual choices about how to manage its facilities and control risk, and these choices are particular to its mission and circumstances. At Gore Place, an early 19th-century historic site in Waltham, Mass., we feel that accurate period interpretation requires using open flames because fires and candles were an important part of the early 19th-century lifestyle. Today, however, they present a major fire risk, particularly if there isn't a suppression system in place. In addition, there are resource constraints. Ideally, our 1806 mansion should be protected by both fire detection and suppression systems, but at this time we only have heat and smoke detection devices.

To determine whether open flames could be included in our interpretation plan, Gore Place asked a team of specialists to prepare a fire-protection appraisal and a comprehensive fire-safety plan for the museum. The team included architects trained in historic preservation and/or specializing in safety assessment, a fire safety engineer, and the local fire department fire-prevention officer. Their assessment included the identification of ignition threats, the evaluation of the fire-prevention and risk-control options, the evaluation of the building for egress, and recommendations for fire detection and automatic fire-suppression systems. The team's conclusion was that fireplaces and candles could be used in the mansion if appropriate fire-prevention strategies were followed carefully. A board and staff task force worked with the team to devise the fire-safety strategies, which included both low-cost steps that could be implemented immediately and plans for the complex and costly new fire-detection and suppression systems. The open-flame policies of Gore Place's overall fire safety plan are as follows:

•Fire extinguishers, serviced annually, are placed throughout the building, and staff is trained in the location and use of such devices. Fire drills are scheduled periodically to familiarize staff with fire-safety procedures and to review evacuation plans.

•Draperies and bed hangings are made from natural fibers that have a "low burn rate" or fabrics that have been treated with a flame retardant.

•Floral decorations are limited to fresh or flame-retardant plant materials.

•Real candles may be used if they are placed in glass hurricanes and are always monitored by a staff person while burning. Battery-operated candles are used whenever possible.

•Only one fireplace—the one that provides the greatest visual impact for visitors—is used on a limited basis, although Gore Place has many fireplaces and stoves. Before the fireplace was put into use, a qualified architect inspected its construction and its chimney for safety. The fireplace is cleaned and inspected annually by a qualified chimney sweep, and large fires are not allowed.

•When any open flame is in use, a staff person is assigned to monitor the room continuously until the flame is extinguished and cold to the touch or, in the case of a fireplace, until the fire is cold and the ashes are removed.

•Smoking is not allowed in or near the building.

•Chafing dishes may be used with supervision.

The installation of a fire-suppression system is now of the highest priority in the conservation needs of the Gore mansion. The board and staff have begun action to fund the installation as quickly as possible. However, even after the suppression system is installed, the current fire-safety policies will continue to be observed because they help ensure the safety of the building and its staff and visitors.

Many historic homes struggle over how to accommodate open flames while controlling risk. We believe the Gore Place approach also can be used for other risk-management problems: weigh the risk against the importance of the activity, use mission as a starting point; assess how the activity under consideration contributes to overall risk; and create a comprehensive management plan that mitigates the risks. ■

Integrated Pest Management (IPM)

Many of the policies we discuss in the previous section (whether or not to allow food, drink, live plants, dried flowers and in what areas of the building) are aimed at least in part at reducing the risk of pest infestations in the museum. Red wine is a risk to the carpet; canapés not only stain, but raise the possibility of mice coming to glean after the reapers (or the cleaning crew). Pests not only damage the buildings, exhibits, collections, they also pose a risk to human health. Rodents may carry the risk of hanta virus. Some museum workers develop severe allergies to dermestid beetles. It is short-sighted, however, to focus exclusively on the oft-contested issue of "will we allow x in the building, the exhibits, the collections" without looking at the bigger picture. Tom Strang of the Canadian Conservation Institute offers his thoughts on how to focus on the "big picture" of pest control and devise a response that makes efficient use of the museum's resources while posing minimum risk to human health.

I've Got Bugs in My Pockets and I Don't Know What to Do with Them

By Tom Strang, Senior Conservation Scientist, Canadian Conservation Institute, Department of Canadian Heritage, Ottawa

You have pests? First, get over the feeling of being stigmatized. Most museums have pests at one time or another; some have them all the time. You can either live with them and hope for the best, or you can fight them off. It really is your choice as the current caregiver of your collections. Given what you know about the pests' behavior, where you find them, and their numbers, you think you need to do something? Good. With that information you are probably drawing a correct conclusion. How far have they spread? You can't tell for sure? That is common. You have several methods for cleaning up the objects you know are infested, and that will take a bit of effort to do properly. What do you do after that? Do you want to avoid being blindsided by another little crisis like this again? If so, your museum should implement Integrated Pest Management (IPM).

The term "Integrated Pest Management" was coined to refer to a method of pest control that integrates knowledge in developmental biology of agricultural pests with effective timing of response methods. The original goal was to find the lowest-cost, highest-return (yield or quality) farming production model for agricultural crops. It's most significant contribution has been to reduce pesticide use from a broadcast prophylactic to a more effective tactical application. The concept adapts beautifully to museum pest control. In collections care, we integrate several modes of action to reduce pest pressure on stored objects. We learned these lessons from a wealth of experience developed in the field of stored food products, as well as our own work with collections.

IPM is a layered approach that tries for the greatest hazard reduction with available resources and effort. Unlike farms, museums are not always driven by hard-nosed "lowest cost" economics in each decision because of the tangible/intangible values of our collections, which, ethically, we avoid compromising. But as a profession we generally don't have a lot of money to throw around so we try to be sensible in allocating resources. IPM helps us make these choices wisely and also tries to increase what we know about pest activity. This information either reinforces our comfort or heightens our awareness of hazards. To do IPM well we need actions to forestall disaster (save resources) and to decrease the number of actions needed to curtail disaster (restrict losses).

You have a choice between "pro-active management" and "crisis management" (to use buzzwords) as endpoints to the question, "When do I act . . . before, now, or later?" Avoiding pest hazards and blocking them are all about trying to be "pro-active," meaning we take some action about serious things before the worst happens. This requires a sensible model of predicting the future outcomes from your present actions. An accurate model requires a systematic survey of our facilities. This survey can produce straightforward reactions to obvious situations. ("Oh, the rain gutter is dumping against the foundation, maybe that is why we have so many damp-loving book lice. We should fix that someday soon.") Indirect connections (indirect to us anyway) are tougher sells but by noticing coincidences, you have somewhere to start an examination. ("You remember the cleaning staff hours you cut back on, sir? Well the bugs are taking over their jobs in the back hall.")

Proactive management includes minimizing hazards from pests by reducing the frequency and intensity of the pest interaction with objects. This creates the outermost shell of preventive conservation. For example, we enforce basic sanitation. Why? Because it reduces the ability of pests to find unseen harborage, food, and water. Don't leave the interior lights on all night near a hole in the wall (leaky door or window). Clean up long-term clutter and other such situations that draw pests inside. By "pushing back" in this way, you will reduce some pest hazards. Even if one is using pesticides indoors, basic sanitation is a prerequisite of their effectiveness. If pests are forced to roam further for sustenance, they'll take the baits, bump into the traps, touch the sprayed baseboards, and die.

Another control method is to block the pests. Without barriers to movement, your entire collection may as well be outside in the field or forest. Containment is useful for many reasons—protection from outdoor weather, fire safety, refining the interior environment—including reducing pests. There is a trade-off; putting objects into closed containers hides any pest activity "behind closed doors." Create effective inspection methods that match your level of containment. If you know the containers are reasonably pest resistant (tightly sealed doors, polymer bags, tight-lidded containers), the objects were pest free before they went into the containers, and you have done nothing to compromise the situation, then you are justifiably less stressed about detection. Reverse any one of these conditions, and you ought to take a look now and again.

When prevention fails or you are handed an infestation (the proverbial Trojan horse) you are in crisis-management mode. Protect yourself by detecting the pests and then responding. Managing big pest infestations is all about ensuring effective suppression. Picking an appropriate method, making adjustments to ensure the technique works, etc., are all important skills to have, and take experience to gain and objective measurement to confirm. Beginning with understanding of the pest's biology, behavior, and susceptibilities we often can modify the situation to lower the pest's success (including avoid and block responses) or kill it outright.

However, it is still a hazard and risk game. (If I treat with X, I attack the ozone layer; if I treat with Y, I wait three times longer with people yelling at me for the objects. Which is better?) Any risk from treatment methods is balanced against the hazard posed by the pest. Consider the use of arsenic in collections—it has moved from a widely used stalwart preserver to a manageable health risk. Or consider the removal of pesticides from our food chain and the restriction on using ozone-depleting fumigants, methyl bromide in particular. We are constantly readjusting our perceptions of acceptable pest-control practices based on increased knowledge and recognition of downstream effects.

Fortunately, we now have a number of nontoxic or low-toxicity options for pest control in collections. We can use low temperature, below 20°C for a week or more to kill insect pests; moisture-resistant bagging and careful handling of the objects prevents most hazards. We use controlled atmospheres (an agricultural term) to asphyxiate insects. Carbon dioxide and low oxygen are the two most common, and we can use these on a large or small scale, adapting to delicate collections or sheer industrial volume to be treated. We use heat to kill insects, from treating whole buildings to using a small oven. This gives us a fast and certain kill, and with bagging or engineered humidity control very delicate objects are not appreciably affected by the process. We use traps and limited bait deployment to kill rodents, but must combine this activity with blocking for it to be effective. We use pesticides, but where human health concerns are high we use tactical approaches like baseboard sprays, and this often is where they are most beneficial and cost effective. We reduced the use of preventative chemical fogging of collections. All treatment methods can be hazardous; nothing is foolproof because fools are so ingenious. But we have a lot more knowledge and professional comfort in these methods now than we did 15 years ago. Early adopters in our profession took managed risks and demonstrated the way for others. Find colleagues with experience in pest management, talk to them, and share your experiences.

Determining an appropriate response is difficult at times when you do not know the extent of the hazard. When the problem is obvious and well contained, this is not difficult. ("Thanks for the moth-eaten fur stole, We'll just pop it in the freezer for now.") It helps to enlist all museum staff in this effort. Early on in your IPM process, involve the staff, including cleaners and security, and increase their concern to such a reasonable level that they accede to sensible pest-control requests: "Please remove garbage promptly. Please inspect and allow treatment for pests before putting new material in collection storage." They'll also give you information: "You know that farming exhibit? I saw something crawl under the grain bags."

Integrating pest-managing activities into our work and pest-managing structures into our workplace buys us more time over the long term. Time for the objects to entertain and inform us. Time for us to enjoy a more healthy life by reducing our chronic exposure to toxins. Time to do other tasks that our paying public can appreciate. ∎

Unfortunately, only 54 percent of respondents report that they practice IPM, and only 39 percent report having an IPM plan. We fear that the other 15 percent may embrace the philosophy, but not actually implement it in a systematic manner. Larger museums (in space or budget) and government museums are more likely to report that they practice integrated pest management. (See table titled "Practice Integrated Pest Management" on page 36.)

Space Rentals

Space rental is a major reason to allow food, drink, flowers, etc., into museums. After all, who would schedule a wedding or bat mitzvah at the museum without them? In addition to the direct revenue the institution receives, space rental also can drive sales at the store (if the store is open during the event), introduce new audiences to the museum, and increase the affection of existing audiences. As one museum director remarked to me, "couples who get married in the museum are more likely to think of us fondly and remember us in their wills." The great majority of museums do rent space (see next page), though museums that are small, in terms of space or budget, are less likely to do so.

Museum policies usually specify to whom the museum will or will not rent. Perhaps because of the role that rentals play in cultivating relationships, private and corporate groups rank second and third as "groups museums rent to." Fewer museums rent to religious (64 percent) or political (51 percent) groups, perhaps because such rentals may imply that the museum agrees with or endorses the positions of the renters. Some years ago, for example, one museum realized it needed to develop a rental policy after it rented the auditorium for a lecture on "defending pornography" (this in a conservative mid-Western town). Not that a museum should never rent to groups with controversial identity or content, but having a policy both guides those choices, based on a museum's mission and values, and is a cornerstone of building a communications plan for answering questions like "Why would you rent to them?"

9.1 Practice Integrated Pest Management

	Yes	No	No response
Overall	**53.6%**	**40.1%**	**6.4%**
Arboretum/botanic garden	82%	9%	9%
Art museum	62%	32%	6%
Children's/youth museum	50%	36%	14%
General museum	66%	28%	6%
Historic house/site	52%	42%	6%
History museum/ historical society	44%	49%	7%
Natural history/anthropology museum	74%	20%	7%
Nature center	47%	53%	0%
Science/technology center/museum	50%	45%	5%
Specialized museum	42%	52%	6%
Zoo/aquarium	79%	21%	0%
Government	65%	30%	6%
Private nonprofit	49%	44%	7%
Dual	63%	33%	4%
Under $125,000	38%	57%	6%
$125,000–$400,000	48%	48%	4%
$400,001–$1,750,000	61%	34%	5%
$1,750,001+	75%	20%	5%
Under 8,000 sq. ft.	41%	53%	6%
8,000–20,000 sq. ft.	49%	47%	4%
20,001–55,000 sq. ft.	57%	38%	5%
55,001+ sq. ft.	75%	20%	5%

10.1 Does Institution Rent Space to Outside Groups

	Yes	No	No response
Overall	**70.4%**	**28.4%**	**1.2%**
Arboretum/botanic garden	91%	9%	0%
Art museum	75%	25%	0%
Children's/youth museum	82%	11%	7%
General museum	68%	31%	2%
Historic house/site	72%	27%	1%
History museum/ historical society	68%	30%	2%
Natural history/anthropology museum	63%	37%	0%
Nature center	77%	23%	0%
Science/technology center/museum	85%	15%	0%
Specialized museum	60%	40%	0%
Zoo/aquarium	93%	7%	0%
Government	62%	36%	1%
Private nonprofit	74%	26%	1%
Dual	71%	25%	4%
Under $125,000	54%	45%	0%
$125-$400,000	67%	32%	0%
$400,001-$1,750,000	85%	15%	0%
$1,750,001+	88%	12%	0%
Under 8,000 sq.ft.	54%	46%	0%
8,000-20,000 sq.ft.	72%	29%	0%
20,001-55,000 sq.ft.	79%	21%	0%
55,001+ sq.ft.	90%	10%	0%

10.2 Groups Space Is/Would Be Rented to

	Would rent to	Have rented to in past 5 years
Religious groups	63.5%	36.3%
Political groups	50.9%	30.0%
Private groups (weddings, parties, graduations, etc.)	84.5%	69.5%
Corporate groups	89.0%	69.0%
Non-religious nonprofit groups	93.1%	75.4%
Other	12.4%	10.6%

"Other" includes school groups, university groups, university departments/functions, military groups, government groups/agencies, and community groups and clubs.

For 85 percent of those respondents that do rent, rental revenues go to the institution's budget while 12 percent send the revenue to the general fund of their parent organization. This does not vary much by discipline, budget, or space size. However, it does vary greatly among museums in parent organizations, depending on the type of parent

10.3 Rental Revenue Goes to

	Institution budget	General fund of the parent	Other	No response
University parent	84	17	0	1
Museum system/museum parent	61	35	11	0
Other non-governmental parent	65	37	2	3
State	73	25	11	0
Municipal/county	56	33	12	5

2003 *Museum Financial Information* shows that 60 percent of museums have income from space rental, contributing a median of 1 percent of operating income. For 10 percent of museums, space rental contributes over 6 percent.

This survey asked specifically about catering and catering revenue. More than one quarter of respondents overall have an exclusive arrangement with one or more caterers, with the practice most common among large museums (as measured by interior space or operating expenses). The average commission is 5.5 percent. We report the average, rather than the median, in this case because a very large number of museums charge no commission, so the median for the overall sample and many of the subsets is zero. (See "Catering" table on the next page.)

In deciding whether or not to rent space, and to whom, museums think through what they want to achieve from the rentals. Then staff determine how to manage the events as smoothly as possible. On page 39, Janet Van Delft, operations manager at Chicago's Robie House, offers some tips about the particularly difficult challenge of renting space that is under renovation.

| | Have Exclusive Agreement with Caterer(s) | | | | | |
	Yes, one caterer	Yes, maintain a list of accepted caterers	Average commission taken by institution	N for mean/ median	No	No response
Overall	10.9%	16.4%	5.5%	231	70.4%	2.3%
Government	13%	12%	4.1%	54	73%	2%
Private nonprofit	10%	18%	6.1%	164	70%	2%
Dual	16%	20%	3.1%	11	57%	6%
Under $125,000	5%	4%	0.8%	15	90%	2%
$125-$400,000	6%	14%	3.7%	41	78%	2%
$400,001-$1,750,000	10%	22%	3.8%	56	68%	0%
$1,750,001+	24%	31%	8.0%	111	44%	1%
Under 8,000 sq.ft.	7%	7%	0.6%	28	84%	2%
8,000-20,000 sq.ft.	5%	12%	2.0%	34	81%	2%
20,001-55,000 sq.ft.	8%	21%	4.2%	48	70%	1%
55,001+ sq.ft.	27%	32%	8.1%	109	41%	0%

Room for Rent

By Janet Van Delft, Operations Manager, Robie House, Chicago

Twice voted by the American Institute of Architects as one of the 10 most important buildings of the 20th century, the Robie House on the campus of the University of Chicago attracts visitors from all over the world. The Frank Lloyd Wright Preservation Trust has managed the property since 1997 and is solely responsible for the $8-million restoration of this National Historic Landmark. The project is only half complete; raising another $4 million is high on our priority list.

One small but important way we raise funds is by opening the house for special events before or after hours. Gleaning from the wisdom of the Preservation Trust's other site, the Frank Lloyd Wright Home and Studio in Oak Park, Ill., we follow its guidelines for special events. The Robie House's special-event policy puts the organizational mission and good stewardship of the building first and honors our mission to restore, preserve, and educate.

Allowing interested groups to experience the building helps us support our mission by:
• cultivating new friends
• raising funds
• educating the community
• increasing our membership, donor, and volunteer base
• becoming an active participant in the community

If you are considering renting a historic building for special events, be aware that there is a conflict of interest between the building's preservation and using the space for breakfasts, dinners, cocktail parties, and corporation recruitment. This conflict can be managed, however, with the help of the board of directors and experienced management, by writing down the rules, giving them to the person requesting the rental, explaining the rules, if necessary, and upholding them without exception. Here are some of the things we have learned at the Robie House about managing special events smoothly. (For a complete list of what you might include in a space rental policy, see Facilities Use Agreement Policies, below.)

Be Clear about the Event Request Procedure

Send out the policy ahead of time for the renter to review. Designate one staff person to review all rental requests, keep a record of dates requested, and keep track of signed forms from the renter and caterer. Make sure that staff person knows the rental fee structure and the deposit amount required to reserve the space. Compile a list of caterers who will follow the rules set forth in your policy. Send a confirmation to the person requesting the special event.

Provide Tours and Monitors

In keeping with the education component of our mission statement, we choose to have volunteers and/or staff present during the event to provide information about Robie House. They also ensure the safety of guests and of collections. You may choose to do this, too. In any case, one staff person should serve as a liaison and be on hand to field requests, resolve problems, and ensure compliance with your policies.

Building Restrictions

Your special-event guidelines should include a list of all the museum's restrictions, not just those particular to special events. For example, if photography is not allowed during a regular working hours, make sure that is on the list. Even if your historic building renovations are not yet complete, set your limits now; that way the restrictions do not have to be revised and you can

begin educating renters about the behavior you expect. This also eliminates confusion arising from the memory that "but you used to let us. . . ." Be very specific—if renters want to be in your building, they will honor and follow your policies.

Logistics

Have a preliminary run-through of the building with the person planning the event. This allows you time to go over the details that help create a favorable impression of the building. Be sure to review the:
•main entrance
•guest list
•restrooms
•times of arrival—caterer and guests
•length of event, including set-up and clean-up
•areas of the museum available to guests
•any restrictions involving the building

Liability

Require both the renter and caterer to furnish special-use liability insurance prior to the event. Ask your insurance agent to furnish applicable information about additional coverage.

Signed Agreements

By providing your forms to the renter and making certain that the forms are signed before the event, you ensure that everyone knows the museum's expectations. It is easier to enforce a rule or restriction if you can point to a signed agreement confirming compliance with all the rules.

Opening an historic building for a special use offers a unique experience to see a masterpiece in a totally different setting. Hearing the story, moving

---

Facilities Use Agreement Policies: Outline of Typical Contents

Who supervises the museum's facility-use program.

Any kinds of functions prohibited by policy:
Weddings:
  Commercial photography/filming
Political Events:
  Fundraising for other organizations
Marketing Events:
  Children's Parties

Usually addressed in most policies (typically in this order):
Museum's mission, significance of site and/or collection
Membership requirement
Fees: deposits, payment, refunds
Capacity
Hours
Caterers/Equipment Rental:
  Must select from approved list
  Permits
  Deliveries and clean-up

Also addressed in policies:
Alcohol
Availability of docents, guided tours
Disclosure on handicapped accessibility
Flowers, potted plants
Gratuities
Insurance
Live animals
Media coverage of event
Movement of museum objects
Music, dancing
Parking
Smoking

Specifications for use of museum name on invitation, written materials
Use of candles
Use of museum image
Use of rice, confetti, bird seed, balloons

American Association of Museums

through the space, seeing the restoration work that has been completed and realizing the extent of the work that remains to be done enriches the guest's experience. It can also generate commitment to your historic building and inspire people to support its preservation. ■

One impact of the choices a museum makes regarding amount of space, allocation of space, and facilities use is the number of staff needed to maintain that space. The data below show that respondents overall don't usually have a full-time person devoted to maintenance until their operating budget is over $400,000 or their space is over 20,000 square feet; or a part-time person until they reach $125,000 or 8,000 square feet. Zoos/aquariums tend to have the largest maintenance staff, followed by arboreta/botanic gardens and science/technology centers/museums.

11.1 Number of Full-time/Part-time Maintenance Staff

	10th percentile	25th percentile	50th percentile	75th percentile	90th percentile	Number of responses
Overall	0/0	0/0	0/0	2/1	6/3	1,119/1,112
Government	0/0	0/1	0.5/3	2/9	6.5/24.3	274/286
Private nonprofit	0/0	0/1	0/4	2/11	6/35	788/839
Dual	0/0	0/1	1/6	4.5/10	14.4/31	45/47
Under $125,000	0/0	0/0	0/1	0/2	0/4	241/263
$125,000–$400,000	0/0	0/1	0/3	1/6	1/10	257/269
$400,001–$1,750,000	0/1	0/3	1/5	2/11	3/20	252/259
$1,750,001+	1/5	2/10	5/22.5	8.5/48.5	29/104.4	257/256
Under 8,000 sq. ft.	0.0	0.0	0.0	0.0	1.0	226
8,000–20,000 sq. ft.	0.0	0.0	0.0	1.0	2.0	250
20,001–55,000 sq. ft.	0.0	0.0	1.0	2.0	3.0	240
55,001+ sq. ft.	0.0	2.0	4.0	8.0	29.0	239

Who Is Responsible for Risk Management?

Museum staff usually do a good job performing their assigned responsibilities. And usually there is some person, or group of people, who has responsibility for facilities management. It may be a chief financial officer, a custodian, a building manager, or the director herself. However, it is rarer for someone to be given overall responsibility for a museum's risk management. You might start by asking, Who is responsible for risk management at your museum? Is it in her job description? If no one is responsible for assessing overall risk and coordinating risk management, will it get done? Will it get done well? If it is partitioned into separate responsibilities (the collections manager managing risk for the collection, the building and grounds manager managing risk for the building and visitors) will it be done in an integrated way?

Overall, 94 percent of respondents identify some staff member as having primary responsibility for risk management, but only 36 percent say that risk management is listed in that person's job description. This figure falls below 20 percent for the smallest quarter of museums (in budget or physical size). Often, staff's performance is evaluated against the responsibilities assigned in their job descriptions. If risk management is not in anyone's job description, will they get kudos for doing it well? Will they be held to a higher standard if they are doing it poorly? Will you only notice whether they are doing it well or poorly when something goes wrong?

12.1 Is Risk Management Identified in the Job Description of the Position Primarily Responsible for This?

	Yes	No	No response
Overall	36.4%	57.4%	6.3%
Under $125,000	17%	76%	8%
$125,000–$400,000	25%	71%	4%
$400,001–$1,750,000	46%	50%	4%
$1,750,001+	64%	32%	4%
Under 8,000 sq. ft.	19%	73%	8%
8,000–20,000 sq. ft.	32%	64%	4%
20,001–55,000 sq. ft.	44%	53%	4%
55,001+ sq. ft.	61%	36%	3%

Respondents most often listed the director as being responsible for risk management, but this position is the least likely to have risk assessment included in the job description. This is probably a case of "the director is ultimately responsible for everything, so he or she must be responsible for this, too." Here are the figures for inclusion of risk management responsibilities in various job positions.

12.2 Risk Management in Job Description by Position Title (for the position identified as responsible)

	Yes	No	No response	N
Director/CEO/head of museum	23.6%	73.9%	2.5%	635
Collections staff	46.3%	49.5%	4.2%	95
Manager/administrator	49.5%	45.9%	4.5%	111
Security	82.7%	17.3%	0.0%	52
Facilities manager	64.5%	32.3%	3.2%	93
Other	55.8%	38.0%	6.2%	129

While overall, most often it is the director/CEO who is assigned responsibility for risk management, the bigger the museum (in budget or size) the more likely it is that this responsibility will be given to someone else. In mid-sized museums this is usually someone on the collections or facilities management staff or sometimes a chief financial officer (CFO), chief operating officer (COO), or an associate or deputy director. In the largest museums, it is usually a vice president for finance or operations, CFO, COO, a deputy director, or occasionally a specialized risk or safety manager. In museums with parent organizations, risk management often is handled by a safety or risk management office or some other section of the parent's staff.

12.3 Primary Responsibility for Risk Management

	Director/CEO/ Head	Collections staff	Manager/ administrator	Security	Facilities manager	Other	No response
Overall	52.5%	7.9%	9.2%	4.3%	7.7%	10.7%	5.9%
Under $125,000	68%	7%	5%	0%	3%	8%	9%
$125,000–$400,000	77%	5%	6%	1%	2%	4%	3%
$400,000–$1,750,000	51%	12%	5%	3%	14%	10%	2%
$1,750,001+	15%	8%	21%	15%	16%	22%	2%
Under 8,000 sq. ft.	68%	7%	6%	1%	2%	9%	6%
8,000-20,000 sq. ft.	69%	9%	5%	2%	5%	5%	4%
19							
20,001-55,000	54%	10%	8%	3%	12%	9%	3%
55,001+ sq. ft.	21%	6%	18%	14%	16%	21%	2%

Note: respondents also were given the choice of development/marketing/PR/membership staff; conservators; visitor services; exhibition staff; and educators. These positions were omitted from the table because they were selected 1 percent or less of the time.

One reason large museums often give overall responsibility for risk management to the CFO or COO is that it has profound financial implications. Making thoughtful risk management decisions is an important way to control costs. Here J. W. Croft and Alexander Sherman discuss how to integrate risk management into financial planning.

Avoid, Transfer, Assume, or Insure?

By Jim Croft, Vice President, Finance and Administration, Field Museum, and Alexander Sherman, Consultant, The Ulanov Partnership

Introduction

During the past three years, many museums have seen insurance rates more than double. World events and changes in the insurance industry have largely driven this financial challenge for museums. Nonetheless, museums retain some ability to affect this trend. The corporate world generally and some museums have a proven strategy for controlling insurance costs to a degree: integrating risk management into financial planning.

The integrated approach generates three prime benefits for museums:

1. Involving more people in risk management can lead to avoiding some risks altogether and to a culture of risk management.

2. Holistic planning for risk can develop non-insurance options.

3. Involvement in, a culture of, and planning for risk management ultimately can help museums find cheaper solutions.

This essay outlines the broad steps of financial planning, then locates risk management within this exercise, and provides some practical steps for applying an integrated approach.

Financial Planning

Through financial planning, institutions ensure that their resources are properly deployed. Broadly speaking, financial planning begins with a clear understanding of the institution's goals and objectives and with the guidelines for allocating resources. A recent study on the challenges facing the 21st-century museum cited financial planning, including strategic planning and operational planning, as a prime concern. Plans that apply to the entire museum, establish overall institutional objectives, and seek to position the organization in terms of its environment are known as strategic plans. Operational plans detail how the institutional objectives are to be achieved.

Generally, one recognizes seven key elements of operational and strategic planning:

• Coordinate departments. When managers understand the organization's direction, they are better able to help achieve those goals. Without planning, departments and individuals in the organization might be working at cross-purposes, preventing the organization from moving toward its objectives.

• Reduce uncertainty. Planning forces staff to look ahead, anticipate change, consider the impact of change, and develop an appropriate response.

• Gather information. External information includes environmental scanning: the systematic analysis of technological, demographic, political, and economic environments in which the institution operates. Internal information includes trends in attendance, head count, and other key areas of performance and resource allocation. Together, these two types of information enable managers to understand the trade-offs the museum must make.

• Identify priorities. In the process of identifying and accepting trade-offs, museum leaders determine their priorities. These priorities drive institutional objectives and goals, and eventually efficient resource allocation.

• Improve efficiency. When individuals within an organization see the goal the organization is trying to achieve, inefficiencies become more obvious and can be corrected or eliminated.

• Promote control and accountability. The museum's planned objectives become a tool to compare actual performance to the plan. If there are significant deviations between actual performance and the planned objectives, the museum leadership can take the necessary corrective action.

• Support continuous improvement. Planning provides a method for actively seeking best practices and encourages teamwork and new partnerships within and outside the organization. Planning can create new ways of looking at things, and ultimately serves to commit members of the planning team to accomplishing the goals they have helped to identify and determine.

In addition, museum leaders have the responsibility to develop scenarios. Scenario planning involves, first, identifying possible situations the institution might face in the future and, two, determining appropriate responses. With attendance, for example, how will the museum control cost if admission revenue is lower than predicted? Alternatively, how will the museum increase staffing if attendance is significantly higher? Or with local government regulations, how will the museum react to changes in permitting or other regulations that impact operations? Scenario planning leads naturally into risk management.

Risk Management

Our corporate colleagues have seen an evolution of risk management. In the 1960s corporations had insurance buyers. By the middle 1970s the insurance buyer was required to take a broader perspective of the company's risk exposure: purchasing insurance and alternatives such as self-insurance and risk-retention groups. Today, corporations are taking an even more holistic approach to risk management, and risk managers are involved in areas as wide-ranging as asset management, corporate liability, and corporate governance.[1] Even as the field of risk management has widened, it has remained at its core a question of scenario planning, of considering the impact and the likelihood of different outcomes.

Scenario planning for risk management begins with developing a comprehensive list of threats.[2] What major interruptions to business could occur, such as natural disasters or facility collapse? What threats are there to the health and safety of staff and visitors, such as slips and trips or dangerous chemicals? Are the collections at sudden risk in any way, such as power failure or theft? With each item on this list, one should consider the impact of the event—how damaging will it be to finances, mission, and reputation—and the likelihood—how often does such an event occur?

The museum leadership, including management and board, must determine their comfort with the risk these threats present: how much insurance can you afford? How great a misfortune can you afford? In answering these questions, the following options should be considered in order of preference to:

•Avoid risk, either by changing the program or the facility, so that the threat no longer exists. Try to avoid risks whenever possible.

•Transfer risk to a third party, often through a contract, so they assume the costs should the threat occur.

•Assume risk, accept the threat as a normal part of doing business (typical for low-impact, high-frequency risks).

•Buy insurance if the risk cannot be avoided or transferred and is too great (either impact or frequency) to assume.

Typically, the result of not considering the four options is to assume the risk.

Guide to Practice

In practice, these are very tough decisions to make. Often, the museum's general counsel or chief financial officer may be more adverse to risk than many of the program managers. Ultimately, management will have to determine whether the benefit to the mission justifies the risk, whether the operating budget can afford the desired level of insurance, whether reserves can cover lower deductibles, and whether the board agrees to the proposed risk portfolio.

You will find different perspectives on buying insurance throughout the rest of this volume. For the other three options—avoiding, transferring, and assuming risk—you may find these pointers practical and useful.

•Invite your underwriters in for an annual walkthrough. They can make suggestions for changing either your facility and operations to lower risk. Moreover, their feeling of partnership may well lead to lower rates!

•Check weather conditions that affect the visitor. There may be relatively inexpensive remedies to potentially costly lawsuits, such as covering the entrance to keep it dry in the rain and snow.

•Have a disaster plan and rehearse it. If the staff know where to go, where to direct the visitors, and whom to call, an emergency can be brought into control much faster.

•Write "hold-harmless" and indemnification clauses into contracts. This is an effective way to manage risk during special events when outside organizations use the museum and during construction projects.

•Increase insurance deductibles. For less frequent threats, management and board may be more comfortable hoping it will not happen than by paying a premium for insurance.

•Develop financial reserves. In an ideal situation, losses not covered by insurance should be covered by unrestricted reserves, as opposed to debt or restricted endowment.

Conclusion

This essay has outlined the broad steps of financial planning and the benefits of taking an integrated approach to risk management. Like planning in general, risk management is an issue for staff and trustees, as well as managers. Involvement in, culture of, and planning for risk management ultimately can help museums find the most economical solutions. Risk cannot be avoided altogether, so, to adapt Ogden Nash, if some kind of risk you must be pursuing, well, remember to do it by doing rather than by not doing.

References

1. Nolan, H. (2004, June). "Crisis Planning Must Include Routine, Extreme." *Business Insurance* 38, no. 25, 10.

2. Foster, J. S. (2004). "Risk Management and Insurance." *Meeting News* (2004 Meeting Planner), 82-87.

Assessing Risk

One of the key responsibilities for the staff member assigned the task of overall risk management is to assess the "big picture" of risk for the museum. When the responsibility for risk management is unclear or divided among several people, the museum's response to risk tends to be fragmented as well. If someone looks at all risks, assessing likelihood each might occur, the impact it would have, and the resources needed to mitigate it, the museum can make wise choices about where to allocate its time and money to reduce risk. Otherwise the registrar, working from her area of knowledge and expertise, might advocate for a better climate-control system while the building manager, who knows the roof needs to be replaced next year, has yet to be heard.

There is an extensive literature regarding risk assessment and management of facilities (see Resources). However, museums are unique in that they must assess and manage risk in collections. Robert Waller of the Canadian Museum of Nature describes the evolving field of quantifying risks to collections to make resource allocation choices.

Know Thine Enemy: Be It Fire, Pestilence, Rot, or Other

By Robert Waller, Ph.D., Chief, Conservation Section, Canadian Museum of Nature

Peering into a murky future. . . .

In ancient times, realizing their inability to foresee, let alone influence, the future, humans left all such matters to the Gods. But beginning with Pascal, who was the first to apply mathematics to games of chance, humans developed formal means of calculating probabilities of uncertain outcomes. With this came the ability not just to forecast but also to influence an uncertain future. Likewise, preservation of cultural property requires not just forecasting the future (assessing risks to collections) but also determining how one can influence the future (reducing risks) with the minimum possible investment.

The goal of preservation planning is to maintain the value of the collection over time. A fully rational approach would require all current and future parties who benefit from the collection's existence to understand the complete value attributed to that collection. It also would require identifying and quantifying all the ways this value might be reduced over time by various processes (like fading) and events (like hurricanes). Finally, it would require complete knowledge of all possible interventions in the collections care system (such as better cases or fire suppression systems) and how they interact with each other, so that the most effective methods of reducing risk could be chosen and applied.

Yikes. . . .

This is quite an order! Of course, we will never have complete knowledge or the ability to integrate and manipulate that knowledge, yet we have to plan preservation strategies. Furthermore, many processes are too slow and many events too infrequent to provide meaningful feedback on the results of our preservation activities. (How often do you find out how well your museum survives a 100-year flood?) Consequently, we can't learn what is best for a collection just by observing what happens to it over time: we may overestimate the threat from a rare event just because we were unlucky enough to experience one; or underestimate the threat of common occurrences, because we have not noticed their effect.

To the rescue. . . .

Fortunately, the field of risk assessment and management provides tools to help museums invest our limited resources to achieve good results despite our incomplete and uncertain knowledge. The first step is to define the scope of the assessment including, but certainly not only, which collections will be included. For most museums, this will include the formally accessioned objects as well as their value-enhancing documentation (e.g., accession and catalogue records). Second, the risks to these collections are identified as comprehensively as possible. Several frameworks for identifying and organizing possible risks are now available—for example, the Canadian Conservation Institute's "Nine Agents of Deterioration" (see Resources). These frameworks help organize quantitative information about risks to collections given your museum's location, building, and collection care policies, procedures, and resources Finally, staff determine the probability of each risk and the likely extent of resulting damage. The results are compiled into an overall assessment of the risks to the collection— these will be both uncertain and complex, but will provide a common basis for decision-making among the staff. Interpreting and presenting these results to decision-makers in a format they recognize as relevant to their responsibilities can be a powerful way to get museum management to devote needed resources to risk-abatement for collections.

This technique is powerful because it takes something that is relatively intangible (the risk to the collection) and expresses it as a number—something concrete and simple that people can debate objectively. In the Canadian Museum of Nature's system of risk assessment, staff determine or estimate numbers that represent the fraction of each collection susceptible to a given risk, the loss in value that would result from damage from that risk, the probability of that risk occurring, and the extent to which the collection is expected to be affected. By deciding what numbers to assign to these variables, staff come to agreement on the size and importance of each risk. Using the results, management can decide where it should apply the museum's resources to achieve the greatest reduction to risk.

The Canadian Museum of Nature has developed a comprehensive collection risk assessment and management process and offers training and support to institutions undertaking their own assessments. As more museums, libraries, and archives embrace this risk-based approach to preservation planning, and collect and share data, more baseline information about the probability and effect of risks will become available. This, in turn, will improve our ability to preserve our collections.

But does it help?

In the meantime, the benefits of adopting a risk-based approach to preservation planning are plentiful:

•The risks expected to cause the greatest loss of value to the institution's collections are identified.

•One or a few outstanding risks become obvious priorities for mitigation.

•The data provide a base for evaluating the impact of undertaking a project that affects many risks, for example, improving the seal-integrity of the building envelope.

•Attention, anxiety, and resources directed to quantitatively insignificant risks can be freed for more productive application.

By defining the scope of the assessment and identifying the actual risks, staff identify the boundaries of preservation issues. Consequently, risk management becomes concrete and realistic, and collections care is not seen as a bottomless pit for resources. Staff can identify, evaluate, and debate possible decisions regarding how much to invest in preservation, looking at the curve of diminishing returns. Communication and, hence, collaboration between components of an institution—such as collections management and facilities management—are improved. More to the point, by conducting a risk assessment and using the information to inform risk management, the institution is seen by its governance, auditors, and staff to be proactive in striving to fulfill its preservation mandate. ■

Emergency Preparedness and Training

Many of the issues we have discussed so far involve managing the day-to-day, incremental processes that affect facilities and risk management: allocation and use of space, pest control, etc. Now we come to the big, scary "end of the world" scenarios, events worthy of separate attention in a plan to respond to what are variously called emergencies or disasters.

The idea of emergency preparedness and planning has been around for a long time. However, the field evidently is far from full implementation of this concept. Only 66 percent of respondents report having an emergency response/disaster plan, and only 60 percent of those report ever conducting a practice or drill for it.

Maybe preparing for an emergency seems like a big use of time that could be better spent on day-to-day operations, fund raising, or other types of planning. However, when disaster does strike, emergency planning may determine whether you will have a functional institution to plan for, fund, or operate. On the following page, Courtney Wilson, director of the B&O Railroad Museum in Baltimore, recounts his museum's experience with emergency preparedness planning and implementation.

13.1 Emergency/Disaster Plan

	Have a plan	Practiced the plan	Never Practiced the Plan	Not sure about practicing
Overall	65.8%	59.7%	23.2%	16.6%
Under $125,000	40%	40%	43%	16%
$125,000–$400,000	60%	52%	31%	17%
$400,001–$1,750,000	80%	64%	18%	17%
$1,750,001+	94%	76%	12%	12%
Under 8,000 sq. ft.	47%	44%	36%	19%
8,000–20,000 sq. ft.	65%	54%	28%	19%
20,001–55,000 sq. ft.	75%	65%	19%	16%
55,001+ sq. ft.	90%	40%	43%	16%

It's All in the Planning Not the Plan

By Courtney B. Wilson, Director, Baltimore & Ohio Railroad Museum

American history buffs, architectural historians, and railroad aficionados are celebrating a National Historic Landmark building in Baltimore, Md.—a grand structure, completed in 1884, rising 122 feet above the city's landscape, and crowned by a dome. This 22-sided polygon of brick covering an acre of ground is lit by monumental windows and holds America's premier collection of railroad locomotives and rolling stock. Known to nearly all as the B&O Roundhouse, its paint is fresh, its windows sparkle, and its industrial magnificence is apparent.

Inside, however, are sights out of sync with the sparkling building. As your eyes pass from the building's interior dome and great clerestory windows down toward the historic trains arranged neatly on tracks around the circular room, you can see that something is not quite right. Some appear just fine—clean-cut machines of a previous age on exhibition for all to see. But others are nothing more than wrecks. Paint has peeled, glass is smashed, wooden locomotive cabs are crushed, broken parts are stacked neatly at their sides, and a few of their once-stoic bodies now list precariously to one side.

On Feb. 16 and 17, 2003, a record-breaking snowstorm brought down one-half of the roof of the B&O Roundhouse, the Baltimore & Ohio Railroad Museum's largest exhibition building. More than a half an acre of wood, wrought iron, slate, and snow came crashing down from as high as 65 feet in the air. A reporter from United Press International declared the event to be "the most catastrophic natural disaster in the history of American museums." Two months later, when the damage estimates began to arrive, it was clear that other challenges loomed on the horizon. Though there was more than $30 million in building and collections damage, our insurance would cover only slightly more than $20 million. It became clear that in the midst of Herculean efforts to recover from the storm, we would have to raise an additional $10 million.

About three years earlier, museum staff had written a disaster plan. The process, utilizing existing examples from similar institutions and government agencies, took nearly a year to complete. Curatorial staff guided the process, and a combination of staff and volunteers wrote the final document. Everyone on staff—from housekeeper to executive secretary—was involved in its preparation, which required thought, research, hours of staff interviews, and the gathering of technical and practical information from everywhere, including the Yellow Pages. In the end, the final product weighed in at several pounds. Training sessions were held, and each staff member was provided with an abbreviated desk-top reference that had tabs labeled with chapter headings such as FIRE, THEFT, MEDICAL EMERGENCY and other subjects that most museum professionals would rather not have in their vocabulary. And so it was complete.

Slightly before midnight on Feb. 16, 2003, the first alarm sounded at the museum, signaling the first of three partial roof collapses that would take place over the next 12 hours. The snow depth was reaching its zenith of 28 inches, and sleet was beginning to fall from the sky. Only two of us were able to reach the museum in the early hours of the morning. It became apparent that the damage to the building was so overwhelming and its condition so unstable, we couldn't rescue artifacts from the piles of rubble and melting snow without risk to life and limb. Weeks passed before the structure was stable enough to allow staff inside. Yet decisions had to be made, planning completed, and technical references consulted in anticipation of that moment of entry.

But no one had a copy of the disaster plan at home. Thus we had to rely upon our experience of researching, creating and writing the disaster plan. Lessons learned during the process of creation guided important decisions and curatorial planning efforts. Other decisions clearly outside of the disaster plan's scope were made in consultation with trusted senior staff, board members, and, well, by the seat of our pants.

The process of structural stabilization, artifact extrication, emergency conservation, planning, rebuilding and restoration has been a saga lasting nearly two years. We anticipate that another six years will pass before all of the damaged locomotives and rolling stock are restored. But we will make a full recovery, and the disaster has given us an opportunity to examine the institution's core values and plan for expansion and renewal. There were losses of important and treasured artifacts that are extremely painful to acknowledge, yet no loss of life or personal injury occurred.

My experience through this chapter of tragedy and triumph in the museum's history leads me to present a short list of annotated thoughts about the importance of disaster preparedness and planning efforts.

The preservation of life and the prevention of injury are of the utmost importance. (We refused to let one staff member enter the unstabilized building and retrieve a copy of the museum's disaster plan from his desk.)

The decisions made in the first 48 hours following an incident will have long-lasting implications on how your institution is perceived. (Media rained down upon us within hours of the incident's "discovery." Presenting the facts, without speculation, in a manner that evoked strength, confidence, and control produced media coverage that has been positive and sympathetic over the long term.)

Universal staff participation in the creation of a unique disaster plan is essential. (Simply "adopting" a plan from a similar institution would not have created a body of critical knowledge among staff members in the absence of the actual document.)

Create a plan that, in addition to specific technical direction and procedure, has universal application. (For example, our plan did not have a chapter tab titled ROOF COLLAPSE.)

There are challenges ahead, but we have ventured a great distance. Since the museum's disaster plan was approved in January 2000, some staff have moved on to other institutions, we've reorganized the staff several times, and new and energetic staff have come aboard. The body of knowledge garnered from the year-long process of creating the disaster plan so long ago is certainly not as sharp as it was on the morning of Feb. 17, 2003, and is completely foreign to approximately half of my colleagues. Therefore, soon we will open up the plan and start the process all over again. ■

While the B&O Railroad Museum's experience was particularly traumatic, in most museums emergency preparedness plans do not just sit on the shelf. Thirty four percent of respondents with plans report having implemented them, most in the last 15 years.

13.2 Implementation of Emergency/Disaster Plan

	Yes	Year(s) implemented						
		Before 1990	1990-95	1996-99	2000-02	2003	2004	Year not specified
Overall	34.4%	9.5%	37.2%	36.5%	18.6%	8.0%	4.4%	6.6%

This was most often for severe weather, followed by fire and flood. Other incidents ran a distant fourth, with power outage the most frequent among them.

13.3 For What Events Was Plan Implemented?

	Fire	Flood	Severe weather	Earth-quake	Bomb threat	Civil unrest	Terrorism	Theft	Toxic chemical/ gas spill	Other	No response
Overall	20.1%	18.2%	49.3%	6.6%	6.2%	0.7%	4.4%	3.3%	4.0%	13.9%	1.5%

So what do museums cover in their emergency preparedness/disaster plans?

13.4 What Does the Emergency Plan Cover

Fire	93.7%
Flood	64.3%
Severe weather	80.5%
Earthquake	39.6%
Bomb threat	59.2%
Civil unrest	27.8%
Terrorism	34.4%
Theft	55.0%
Toxic chemical/gas spill	39.2%
Other	13.6%
Power outage/power problem	5.2%
Medical/trauma/injury/accident	6.3%
No response	1.5%

"Other" consists of animal escapes/bites/incidents; lost or missing children; and building/systems failures. Some respondents list miscellaneous other incidents, many of which are particular to specific museums: man overboard, tidal waves, nuclear power plant explosion, train derailments, radiological emergency. Therein lies the heart of an emergency response plan: it has to be written to account for risks faced by your particular museum, which may be unusual or uncommon. Museums developing emergency plans are advised to study national data on the potential risks to their geographic area for flood, wildfire, earthquake, tornados, etc., and study their immediate surroundings for other threats. Maybe you have a nuclear power plant in your backyard or a biohazard facility or high-security prison. This is one reason that taking an "off the shelf" model plan and adapting it can be dangerous. Wilson persuasively argues that the process of planning is more important than having the plan, as planning embeds knowledge in the organization. Without a personalized assessment of your museum's risks, you won't know whether your plan covers the relevant issues.

Health/Safety/Emergency Training
Almost half of respondents provide training on a variety of basic health, safety, and emergency issues to their staff.

14.1 Types of Training Provided to Staff

	Training is provided	Training is mandatory for all staff	For those who provide training		
			Training is mandatory for some staff	Training is optional	No response on mandatory/ optional status
Emergency response	47.8%	42.9%	41.9%	10.9%	4.3%
First aid/CPR	41.2%	16.4%	57.7%	22.4%	3.4%
General health and safety	47.9%	45.3%	33.5%	15.4%	5.9%
Hazardous material handling	33.8%	17.1%	68.9%	10.8%	3.2%

Some data on training by governance type, discipline, etc., are provided in "Specialized Breakouts." The largest quarter of museums (in size and budget) are roughly three times more likely to provide training than the smallest quarter of museums. For hazardous material training, the difference is even greater.

Insurance

In the best of all possible worlds, museums would do such a great job managing risk that nothing bad would ever happen. Then we wouldn't need insurance. But this is the real world; bad things do happen. And prudent museums have insurance to make sure that they get financial compensation for their loss. Having the money to rebuild, compensate someone for an injury, or "replace" a collections object is far inferior than a situation in which the building did not burn down, the person did not fall, or the object did not shatter. But it is better than nothing. Budgeting for risk management is a balancing act between allocating time and money to policies and procedures that avert bad things (sprinkler systems, salt for the sidewalk, training on object handling) and insurance to make up for the ones that happen anyway.

Eric S. Fischer, senior vice president of Willis Fine Art, Jewelry & Specie, contributes this overview examining the place of insurance in museum risk management and the kinds of insurance museums carry.

What Part Does Insurance Play in Overall Risk Management?

By Eric S. Fischer, Senior Vice President, Willis Fine Art, Jewelry & Specie

Insurance is the substitution of a small certain expense for a large uncertain loss. It also transfers the risk, protects against uncertainty, shares the loss, and reduces anxiety.

One can separate risk into two types: 1) Speculative (gambling) and 2) Pure Risk (possibility of damage from windstorm, fire, etc.). Insurance is designed to respond to pure risk.

The first step in risk management should be to identify and analyze hazards that threaten the collection and building(s). This should be a survey of the museum's operation conducted by staff and external experts, each identifying possible losses from such causes as human interaction (vandalism, theft . . .); natural disasters (floods, earthquake, hurricanes, tornados, snow . . .); physical plant mishaps (fire, HVAC failure, sewer back ups . . .), and accidents (a car crashes into the museum, power lines are down . . .). Then the museum should consider the various methods of handling those risks.

The first and most important method is to try and reduce the likelihood of a loss. Techniques for preventing a loss or reducing the likelihood of a potential loss can include such actions as installing sprinkler systems, maintaining central station burglar alarms, and keeping work areas clean and free of any combustible materials, to name but a few.

Insurance, which is only a part of the overall risk management process, is a transfer of the potential financial loss to an insurance company through the payment of premiums. In the event of a loss, the company provides funds through a claim payment that hopefully will return the museum to its original position (or as close as possible given the circumstances). The real key is to understand the type of policy you have purchased and how the policy covers your potential losses.

Selecting an insurance agent/broker who understands your institution's particular needs is an integral part of the risk-transfer process. A knowledgeable agent/broker will point out the best insurance products available, access loss-control services (such as consulting, surveys, training) provided by the insurance companies, and keep you up-to-date on changes that may affect museums and cultural institutions.

Basic Types of Insurance?

"Property Insurance" incorporates various coverages such as insurance for the contents contained within your building—including desks, chairs, computers, valuable, papers, and any other non-collection items—as well as the building itself. The construction of the building has a lot to do with your premium; fire-resistant construction poses less of a risk to an insurer than a wood-frame building does. Carefully examine the method of valuation for losses under this coverage. Will the policy provide complete coverage in the event of a loss? Will the insurance funds pay for materials that reflect the historic nature of the building? Work with your agent/broker to ensure that you have the coverage that best fits your institution. Ask questions until you understand exactly what the policy will and will not cover.

Other coverages provided by "Property Insurance" include:
•"Builders Risk" for building expansions/new construction
•"Business Income" for income lost during a renovation after a covered loss
•"Extra Expense" for any additional expenses necessary to continue operating
•"Boiler and Machinery" for any pressure device (e.g., steam heat) or operating machine that has a sudden and accidental breakdown

Commercial General Liability may be the most important coverage a museum purchases. This covers your liability as a public institution with regular visitors. This will protect you against claims for medical expenses a visitor makes after an accident on the premises; damage to property owned by others or an employee (this also can include automobile liability); personal injury; and advertising injury (e.g., claims of damage arising from your marketing activities—copyright infringement, unfair competition, etc.).

Directors and Officers insurance covers liability arising out the actions and decisions made by the directors and officers in your institution. (See Margo Dundon's essay on this topic.)

Workers' Compensation benefits are paid for on-the-job injuries, regardless of negligence on anyone's part. Even employees injured as a result of their own negligence are entitled to benefits and cannot sue the employer. Depending on the state you live in, workers' compensation insurance is available either through a state fund or private insurance (most states). If you are a federal employee, please see the Federal Employees Compensation Act.

An Umbrella Liability policy is written over a primary policy to increase the overall amount of protection. There are three reasons to purchase this coverage. It 1) provides coverage in excess of an underlying policy at an affordable price, 2) covers losses not covered by other policies, and 3) replaces coverage for underlying polices when an underlying limit is exhausted.

A museum looking to purchase Fine Art and Collections insurance should look for the broadest coverage available—an all-risk policy with only the following exclusions: gradual deterioration, inherent vice, moth, vermin and rodents, war, government action, nuclear contamination/radiation, and shipments by regular U.S. mail. Depending on the size of your collection, you may want to insure at a Probable Maximum Loss (PML). Since the premium is based on the limit of insurance you purchase, this method allows you to set a loss limit that is not the value of your entire collection but rather represents what you believe would be lost in event of a major loss (fire, flood, theft). You also may want to insure collection objects at the "current market value" at the time of the loss rather than schedule your collection and update the values on a regular basis, which can get rather expensive.

After the terrorist acts of Sept. 11 2001, terrorism was excluded from most, if not all, insurance policies. Because this provided a tremendous hindrance to many aspects of business (including museum exhibitions), the Terrorism Risk Insurance Act of 2002 (TRIA) was passed by Congress and signed into law in November 2002. The act requires all companies offering property insurance coverage in the United States to offer "qualified" terrorism coverage. The TRIA coverage was not as comprehensive as the pre-Sept. 11 coverage, but it enabled many projects to continue. As time passed, a few insurance companies once again began to offer a more comprehensive form of terrorism coverage. As stated above, your agent/broker should keep you updated on this and all aspects of insurance as it relates to museums and other cultural institutions (Note: TRIA is due to expire at the end of 2005 and will renew only if Congress passes legislation to continue it.)

Event/Exhibition Cancellation insurance is also available. This coverage will reimburse you for your expenses and any unrealized profit for the cancellation/curtailment of an exhibition for events beyond your control (airline strikes, flooding, snow storms, etc.). But it does not cover losses from poor attendance or contractual problems with organizers/lenders. ■

Types of Coverage

Ninety-one percent of the museums responding to the survey have some type of insurance. Most of the remaining nine percent did not provide information about their coverage, though they presumably have some. (Most are, for example, inside larger parent organizations that are presumably insured). The most common types of coverage reported are commercial/general liability, collections/fine arts, directors & officers liability, and exhibitions/loans.

15.1 Insurance Coverage Held by Respondents

	Presently carry	Presently carry but considering dropping	Investigating/ planning to carry by 2005	No response
Commercial/general liability	75.9%	0.1%	0.3%	23.7%
Automobile	44.9%	0.1%	1.1%	54.0%
Collections/fine arts	62.1%	0.3%	2.0%	35.5%
Directors & Officers liability	59.7%	0.2%	4.1%	36.0%
Event cancellation	3.9%	0.1%	2.0%	94.0%
Exhibitions/loans	49.7%	0.0%	1.2%	49.2%
Transit	18.8%	0.1%	0.8%	80.3%
Terrorism	19.8%	0.3%	1.6%	78.3%
Other	13.5%	0.1%	0.0%	86.4%

Here is a summary of insurance coverage by governance and operating expenses. See the appendices for more details for other segments of the data.

15.2 Insurance Coverage by Governance and Operating Expenses

	Commercial/ general liability	Automobile	Collections/ fine arts	Directors and Officers liability	Event cancellation	Exhibitions/ loans	Transit	Terrorism	Other
Government	59%	43%	58%	35%	6%	50%	23%	14%	5%
Private nonprofit	82%	46%	64%	69%	4%	49%	18%	22%	17%
Dual	74%	43%	65%	43%	0%	59%	14%	14%	4%
Under $125,000	70%	13%	48%	37%	2%	29%	8%	7%	8%
$125,000– $400,000	75%	37%	61%	60%	2%	47%	15%	10%	9%
$400,001– $1,750,000	81%	59%	71%	75%	5%	60%	22%	27%	17%
$1,750,001+	88%	82%	80%	82%	8%	76%	35%	41%	24%

Note that insurance coverage appears to be very stable; few respondents intend to drop or add coverage in the near future. The exception to this is directors and officers liability (D&O) insurance; nearly 4 percent of respondents are considering adding this in the near future. While only 60 percent overall report having D&O, 69 percent of private nonprofit museums have this coverage. It is actually surprising this number is not higher, given the litigious nature of our society today and the legal responsibility board members bear for the actions of their museums. Margo Dundon, president & CEO of the Museum of Science and History, Jacksonville, Fla., contributes these thoughts on the importance of D&O insurance to a museum's risk management package.

Just D&O It!

By Margo Dundon, President & CEO of the Museum of Science and History, Jacksonville, Fla.

In the course of a MAP survey I conducted not too long ago, I discovered that the participant museum carried no form of insurance whatsoever. As I discussed the potential pitfalls of a lack of coverage with the museum's board, I was interrupted by an elderly trustee who said, "Missy, you're talking nonsense. People don't sue museums."

I wasn't sure if I was most stunned by being called "missy," by the pronouncement that my concerns were nonsense, or by the naive belief that museums and their boards are somehow immune from lawsuits.

While surveys indicate that a substantial percentage of museums carry general liability insurance, a significantly smaller number carry Directors and Officers Liability Insurance (D&O). Some boards and directors may not know exactly what D&O is or why it is important for their museums. Others may be aware of D&O but, as they struggle to keep operating expenses as low as possible, see it as a luxury. This is especially true if they possess the mistaken belief that museums, held in public affection just behind the flag, motherhood, and apple pie, do not get sued. The reality is that nonprofit institutions, including museums, can and do get sued, both by their employees and the public.

If someone is injured in a museum, the incident usually is covered by general liability insurance. D&O insurance, which is separate from the general liability policy, protects board members, administrative staff, and the institution from liability created by board actions.

In today's litigious society, lawsuits are sometimes brought in response to actions and decisions made by nonprofit management and governance. The

Insurance Journal reports that these disputes usually revolve around hiring and firing decisions, employee supervision, harassment, the application of nonprofit assets, and interpretation of nonprofit charters. Almost any day-to-day decision or action in a museum can trigger a lawsuit that not only could hurt the organization financially but also might threaten the personal assets of its trustees and executives.

Some museums may operate under the assumption that their state laws protect them from suits against their board members and directors. However, the Nonprofit Risk Management Center reports that in all but a handful of states the doctrine of charitable immunity has been abolished.

While it is true that the lawsuits are seldom successful, the costs to defend against claims, even frivolous claims, can be high. D&O insurance indemnifies directors and officers of nonprofit institutions, including museums, for damages and defense costs arising from lawsuits. These matters often get settled, and the ability to have an insurance company participate in settlement negotiations may be reason enough to carry the appropriate coverage.

Some sought-after board candidates may be reluctant to serve on nonprofit boards if the organization does not provide D&O insurance, since they could be forced to pay for legal fees and damages out of their personal assets. My own experience as a museum director has taught me that most savvy prospective board members ask if the museum has D&O coverage. On at least two occasions I have been asked to provide documentation of such coverage before corporations would allow their employees to serve on our board. In fact, BoardSource's website (www.boardsource.org) provides a list of questions prospective board members should ask when considering service on a nonprofit board. Among those questions is, "Does the organization have directors and officers liability coverage?"

It should be noted that D&O policies are not standard, and coverage varies from one provider to the next. In addition, the market for D&O is competitive, allowing museums of all sizes to obtain coverage at reasonable cost. With access to D&O coverage, no museum should put its board or institution at risk.

Collections/fine arts is another important but contentious area of insurance. It is important because collections lie at the heart of what most museums do. It is contentious because some museum professionals believe that placing a value on collections material is both arbitrary (some collections have no market value) and dangerous (it may tempt a governing authority or parent organization to sell the collections for cash). Here is data by discipline on which museums carry collections insurance, compared to the percent of such museums holding collections (from 2003 *Museum Financial Information*).

15.3 Collections Insurance by Discipline

	% with collections insurance	% holding collections
Arboretum/botanic garden	46%	83%
Art museum	91%	85%
Children's/youth museum	36%	11%
General museum	58%	86%
Historic house/site	66%	73%
History museum/ historical society	52%	84%
Natural history/anthropology museum	57%	79%
Nature center	24%	33%
Science/technology center/museum	43%	48%
Specialized museum	60%	71%
Zoo/aquarium	39%	62%

The following essay examines some of the issues surrounding the selection and use of collections/fine arts insurance.

Knowing Your Collections Are Insured ...Priceless

By Elizabeth Merritt, Director, AAM Museum Advancement & Excellence

Museums hold collections in trust for the public. This stewardship responsibility requires thoughtful resource allocation both to prevent damage to the collections and to make restitution should damage or loss occur. To meet this stewardship responsibility, a museum must devote adequate financial and staff resources to collections care, conservation, and emergency preparedness. A good risk-management plan also includes strategies for repairing or replacing material if damage or loss occurs. This usually involves collections insurance.

How Much Coverage Should a Museum Purchase?

Most museums do not insure for the full value of their collections for two reasons:

•The value is constantly fluctuating, and there is no way to keep it current at every point in time.

•It is not economical. For most museums, insuring for the full value of their collections would be an irresponsible use of financial resources that could go toward preventing loss through other methods, such as fire suppression and conservation.

Therefore, museums usually purchase "blanket insurance"—insurance that covers loss of any covered object up to a given amount—for an amount less than the full value of the collection. This insured value often is determined by calculating "probable maximum loss"—the estimated amount of financial loss that would occur in a single event that did not destroy the whole collection. Each museum has to assess its own collection, storage and exhibit environments, and risk factors to arrive at this amount. For example, a museum in a floodplain might calculate its probable maximum loss by assessing the damage that would occur if its basement storage rooms flooded. A museum in an earthquake-prone area might calculate potential damage to collections based on a scenario in which one wing of the building collapses.

What If the Material Is Irreplaceable?

Some collections material is truly unique and irreplaceable. In a larger sense, however, it constitutes a cultural or scientific asset for the community the museum serves. Even if a loss is total, insurance can enable the museum to purchase a comparable asset, if not a replacement, that can serve the museum's mission and the community's needs in a way similar to the lost material.

How Do We Determine Value?

For the purposes of collections insurance, valuation usually is handled in one of two ways.

•Schedules. Some museums that insure a limited number of objects use a "schedule," listing specific pieces and the values for which they are insured. These values are the basis for compensation at time of loss. Note that such schedules may need to be updated frequently to reflect accurate values and may leave newly acquired material without insurance coverage if it has not yet been added to the schedule. This method is rarely practical for large collections.

•Blanket coverage. Many museums purchase blanket insurance that covers all the collections described, in a general way, in the insurance policy. Usually the insured value for a given piece is specified as "market value at time of loss." The museum and its insurance agent should discuss how market value would be determined by the loss adjuster. The museum may need to be able to produce documentation such as inventories, condition reports, and photographs to support this valuation.

What If the Material Has No Market Value?

While insurance coverage usually is written for "market value at time of loss," some collections have no market value, either because they have no commercial worth (e.g., geological core samples, institutional archives) or because it is illegal to sell them (e.g., endangered species). In this case the museum's collections staff should work with the insurance underwriter to determine an alternate method of valuation. These alternatives can include:

•an amount that reflects the cost of re-collecting and/or preparing and curating the material

•an amount that the museum feels would help "make it whole" again if the loss occurs

The fact that these values cannot be validated in the marketplace should not be a barrier as long as the museum and the underwriter can agree on the basis for valuation and the amount of the premium. Negotiation of a method of determining value should take place before a loss occurs—this is not something to argue about while salvaging artifacts from the rubble.

Note: This essay first appeared as a Fact Sheet in the members-only section of the AAM website. Fact Sheets are an AAM Information Center resource available to all AAM individual and institutional members.

Additional Resources

The American Federation of Arts has an Artsure Insurance Program and answers a series of frequently asked questions on its website: www.artsure-ins.com/co_brand/afa/faq.html.

The Free Management Library, hosted by the Management Assistance Program for Nonprofits, offers several articles on different aspects of insurance and includes a dictionary of insurance terms: www.managementhelp.org.

The Huntington T. Block Insurance Agency website has a series of frequently asked questions about insurance issues specific to museums: www.huntingtonblock.com. ■

Insurance for Museums within Parent Organizations

Museums within larger parent organizations often receive support from the parent—including security, building and grounds maintenance, pest control, development assistance, etc.—that do not appear in their operating budgets. They also often are covered by the parent's insurance or the parent pays their insurance costs, wholly or in part. Here are summaries of insurance coverage for respondents overall and by governance, operating expenses, and interior space. See "Specialized Breakouts" for more details for these segments of the data.

15.4 Parental Involvement in Insurance (for respondents with parent organizations)

	Institution fully covered under parent	Covered under parent, but maintains separate riders	Not covered under parent	No response	Parent has regulations/ guidelines to which museum must adhere
Overall	64.3%	18.7%	9.4%	7.7%	59.6%
Government	63%	21%	7%	10%	64%
Private nonprofit	71%	13%	11%	5%	52%
Dual	41%	41%	15%	3%	68%
Under $125,000	70%	16%	10%	4%	61%
$125,000–$400,000	64%	19%	9%	8%	62%
$400,001–$1,750,000	65%	18%	8%	9%	61%
$1,750,001+	50%	34%	13%	2%	61%

Some museums have separate riders to cover collections, exhibitions, and/or incoming or outgoing loans of objects.

15.5 Does the Parent Organization Pay for Insurance

	Pay all costs	Pay some costs	Not pay	No response
Overall	59.1%	16.0%	13.2%	11.7%
Government	57%	18%	9%	16%
Private nonprofit	66%	11%	17%	6%
Dual	41%	27%	21%	12%
Under $125,000	69%	11%	14%	7%
$125,000–$400,000	60%	14%	13%	14%
$400,001–$1,750,000	58%	16%	13%	13%
$1,750,001+	40%	34%	20%	6%
Under 8,000 sq. ft.	70%	9%	15%	6%
8,000–20,000 sq. ft.	53%	14%	15%	18%
20,001–55,000 sq. ft.	63%	18%	9%	10%
55,001+ sq. ft.	48%	27%	18%	7%

"Self-insurance"

Twenty percent of respondents "self-insure." Large museums or parent organizations, for example, may maintain an insurance pool and run their own insurance programs with risk assessors and loss adjustors, effectively acting as their own insurance agents and underwriter. However, museums that say they are "self-insured" often they mean they have no insurance and intend to pay for repair or replacement of collections material out of general operating or capital funds. Often this means that the collections are effectively uninsured.

15.6 Meaning of Self-insurance (for the 20% of respondents who self-insure)

	Set aside and manage a designated fund with internal loss assessment/ payment	Replace/ repairs out of general fund budget	Does not replace value of losses	Other	No response
Overall	25.8%	48.4%	11.7%	15.7%	10.1%
Government	31%	43%	11%	16%	11%
Private nonprofit	14%	67%	13%	9%	7%
Dual	26%	26%	16%	32%	11%

There is also the issue of how museums offset the costs of deductibles or small claims that are not worth submitting to an insurance agency. Very few museums maintain a fund to cover such costs.

15.7 Does the Museum Maintain a Small Claims/Deductibles Fund

	Yes	Median fund size	N for median	No	No response
Overall	6.2%	$5,000	37	84.8%	9%

Cost of Insurance

Museums that purchase insurance spend a median of $12,000, 2.8 percent of their operating expenses, on insurance. Of the 470 respondents with parent organizations, 132 (28 percent) have some or all of their insurance costs covered by the parent organization. The median amount covered by the parent (when it covers any of the insurance costs) is 100 percent.

15.8 Insurance Costs—Overall

	10th percentile	25th percentile	50th percentile	75th percentile	90th percentile	Number of responses
Total insurance costs	$1,470	$3,857	$12,000	$41,000	$126,365	883
As percent of total operating expenses	0.8%	1.6%	2.8%	4.8%	9.0%	837
Paid by the institution	$1,500	$3,900	$12,352	$39,722	$120,563	783
Paid by the parent (where applicable)	$1,006	$2,458	$8,800	$42,264	$1,159,674	132

This survey did not deal with the costs of providing health insurance to employees, a significant and growing cost to museums. However, in summer 2004, AAM partnered with the Johns Hopkins Center for Civil Society Studies' Listening Post Project on a survey of nonprofits, including museums. This essay (see next page) by Richard O'Sullivan, assistant director of the Listening Post Project, and Lester Salamon, director, Civil Society Studies, explains the results of that research.

Museums Share in Health Benefits Cost Squeeze. But Who Pays?

By Richard O'Sullivan, Assistant Director, Listening Post Project, and Lester Salamon, Director, Johns Hopkins Center for Civil Society Studies

A recently completed study conducted by the Johns Hopkins Listening Post Project discovered that nonprofit organizations, including museums, have been hit especially hard by today's double-digit increases in health-benefit costs. What is more, while for-profit firms can pass more of these costs on to customers, nonprofits are finding it necessary to shift a disproportionate share of the resulting burden to their already less well-paid employees.

A slightly smaller share of museums than other nonprofits reported increases in health benefit costs that exceeded the national average. But this may be due to the fact that many museums are parts of larger institutions, such as universities, that bury health-benefit costs in broader employee benefit packages. According to Dr. Lester Salamon, director of the Listening Post Project and the Johns Hopkins Center for Civil Society Studies, "This may actually lead to greater trouble for museums since they may not be aware of the impact that rising health-benefit costs are having on their budgets and hence on the ability of their organizations to serve their communities."

Drawing on a national panel of nonprofit organizations serving as organizational "listening posts" on major challenges facing nonprofit organizations, the health-benefits survey found that 63 percent of nonprofit organizations experienced health-benefit cost increases of 11 percent or more over the past year. For 15 percent of those organizations, the increase was over 20 percent. This means that the average nonprofit health-benefit cost increase exceeded the 11.2 percent average for all firms revealed by a recent Kaiser Family Foundation survey. Significantly, moreover, a majority of nonprofit organizations in all size classes reported increases of 11 percent or more, suggesting that even large nonprofits are not large enough to achieve real economies of scale in health-benefit purchase.

These increases are especially significant in view of the relatively high proportions of nonprofits that provide health insurance benefits to their employees. Overall, 93 percent of the listening posts provide health insurance to their employees compared to only 63 percent of all employers. Even among the smallest organizations—those with fewer than 10 employees—76 percent of nonprofit organizations offered employees health benefits compared to 52 percent of all very small employers. Clearly, health insurance is one of the crucial benefits of nonprofit employment, compensating in part for the relatively low wages that nonprofits pay.

Size and Impact of Health Benefit Costs May Be Invisible to Museums

Notably, only 49 percent of museums reported health-benefit cost increases of 11 percent or more, well below the 63 percent for all nonprofits. However, this may partly be explained by the fact that significant numbers of museums are parts of larger institutions that do not break out the health-benefit portion of their benefit packages. This means that fewer museums may be aware of the true costs of the health benefits they offer.

Do Nonprofits Make Better Insurance Customers?

In addition, nonprofit organizations proved very reluctant to eliminate health benefits because of their importance to employees. "Salaries are already so low in the museum field, we do not want to balance the budget by reducing employee benefits if we can possibly help it," noted Deborah Smith, the executive director of the Pejepscot Historical Society in Brunswick, Maine. Several respondents reported asking their employees to consider the trade-offs between health benefits and other compensation, including wages and cost-of-living increases. This resistance to eliminating health benefits coupled with the high incidence of coverage suggests that nonprofit organizations should be extremely attractive customers for health insurers.

The "Silent Tax"

While nonprofit organizations were reluctant to eliminate health benefits, they found it necessary to shift more of the costs to their employees. Thus, three in five organizations reported shifting health costs to their employees by increasing employees' share of prescription drug costs (45 percent), increasing co-payments or deductibles on office visits (40 percent), or increasing employees' share of premiums (36 percent). In addition, a third of respondents reported that they reduced or cut raises, bonuses, or non-healthcare benefits because of rising health-benefit costs. "Shifting more healthcare costs to nonprofit employees may be the path of least resistance, but it may also be the path to oblivion for our organizations, which depend on the dedication of our employees to meet the health and welfare needs of our often-disadvantaged populations," said Peter Goldberg, chair of the Listening Post Project Advisory Committee and president and CEO of the Alliance for Children and Families.

The Last Word

Jill Hartz, director of the University of Virginia Art Museum in Charlottesville, summarized the study's findings for many of the listening posts calling for concerted action by the nonprofit sector when she observed, "These findings clearly show that nonprofits believe that healthcare is an essential benefit for employees and are doing all they can to maintain that benefit in the face of escalating costs, both in healthcare and basic operations. If health costs continue to rise, this challenge may be insurmountable and could result in high employee turnover as well as cutbacks in the services provided by nonprofits."

To learn more about the results of the Health Benefits Sounding and other Listening Post research, visit www.jhu.edu/listeningpost/news. If you would like to become a Listening Post, e-mail listeningpostproject@jhu.edu. ∎

Policies, Plans, and Other Documents

Museums completing self-studies for the Museum Assessment and Accreditation programs often find there is a gap between practice and documentation. They may think that "everybody knows" what to do, how to do it, what the policy is, what the goals are. In fact, board, staff, and volunteers often have their own ideas on these points. Putting policies and plans in writing gives people something to look at and allows them to test their understanding of what "everybody knows."

A policy or plan that is not written down is really an informal understanding, arrived at by one person or a few people without sufficient input or communication from everyone else. Writing it down creates the opportunity for a formal process of involving stakeholders—community, volunteers, staff, members of the governing authority. This increases the chance that it will be a good policy or plan, with more options and better information taken into account. It also encourages stakeholders to commit to implementing the resulting decisions. In addition, approving plans and policies is a key responsibility of the governing authority; how can it formally approve something that has not been presented in writing?

Written documents also create institutional memory. In one recent three-year period half the directors of accredited museums changed jobs. Some museums may lose half to three-quarters of their staff in one year, particularly if they are going through major changes such as new building projects, moving, altering their governance structure, creating a new mission, merging, etc. Most governing authorities have term limits and regular turnover of the members, sometimes on a yearly schedule. When people leave, they take with them an immense amount of institutional memory. If a really good policy or plan is not in writing, how do you pass it on to the new people? How do you orient incoming board members and staff?

Written documents also provide accountability. There is an ever greater expectation that museums be transparent in their operations. People who support the museum—private donors; city, state, or federal government; corporations and foundations—want to see evidence of good management and sound decision making, often in the form of written policies and plans. Museum accreditation revolves around the institution's written documents as well as an examination of how they were developed and how they are implemented.

16.1 Policies/Plans

	Have	Do not have	In development	No response
Facilities use policy	56.6%	26.2%	6.4%	10.7%
Building rental policy	57.0%	28.9%	5.5%	8.5%
Special events policy for outside groups	51.3%	32.6%	5.5%	10.6%
Special events policy for museum-sponsored events	36.2%	45.0%	6.4%	12.4%
Filming policy	39.4%	43.6%	6.3%	10.7%
Filming agreement	24.6%	54.6%	5.6%	15.1%
Policy on use of funds resulting from insurance claims on losses to collections	17.7%	63.0%	3.9%	15.5%
Cyclical maintenance plan	38.8%	36.9%	10.5%	13.8%
Emergency preparedness/disaster plan	60.0%	23.9%	8.8%	7.4%
Historic structure master plan	21.7%	56.7%	7.9%	13.8%
Integrated pest management plan	39.2%	43.7%	6.4%	10.7%

It is equally important to review these documents on a regular basis. An out-of-date policy or plan can be worse than none—creating the illusion that you have what you need when, in fact, it doesn't reflect your current circumstances. The majority of respondents report updating their policies and plans "as needed." About 37 percent could give the date of the last update, with the median date reported being 2003 (the year previous to the survey).

16.2 Policy Update Schedule (% base are those who have the policy)

	Monthly	Quarterly	Annually	Other regular	As needed	No response
Facilities use policy	0.4%	0.4%	19.4%	3.9%	60.1%	15.6%
Building rental policy	0.9%	0.3%	22.0%	2.9%	58.1%	15.8%
Special events policy for outside groups	0.8%	0.2%	20.9%	2.9%	58.8%	16.4%
Special events policy for museum-sponsored events	0.7%	0.0%	21.2%	3.0%	58.4%	16.7%
Filming policy	0.6%	0.2%	9.0%	4.4%	65.6%	20.1%
Filming agreement	0.3%	0.0%	7.0%	4.4%	64.4%	23.8%
Cyclical maintenance plan	2.8%	2.3%	29.1%	4.3%	43.4%	18.1%
Emergency preparedness/ disaster plan	0.1%	1.0%	27.4%	3.4%	49.4%	18.6%
Historic structure master plan	0.4%	0.8%	14.1%	7.3%	56.5%	21.0%
Integrated pest management plan	4.0%	1.7%	21.3%	2.7%	53.2%	17.1%

Whether and when a policy is written and updated frequently depends on who is responsible. As with overall responsibility for risk management, it also depends on whether this responsibility is explicitly assigned to that person. The director is cited most often as the position responsible for policy development.

Table 16.3, "Responsibility for Policy/Plan Development" (see next page), omits the columns for educators, conservators, security, and exhibition staff as the values were always under 2 percent, with the following exceptions: Conservators are responsible for integrated pest management plans 3.6 percent of the time, and security staff are responsible for emergency/disaster preparedness plans 7.8 percent of the time.

The numbers are very similar for responsibility for implementation, with slightly more respondents reporting that the responsibility is delegated to staff other than the director.

16.3 Responsibility for Policy/Plan Development

	Director/ CEO/ head of museum	Collections staff	Develop-ment marketing/ PR/ membership	Educator	Manager/ administrator	Security	Facilities manager	Visitor services	Governing authority	Other	No response
Facilities use policy	39.6%	1.6%	4.3%	0.8%	12.3%	0.4%	6.2%	2.2%	11.3%	2.6%	18.5%
Building rental policy	35.9%	0.9%	8.5%	0.9%	13.1%	0.1%	5.0%	3.3%	10.7%	3.8%	17.4%
Special events policy for outside groups	35.8%	0.9%	9.3%	1.0%	13.5%	0.4%	4.8%	3.9%	9.2%	3.2%	18.0%
Special events policy for museum-sponsored events	35.1%	0.8%	10.5%	1.7%	11.8%	0.4%	4.8%	2.3%	7.6%	2.7%	22.3%
Filming policy	28.0%	13.4%	13.6%	0.5%	6.9%	0.2%	1.1%	0.7%	9.8%	2.5%	21.9%
Filming agreement	23.2%	15.6%	13.7%	0.5%	4.1%	0.3%	1.1%	0.3%	9.6%	3.8%	26.8%
Cyclical maintenance plan	22.3%	5.2%	0.2%	0.3%	6.4%	0.3%	31.2%	0.3%	8.0%	2.8%	22.3%
Emergency preparedness/ disaster plan	30.3%	11.7%	0.2%	0.4%	9.1%	7.8%	9.5%	0.7%	5.3%	3.1%	20.2%
Historic structure master plan	36.1%	5.6%	0.8%	0.3%	5.6%	0.0%	5.3%	0.3%	11.5%	6.7%	26.3%
Integrated pest manage-ment plan	17.2%	23.2%	0.2%	0.4%	5.3%	0.7%	20.1%	0.5%	6.4%	3.4%	18.5%

The "Responsibility for Policy/Plan Implementation" table omits the columns for educators, conservators, security, and exhibition staff as the values were always under 2 percent, with the following exceptions: Conservators are responsible for implementation of integrated pest management plans 2.4 percent of the time, and security staff for filming policies 3.4 percent of the time and emergency preparedness/disaster plans 10.6 percent of the time.

16.4 Responsibility for Policy/Plan Implementation

	Director/ CEO/ head of museum	Collections staff	Develop- ment marketing/ PR/ membership	Manager/ administrator	Facilities manager	Visitor services	Governing authority	Other	No response
Facilities use policy	33.7%	2.2%	5.4%	14.2%	10.2%	4.5%	2.4%	4.1%	21.8%
Building rental policy	27.1%	1.1%	10.3%	15.7%	9.0%	6.2%	2.4%	5.5%	21.0%
Special events policy for outside groups	27.2%	1.3%	11.9%	14.5%	7.8%	7.0%	1.7%	5.7%	21.1%
Special events policy for museum-sponsored events	26.2%	2.1%	13.0%	13.4%	7.0%	4.5%	1.7%	5.0%	25.4%
Filming policy	22.6%	12.5%	15.0%	8.7%	2.4%	4.2%	2.5%	2.9%	24.6%
Filming agreement	18.3%	13.9%	15.0%	8.5%	1.6%	2.7%	3.3%	2.7%	30.6%
Cyclical maintenance plan	16.1%	5.2%	0.2%	5.2%	39.9%	0.8%	3.5%	4.2%	23.8%
Emergency preparedness/ disaster plan	29.0%	10.0%	0.6%	7.9%	11.4%	1.7%	1.8%	3.2%	22.7%
Historic structure master plan	39.2%	5.6%	0.0%	5.9%	7.0%	0.3%	5.6%	5.0%	29.4%
Integrated pest management plan	16.5%	20.9%	0.0%	5.6%	25.6%	0.7%	2.2%	3.8%	21.1%

Consult "Specialized Breakouts" for details about these policies/plans by discipline and some other breakouts. Here is a breakdown of presence of these policies/plans by governance, operating expenses, and interior square feet.

16.5 Presence of Policies/Plans by Governance, Size

	Facilities use policy	Building rental policy	Special events policy for outside groups	Special events policy for museum-sponsored events	Filming policy	Filming agree-ment	Policy use of funds from insurance claims on collections	Cyclical mainten-ance plan	Emergency prepared-ness/disaster plan	Historic structure master plan	Integrated pest management plan
Government	63%	55%	56%	43%	47%	29%	20%	48%	73%	22%	53%
Private nonprofit	54%	58%	49%	33%	36%	23%	17%	36%	55%	20%	33%
Dual	78%	63%	63%	49%	51%	27%	27%	61%	71%	37%	59%
Under $125,000	49%	40%	36%	29%	24%	14%	10%	26%	32%	18%	24%
$125,000–$400,000	51%	49%	41%	28%	36%	19%	15%	35%	53%	23%	34%
$400,001–$1,750,000	66%	75%	65%	39%	47%	34%	24%	47%	78%	25%	45%
$1,750,001+	70%	73%	72%	56%	58%	36%	25%	57%	87%	22%	49%
Under 8,000 sq. ft.	47%	41%	37%	25%	31%	21%	10%	26%	38%	15%	29%
8,000–20,000 sq. ft.	56%	53%	45%	31%	34%	21%	17%	38%	58%	26%	33%
20,001–55,000 sq. ft.	63%	69%	61%	41%	45%	28%	20%	44%	72%	21%	39%
55,001+ sq. ft.	70%	75%	74%	53%	53%	33%	28%	56%	83%	22%	62%

On the following page, Elise LeCompte of the Florida Museum of Natural History, writes about developing and implementing museum policies.

Why? Because We Said So!

A Guide to the Development, Implementation, and Enforcement of Museum Policies

By Elise V. LeCompte, Registrar and Assistant Chair, Florida Museum of Natural History

The Importance of Policy

With all of the complex legal and ethical issues that museums now face, policies provide direction on how to proceed in legal and ethical ways. Policies define areas of responsibility and set guidelines, both for those charged with making decisions regarding specific functions of the museum and for those who carry out various activities within the museum. They serve as formal delegations of responsibilities, sanctioned activities, and approved behavior. They enhance the integrity and credibility of important operational decisions.

Written policies provide:

• direction, continuity, and predictability

• accountability for standards and service

• standardized methods for institutions to comply with legal and ethical expectations

• guidelines for all levels of museum staff, volunteers, and visitors regarding expectations, obligations, and rights

• uniformity, by establishing consistency in operations

Policy Development

Drafting a policy requires communication and discussion among members of the governing authority, management, staff, volunteers, and sometimes the constituents that the museum serves. This is rarely easy. There will be varied opinions regarding what should be covered in the policy, how it should be implemented, and who should have responsibility for implementing or enforcing it. Policy development often takes a lot of negotiation, as the museum works through uncertainty and disagreement. It is a time-consuming process that should not be rushed — working through issues is as important as the finished policy.

In some cases a policy can be drafted by one person. Most often, however, policies are best developed by a committee that consists of a broad mix of the constituents listed above. Include staff members from the areas within the museum that will be affected by the policy. If the policy may be controversial, it helps to include a staff member from a division other than that affected, in order to provide objectivity. Usually the director and governing authority, or a representative or committee of the governing authority, reviews a draft, as these are the parties that will be responsible for final approval of a policy.

Before drafting any policy, the committee reviews professional standards, institutional mission and goals, available institutional resources, personnel responsibilities and expectations, and institutional strengths and weaknesses. This helps the committee set priorities and develop effective policies that will work for its specific circumstances. The goal is to end up with policies that reflect the museum's capabilities and can be realistically implemented.

Developing the content of a policy requires attention to:

• mission of the institution

• organizational structure of the institution and available resources

• purpose and objective of the policy (including defining areas of responsibility clearly)

• authority for implementation (including delegating final decision-making authority to one individual or group) and enforcement (including permitting the decision-making authority to grant exceptions in unusual circumstances)

• levels of approval required for the policy

• laws, professional guidelines, and ethical standards that would regulate the policy

People are more likely to comply with policies that are easy to read and understand. Avoid jargon. Short sentences work best. Clearly define terms. State rules in a positive way and explain the reasons for any restrictions.

If the museum includes departments or divisions, develop policies at the broad institutional level first before working on department-specific issues. For example, at the Florida Museum of Natural History the institutional collections policy is supplemented by policies specific to each of its divisions. Each divisional policy covers situations that are unique to that division. However, none of the divisional policies contradicts the institutional policy in any way. All of a museum's policies should complement and support each other.

Policies	Procedures
•General guidelines to regulate the activities of the organization	•Detailed methods for performing an action
•Standards for exercising good judgment	•Protocols to follow when implementing a policy
•Delegate authority for implementation	•Succinct directions to accomplish a specific task
•Not inherently time-limited—endure until circumstances require change	•Step-by-step "how to"
•Approved by the governing authority	•Approved at the staff level

From *Collections Management Policies* by John Simmons, forthcoming from AAM in 2005.

Policies versus Procedures

Policies supply the standards for decision-making and the guidelines for taking action in a given situation. They provide useful guidance, but do not stifle the flexibility needed for ad hoc decisions. Procedures, on the other hand, specify the mechanism and details needed to implement policy. Because procedures are subject to frequent revision and staff usually have the authority to change them, they should be set down in a separate document from the policy itself.

Policy Approval

Policies are approved by the museum's governing authority, as it is legally and ethically accountable for the museum's actions. The governing authority is responsible for ensuring that policies reflect the goals of the museum and that there are resources available to carry them out. In a museum within a larger organization (e.g., city, county, or state government; university; foundation), the governing authority may delegate policy approval down the chain of command, for example to a department head, university president, or provost.

Implementation and Dissemination

Even the best written policy is only effective if it is well implemented and widely disseminated. Once approved, a policy should be distributed to all staff, members of the governing authority, and other affected parties. This might be accomplished through written and electronic formats (i.e., printed documents, e-mail, website) as well as through museum-wide meetings. You may want to schedule training sessions to explain how to comply with the policy. Some policies that address mandated legal procedures for compliance (like those related to the generation and disposal of hazardous waste) may require detailed training sessions that teach museum staff how to comply with the law.

It is a good idea to prepare a cover memo that gives some context for why the policy was developed, who needs to abide by the policy, and how it will affect them. Consider including policies in an orientation packet for incoming members of the governing authority and new staff and volunteers. Some institutions require that staff and volunteers sign a document stating that they have read and will adhere to the museum's policies.

Policy Enforcement

Enforcing policies in a fair and consistent manner helps ensure that they are effective. It is a good idea to delegate responsibility for this to one individual or a small group. It might be the director, one or two board or staff members, or a chair of an appropriate museum committee. For example, at the Florida Museum of Natural History, the chair of the museum's health and safety committee (with backup from the associate director and director) is responsible for the implementation and enforcement of the museum's policies related to health and safety issues.

Establish procedures for reviewing activities to make sure that policies are being followed and are working well. Clarify who has the authority to interpret a policy, to judge when an infraction has occurred, and to decide whether disciplinary or corrective actions will be taken. Establish a procedure for reporting infractions. Some museum personnel manuals specify that willful disregard of the institution's policies may result in disciplinary action or termination of privileges. Requests for exemptions from the policy should include a formal, written petition to the party responsible for its enforcement.

Updating Policies

Policies are not set in stone—developing and revising them is an ongoing process. They have to change as the needs of the institution evolve. Reviewing policies on a regular schedule ensures that they are effective and up-to-date. For example, a disaster-preparedness policy for a museum subject to hurricanes could be reviewed annually prior to the start of the hurricane season. An investment policy may need to be reviewed at the beginning or end of each fiscal year. Policies also should be reviewed and updated whenever any significant changes occur at the museum, even if the review falls outside the normally planned schedule. For example, a construction project (such as the addition of a new wing or a move to a new building) would necessitate a review of policies related to access, security, and health and safety. As new scientific techniques are developed (e.g.,

new and better methods for genetic testing), many natural history museums are developing policies related to specimen and artifact sampling, especially for destructive techniques. Periodic reassessment of or change in a museum's institutional mission and goals also may lead to creating or revising policies. Create procedures for conducting this review and designate who is responsible for ensuring it is accomplished. It is a good idea to get museum-wide input whenever a policy is reviewed and updated as well as when it is first drafted.

Conclusion

Policy development is a complex and often difficult process. However, policies dealing with such issues as collections management, health and safety, access and use, and facilities use (to name a few) are necessary to help guide and protect the museum, its collections, its facilities, its administration, and its staff, volunteers, and visitors as it fulfills its mission and accomplishes its goals. In the long run, the development, implementation, and enforcement of institutional policies is a necessary and rewarding endeavor.

Specialized Breakouts

Notes about Interpreting the Data in this Chapter

Many of the breakouts contain relatively few museums. Please read the section on page 8 on sample size and significance for context on how to interpret data for such small samples. In some tables there are blanks where a number cannot be provided because of the small sample size. For example, in percentile tables we can't provide 10th and 90th percentile figures for very small groups (10 percent may be represent less than one respondent!)

For any data related to parent organizations (their involvement in paying for insurance, for example), the numbers reported are for only that portion of the respondents that have parent organizations.

Section A: Aquarium/Zoos

Total responses = 28

This group includes 24 zoos and four aquariums. Thirty-six percent of these institutions have a parent organization.

A.1

	10th percentile	25th percentile	50th percentile	75th percentile	90th percentile	Number of responses
Operating income	$474,426	$1,419,879	$7,359,646	$16,289,218	$25,044,084	25
Operating expense	$638,194	$2,257,476	$6,085,085	$16,559,889	$24,053,394	26
Attendance	104,000	389,435	602,525	1,039,135	1,387,802	25
Full-time staff	9	39	120	181	231	27
Part-time staff	5.5	15	38	70.5	257.9	26
Maintenance staff full-time	1.0	4.0	13.5	30.8	44.2	28
Maintenance staff part-time	0.0	0.0	1.5	7.8	14.1	28
Total interior square footage	15,000	38,000	113,302	278,621	500,000	19
Insurance costs paid by institution	$9,304	$22,103	$152,691	$267,288	$446,000	18
Insurance costs paid by parent						2
Total insurance costs paid	$9,990	$19,414	$150,383	$270,384	$500,000	19

A.2 Space—presence and allocation as a percentage of total space

	Present in institution (n=28)		10th percentile	25th percentile	50th percentile	75th percentile	90th percentile	Number of responses
	Yes	No						
Exhibitions	71%	0%		31.0%	48.7%	65.5%		8
Collections storage	64%	0%	1.4%	2.4%	4.6%	26.1%	49.5%	10
Non-collections storage	64%	4%	0.8%	1.3%	7.2%	8.8%	17.0%	11
Offices	71%	0%	1.7%	4.5%	6.5%	8.5%	13.9%	12
Education (classrooms)	71%	0%	1.5%	1.9%	2.7%	5.2%	7.6%	13
Library/research	68%	0%	0.1%	0.4%	0.7%	1.0%	1.5%	12
Museum store	68%	4%	0.5%	1.4%	2.5%	6.2%	9.4%	12
Public space/ public functions	54%	4%		8.6%	17.6%	40.0%		7
Food service	68%	0%	1.0%	1.6%	4.3%	8.7%	18.0%	12
Auditorium/ theaters	36%	25%		1.8%	5.1%	17.6%		7
Maintenance	64%	0%	0.7%	3.3%	6.2%	15.2%	19.7%	10
Conservation/ collections prep	39%	14%		0.5%	1.9%	11.6%		6

(*Percentages for yes and no often do not add to 100 percent—the remainder did not answer the question.)

A.3 Space allocation in square feet

	10th percentile	25th percentile	50th percentile	75th percentile	90th percentile	Number of responses
Exhibitions	7,800	46,027	90,000	584,557	1,157,851	13
Collections storage	734	2,215	5,000	20,000	201,350	12
Non-collections storage	290	1,125	2,300	14,625	44,526	12
Offices	550	1,250	4,599	13,762	27,726	14
Education (classrooms)	700	960	2,321	7,000	15,278	15
Library/research	35	175	600	1,250	3,925	14
Museum store	288	600	2,554	5,000	7,027	15
Public space/ public functions		10,500	18,756	147,800		9
Food service	300	475	4,494	10,227	29,361	14
Auditorium/ theaters		3,168	6,140	53,950		7
Maintenance	260	3,070	4,940	13,411	38,056	12
Conservation/ collections prep		1,245	2,725	3,500		6

A.4 What is allowed in building by policy

	Collection areas	Exhibit areas	Staff offices	Public spaces	Grounds
Open flames	4%	7%	11%	7%	36%
Food	29%	54%	96%	89%	93%
Beverages (other than water)	21%	39%	96%	86%	89%
Live plants	57%	79%	89%	79%	82%
Fresh flowers	5%	64%	93%	75%	71%
Dried plant material	61%	79%	79%	71%	75%
Personal artwork	14%	18%	75%	14%	14%
Filming	61%	89%	61%	86%	86%
Photography	57%	93%	71%	93%	93%

Ninety-three percent of respondents indicate that they rent space to outside groups. Eighty-nine percent report that the rental revenue goes to the institution's budget (as opposed to a parent organization or other group).

A.5 Groups space is/would be rented to

	Would rent to	Have rented to in past 5 years
Religious groups	96%	73%
Political groups	77%	46%
Private groups (weddings, parties, graduations, etc.)	96%	81%
Corporate groups	100%	85%
Non-religious nonprofit groups	100%	81%
Other	15%	15%

A.6 Have exclusive agreement with caterer(s)

	Yes, one caterer	Yes, maintain a list of accepted caterers	Median percent commission taken by institution	Average commission	N for mean/ median	No	No response
Overall	32%	14%	12.0%	13.3%	7	50%	4%

A.7 Parking offered

	Have on-site parking	Median number of spaces	N for median	Have off-site parking	Median number of spaces	N for median
	79%	600	21	11%	764	3

Practice and Implementation of the Emergency Plan

Of the 89 percent of zoos/aquaria that have a disaster plan (see last table in this section) 96 percent report having practiced it.

A.8 Year emergency plan practiced

	Year not specified	Before 1996	1996-1999	2000-2002	2003	2004
	8%	4%	0%	8%	32%	48%

A.9 Types of training provided to staff

	Training is provided	For those who provide training			
		Training is mndatory for all staff	Training is mandatory for some staff	Training is optional	No response on mandatory/ optional status
Emergency response	93%	46%	46%	4%	4%
First aid/CPR	96%	4%	89%	4%	4%
General health and safety	82%	57%	35%	9%	0%
Hazardous material handling	93%	31%	58%	8%	4%

A.10 Parental involvement with insurance (for respondents with parent organizations)

Institution fully covered under parent	Covered under parent, but maintains separate riders	Not covered under parent	No response
80%	10%	10%	0%

Seventy percent of respondents indicate that the museum must adhere to the parent organization's regulations or guidelines regarding insurance.

A.11 Does the parent pay for insurance?

Pay all costs	Pay some costs	Not pay	No response
50%	40%	10%	0%

A.12 Insurance types (See also insurance costs figures in first table of this section)

	Presently carry	Presently carry but considering dropping	Investigating/ planning to carry by 2005	No response
Commercial/general liability	82%	0%	0%	18%
Automobile	82%	0%	0%	18%
Collections/fine arts	39%	0%	0%	61%
Directors and officers liability	68%	0%	0%	32%
Event cancellation	4%	0%	0%	96%
Exhibitions/loans	18%	0%	0%	82%
Transit	14%	0%	0%	86%
Terrorism	29%	0%	0%	71%
Other	25%	0%	0%	75%

A.13 Maintain a fund to offset small claims/deductibles

	Yes	Median fund size	N for median	No	No response
	14%	$3,037,500	4	75%	11%

Thirty-nine percent of respondents report being self-insured.

A.14 Meaning of self-insured

	Set aside and manage a designated fund with internal loss assessment/payment	Replace/repairs out of general fund budget	Does not replace value of losses	Other	No response
	55%	55%	9%	18%	0%

A.15 Policies/plans

	Have	Do not have	In development	No response
Facilities use policy	57%	18%	0%	25%
Building rental policy	64%	21%	4%	11%
Special events policy for outside groups	57%	25%	0%	18%
Special events policy for museum-sponsored events	39%	50%	0%	11%
Filming policy	57%	25%	0%	18%
Filming agreement	25%	50%	0%	25%
Policy on use of funds resulting from insurance claims on losses to collections	4%	79%	0%	18%
Cyclical maintenance plan	50%	18%	7%	25%
Emergency preparedness/disaster plan	89%	4%	0%	7%
Historic structure master plan	25%	64%	0%	11%
Integrated pest management plan	64%	25%	4%	7%

Section B: Arboretum/Botanic Gardens

Total responses = 22

Eighteen percent of these institutions have a parent organization.

B.1

	10th percentile	25th percentile	50th percentile	75th percentile	90th percentile	Number of responses
Operating income	$133,000	$502,963	$848,093	$4,293,772	$25,839,117	21
Operating expense	$150,696	$720,856	$1,200,000	$4,299,328	$22,423,889	21
Attendance	15,750	65,000	104,611	292,053	600,000	22
Full-time staff	1	5	13.5	36.8	282	22
Part-time staff	.3	5	11	17.75	67.2	22
Maintenance staff full-time	0.0	1.0	1.5	7.0	34.2	22
Maintenance staff part-time	0.0	0.0	1.0	3.8	9.7	22
Total interior square footage	4,160	15,782	23,000	119,322	422,105	17
Insurance costs paid by institution	$3,281	$13,761	$47,708	$130,113	$705,600	17
Insurance costs paid by parent						0
Total insurance costs paid	$3,281	$13,761	$47,708	$130,113	$705,600	17

B.2 Space—presence and allocation as a percentage of total space

	Present in institution (n=22)		10th percentile	25th percentile	50th percentile	75th percentile	90th percentile	Number of responses
	Yes*	No						
Exhibitions	68%	14%		5.4	12.5	25.8		9
Collections storage	64%	27%		7.8	16.2	30.6		7
Non-collections storage	82%	9%	1.6	8.4	13.1	26.4	30.8	10
Offices	100%	0%	2.5	6.6	11.8	19.2	23.6	13
Education (classrooms)	82%	9%	1.0	3.2	4.8	10.6	40.0	13
Library/research	82%	5%	0.4	0.6	3.3	10.6	17.8	13
Museum store	73%	23%	0.7	2.0	3.0	6.1	10.0	12
Public space/ public functions	82%	9%		10.0	18.8	40.4		9
Food service	46%	50%		1.7	4.7	7.6		6
Auditorium/ theaters	41%	41%		0.7	2.3	4.6		5
Maintenance	86%	5%	0.3	3.3	6.2	15.7	33.2	12
Conservation/ collections prep	68%	23%		2.3	6.2	13.1		8

(*Percentages for yes and no often do not add to 100 percent—the remainder did not answer the question.)

B.3 Space allocation in square feet

	10th percentile	25th percentile	50th percentile	75th percentile	90th percentile	Number of responses
Exhibitions	960	1,836	9,051	47,000	532,320	11
Collections storage		1,829	10,100	38,125		8
Non-collections storage	280	2,673	10,019	22,500	48,000	10
Offices	250	800	2,600	13,500	71,500	14
Education (classrooms)	325	744	2,142	4,625	45,000	14
Library/research	100	120	960	7,452	64,800	13
Museum store	260	946	1,446	3,375	9,400	12
Public space/ public functions	875	2,150	7,995	22,500	48,000	10
Food service		300	2,000	8,500		7
Auditorium/ theaters		725	3,160	6,250		6
Maintenance	120	400	2,000	13,000	21,200	13
Conservation/ collections prep		1,000	4,500	6,600		9

B.4 What is allowed in building by policy

	Collection areas	Exhibit areas	Staff offices	Public spaces	Grounds
Open flames	5%	0%	0%	5%	23%
Food	9%	23%	86%	82%	55%
Beverages (other than water)	9%	18%	86%	91%	50%
Live plants	82%	91%	86%	86%	91%
Fresh flowers	46%	64%	82%	73%	64%
Dried plant material	50%	68%	73%	68%	55%
Personal artwork	9%	32%	82%	27%	14%
Filming	59%	73%	32%	77%	82%
Photography	73%	77%	46%	82%	82%

Ninety-one percent of respondents indicate that they rent space to outside groups. Ninety-five percent report that the rental revenue goes to the institution's budget (as opposed to a parent organization or other group).

B.5 Groups space is/would be rented to

	Would rent to	Have rented to in past 5 years
Religious groups	85%	70%
Political groups	65%	50%
Private groups (weddings, parties, graduations, etc.)	95%	80%
Corporate groups	90%	80%
Non-religious nonprofit groups	95%	85%
Other	0%	0%

B.6 Have exclusive agreement with caterer(s)

	Yes, one caterer	Yes, maintain a list of accepted caterers	Median percent commission taken by institution	Average commission	N for mean/ median	No	No response
Overall	14%	27%	12.0%	10.0%	8	59%	0%

B.7 Parking offered

	Have on-site parking	Median number of spaces	N for median	Have off-site parking	Median number of spaces	N for median
	96%	120	19	5%		1

Practice and Implementation of the Emergency Plan

Of the 59 percent of arboretums/ botanic gardens that have a disaster plan (see last table in this section) 63 percent report having practiced it.

B.8 Year emergency plan practiced

	Year not specified	Before 1996	1996-1999	2000-2002	2003	2004
	10%	0%	0%	0%	50%	40%

B.9 Types of training provided to staff

	Training is provided	For those who provide training			
		Training is mndatory for all staff	Training is mandatory for some staff	Training is optional	No response on mandatory/ optional status
Emergency response	46%	30%	50%	20%	0%
First aid/CPR	73%	19%	63%	19%	0%
General health and safety	86%	32%	47%	21%	0%
Hazardous material handling	82%	11%	89%	0%	0%

B.10 Parental involvement with insurance (for respondents with parent organizations)

Institution fully covered under parent	Covered under parent, but maintains separate riders	Not covered under parent	No response
75%	0%	25%	0%

Fifty percent of respondents indicate the parent organization has regulations or guidelines regarding insurance to which the museum must adhere.

B.11 Does the parent pay for insurance?

Pay all costs	Pay some costs	Not pay	No response
75%	0%	25%	0%

B.12 Insurance types (See also insurance costs figures in first table of this section)

	Presently carry	Presently carry but considering dropping	Investigating/ planning to carry by 2005	No response
Commercial/general liability	86%	0%	0%	14%
Automobile	82%	0%	0%	18%
Collections/fine arts	46%	0%	5%	50%
Directors and officers liability	73%	0%	0%	27%
Event cancellation	5%	0%	0%	95%
Exhibitions/loans	32%	0%	0%	68%
Transit	5%	0%	0%	96%
Terrorism	23%	0%	0%	77%
Other	18%	0%	0%	82%

B.13 Maintain a fund to offset small claims/deductibles

	Yes	Median fund size	N for median	No	No response
	5%		1	86%	9%

Twenty-three percent of respondents report being self-insured.

B.14 Meaning of self-insured

	Set aside and manage a designated fund with internal loss assessment/ payment	Replace/repairs out of general fund budget	Does not replace value of losses	Other	No response
	40%	40%	20%	0%	0%

B.15 Policies/plans

	Have	Do not have	In development	No response
Facilities use policy	64%	27%	0%	9%
Building rental policy	77%	14%	5%	5%
Special events policy for outside groups	64%	23%	0%	14%
Special events policy for museum-sponsored events	36%	45%	5%	14%
Filming policy	41%	41%	5%	14%
Filming agreement	32%	55%	5%	9%
Policy on use of funds resulting from insurance claims on losses to collections	9%	82%	0%	9%
Cyclical maintenance plan	32%	45%	5%	18%
Emergency preparedness/disaster plan	59%	18%	14%	9%
Historic structure master plan	27%	55%	0%	18%
Integrated pest management plan	64%	23%	5%	9%

Section C: Art Museums

Total responses = 250

Forty-four percent of these institutions have a parent organization.

C.1

	10th percentile	25th percentile	50th percentile	75th percentile	90th percentile	Number of responses
Operating income	$109,200	$400,000	$1,409,202	$3,841,660	$9,606,499	227
Operating expense	$93,700	$359,250	$1,321,310	$3,751,335	$9,902,995	232
Attendance	6,800	15,000	40,000	107,123	220,635	225
Full-time staff	1	3	11	30	80.2	248
Part-time staff	1	2	6	16	40	245
Maintenance staff full-time	0.0	0.0	1.0	3.0	8.0	234
Maintenance staff part-time	0.0	0.0	0.0	1.0	2.0	231
Total interior square footage	5,000	13,680	33,000	82,883	168,147	234
Insurance costs paid by institution	$3,617	$11,110	$28,127	$84,634	$184,041	172
Insurance costs paid by parent	$4,500	$18,500	$60,000	$152,790	$1,935,312	37
Total insurance costs paid	$3,890	$12,000	$32,500	$92,275	$265,537	197

C.2 Space—presence and allocation as a percentage of total space

	Present in institution (n=28)		10th percentile	25th percentile	50th percentile	75th percentile	90th percentile	Number of responses
	Yes*	No						
Exhibitions	95%	0%	17.6%	25.8%	34.0%	49.8%	66.6%	208
Collections storage	88%	7%	2.4%	5.1%	8.0%	16.7%	26.7%	181
Non-collections storage	80%	8%	1.5%	2.7%	4.7%	8.2%	13.4%	163
Offices	93%	1%	3.7%	5.1%	8.9%	13.6%	20.7%	195
Education (classrooms)	61%	24%	1.2%	2.4%	5.0%	10.3%	17.0%	131
Library/research	63%	23%	0.5%	1.0%	1.7%	3.2%	5.3%	130
Museum store	64%	22%	0.6%	0.9%	1.7%	2.8%	3.8%	138
Public space/ public functions	63%	21%	2.4%	4.4%	8.5%	13.4%	25.4%	124
Food service	44%	40%	0.8%	1.2%	1.7%	2.7%	4.1%	89
Auditorium/ theaters	43%	38%	1.3%	2.3%	3.5%	6.6%	11.5%	89
Maintenance	63%	21%	0.6%	1.2%	3.0%	9.0%	13.1%	124
Conservation/ collections prep	64%	20%	0.7%	1.6%	2.8%	5.4%	8.0%	131

(*Percentages for yes and no often do not add to 100 percent—the remainder did not answer the question.)

C.3 Space allocation in square feet

	10th percentile	25th percentile	50th percentile	75th percentile	90th percentile	Number of responses
Exhibitions	2,800	4,782	10,642	23,521	57,000	213
Collections storage	500	1,000	3,133	7,308	15,971	187
Non-collections storage	250	500	1,244	3,401	8,070	168
Offices	400	1,000	2,500	7,900	20,000	201
Education (classrooms)	630	1,000	2,242	5,475	11,415	132
Library/research	200	373	900	2,500	5,675	133
Museum store	200	431	900	1,800	3,102	140
Public space/ public functions	694	1,600	3,935	10,000	19,872	126
Food service	141	400	1,187	3,159	5,630	90
Auditorium/ theaters	1,200	1,900	3,150	5,869	9,993	89
Maintenance	100	366	1,800	6,000	19,600	127
Conservation/ collections prep	294	500	1,200	3,535	6,870	134

C.4 What is allowed in building by policy

	Collection areas	Exhibit areas	Staff offices	Public spaces	Grounds
Open flames	1%	2%	1%	14%	20%
Food	6%	22%	82%	78%	79%
Beverages (other than water)	5%	23%	85%	77%	76%
Live plants	6%	20%	66%	59%	68%
Fresh flowers	8%	33%	80%	82%	65%
Dried plant material	7%	20%	53%	51%	44%
Personal artwork	2%	4%	70%	10%	8%
Filming	20%	46%	36%	66%	64%
Photography	27%	52%	44%	72%	70%

Seventy-five percent of respondents indicate they rent space to outside groups. Ninety five percent report the rental revenue goes to the institution's budget (as opposed to a parent organization or other group).

C.5 Groups space is/would be rented to

	Would rent to	Have rented to in past 5 years
Religious groups	50%	27%
Political groups	44%	22%
Private groups (weddings, parties, graduations, etc.)	78%	67%
Corporate groups	94%	77%
Non-religious nonprofit groups	95%	78%
Other	15%	13%

C.6 Have exclusive agreement with caterer(s)

	Yes, one caterer	Yes, maintain a list of accepted caterers	Median percent commission taken by institution	Average commission	N for mean/ median	No	No response
Overall	22%	23%	0.0%	4.7%	82	55%	0%

C.7 Parking offered

	Have on-site parking	Median number of spaces	N for median	Have off-site parking	Median number of spaces	N for median
	64%	78	135	10%	83	22

Of the 74 percent of art museums that have a disaster plan (see last table in this section) 67 percent report having practiced it.

C.8 Year emergency plan practiced

Year not specified	Before 1996	1996-1999	2000-2002	2003	2004
4%	2%	2%	10%	57%	26%

C.9 Types of training provided to staff

	Training is provided	For those who provide training			
		Training is mndatory for all staff	Training is mandatory for some staff	Training is optional	No response on mandatory/ optional status
Emergency response	63%	41%	46%	9%	4%
First aid/CPR	45%	6%	66%	24%	4%
General health and safety	52%	44%	34%	17%	5%
Hazardous material handling	40%	8%	76%	12%	4%

C.10 Parental involvement with insurance (for respondents with parent organizations)

Institution fully covered under parent	Covered under parent, but maintains separate riders	Not covered under parent	No response
56%	28%	8%	8%

Sixty-three percent of respondents indicate the parent organization has regulations or guidelines regarding insurance to which the museum must adhere.

C.11 Does the parent pay for insurance?

Pay all costs	Pay some costs	Not pay	No response
59%	23%	10%	8%

C.12 Insurance types (See also insurance costs figures in first table of this appendix)

	Presently carry	Presently carry but considering dropping	Investigating/ planning to carry by 2005	No response
Commercial/general liability	81%	0%	0%	18%
Automobile	61%	0%	2%	38%
Collections/fine arts	91%	0%	1%	8%
Directors and officers liability	74%	0%	3%	23%
Event cancellation	6%	0%	2%	92%
Exhibitions/loans	79%	0%	1%	20%
Transit	37%	0%	1%	62%
Terrorism	33%	0%	2%	65%
Other	18%	0%	0%	82%

C.13 Maintain a fund to offset small claims/deductibles

	Yes	Median fund size	N for median	No	No response
	7%	$3,000	8	88%	4%

Seventeen percent of respondents report being self-insured.

C.14 Meaning of self-insured

	Set aside and manage a designated fund with internal loss assessment/payment	Replace/repairs out of general fund budget	Does not replace value of losses	Other	No response
	38%	52%	10%	10%	2%

C.15 Policies/plans

	Have	Do not have	In development	No response
Facilities use policy	65%	18%	5%	12%
Building rental policy	64%	19%	4%	12%
Special events policy for outside groups	63%	18%	6%	13%
Special events policy for museum-sponsored events	44%	33%	8%	15%
Filming policy	49%	32%	7%	12%
Filming agreement	27%	47%	4%	22%
Policy on use of funds resulting from insurance claims on losses to collections	26%	51%	4%	18%
Cyclical maintenance plan	47%	29%	8%	16%
Emergency preparedness/disaster plan	74%	11%	7%	9%
Historic structure master plan	17%	58%	4%	21%
Integrated pest management plan	45%	35%	8%	12%

Section D: Children's/Youth Museums

Total responses = 28

Only one of these institutions has a parent organization—for this reason this section does not include data on parent organization support, etc.

D.1

	10th percentile	25th percentile	50th percentile	75th percentile	90th percentile	Number of responses
Operating income	$321,243	$425,916	$1,288,658	$2,294,003	$7,565,287	24
Operating expense	$343,300	$412,960	$1,307,643	$2,134,077	$6,325,172	25
Attendance	40,000	60,461	119,462	195,347	521,802	24
Full-time staff	0.8	5	13	21	55.4	27
Part-time staff	1.6	7	11	24	79.4	27
Maintenance staff full-time	0.0	0.0	1.0	1.3	3.3	26
Maintenance staff part-time	0.0	0.0	1.0	1.0	2.3	26
Total interior square footage	5,490	17,626	26,460	44,250	93,150	26
Insurance costs paid by institution	$3,747	$9,006	$26,561	$42,196	$147,505	21
Insurance costs paid by parent						0
Total insurance costs paid	$3,747	$9,006	$26,561	$42,196	$147,505	21

D.2 Space—presence and allocation as a percentage of total space

	Present in institution (n=28)		10th percentile	25th percentile	50th percentile	75th percentile	90th percentile	Number of responses
	Yes*	No						
Exhibitions	89%	0%	18.6%	37.5%	47.3%	66.7%	80.0%	19
Collections storage	54%	29%		1.5%	2.0%	11.1%		9
Non-collections storage	79%	4%	1.2%	3.8%	9.6%	18.4%	24.6%	12
Offices	82%	7%	4.6%	8.5%	12.0%	17.4%	20.1%	16
Education (classrooms)	71%	11%	0.6%	2.2%	5.0%	6.8%	9.6%	13
Library/research	32%	46%		0.7%	1.5%	3.0%		5
Museum store	86%	0%	1.1%	1.4%	2.1%	3.4%	5.9%	16
Public space/ public functions	71%	14%	3.6%	7.9%	9.1%	10.7%	31.3%	12
Food service	36%	46%		1.4%	1.8%	3.6%		7
Auditorium/ theaters	57%	25%		2.4%	3.9%	4.7%		8
Maintenance	61%	25%		0.9%	3.0%	4.6%		8
Conservation/ collections prep	29%	43%		0.8%	1.3%	1.8%		5

(*Percentages for yes and no often do not add to 100 percent—the remainder did not answer the question.)

D.3 Space allocation in square feet

	10th percentile	25th percentile	50th percentile	75th percentile	90th percentile	Number of responses
Exhibitions	2,500	4,000	12,000	22,500	39,270	19
Collections storage		177	800	3,250		9
Non-collections storage	199	725	2,482	5,603	9,990	12
Offices	635	1,763	2,577	7,801	16,144	16
Education (classrooms)	98	275	900	1,612	10,400	13
Library/research		225	493	2,500		5
Museum store	93	242	526	1,000	6,400	16
Public space/ public functions	405	1,486	2,391	5,810	54,135	12
Food service		588	800	8,850		7
Auditorium/ theaters		679	1,000	2,250		8
Maintenance		323	801	1,000		8
Conservation/ collections prep		100	550	4,050		5

D.4 What is allowed in building by policy

	Collection areas	Exhibit areas	Staff offices	Public spaces	Grounds
Open flames	0%	0%	0%	4%	0%
Food	0%	25%	82%	57%	54%
Beverages (other than water)	0%	18%	86%	54%	50%
Live plants	0%	36%	75%	50%	54%
Fresh flowers	4%	21%	79%	57%	50%
Dried plant material	4%	29%	50%	29%	25%
Personal artwork	4%	25%	89%	14%	14%
Filming	25%	79%	32%	71%	54%
Photography	32%	79%	43%	75%	61%

Eighty-two of respondents indicate they rent space to outside groups. One hundred percent report the rental revenue goes to the institution's budget (as opposed to a parent organization or other group).

D.5 Groups space is/would be rented to

	Would rent to	Have rented to in past 5 years
Religious groups	74%	22%
Political groups	57%	22%
Private groups (weddings, parties, graduations, etc.)	100%	74%
Corporate groups	100%	70%
Non-religious nonprofit groups	100%	74%
Other	4%	4%

D.6 Have exclusive agreement with caterer(s)

	Yes, one caterer	Yes, maintain a list of accepted caterers	Median percent commission taken by institution	Average commission	N for mean/ median	No	No response
Overall	7%	14%	10.0%	7.4%	5	75%	4%

D.7 Parking offered

	Have on-site parking	Median number of spaces	N for median	Have off-site parking	Median number of spaces	N for median
	57%	140	11	4%		0

Practice and Implementation of the Emergency Plan

Of the 75 percent of children's/youth museums that have a disaster plan (see last table in this section) 91 percent report having practiced it.

D.8 Year emergency plan practiced

	Year not specified	Before 1996	1996-1999	2000-2002	2003	2004
	5%	5%	0%	10%	40%	40%

D.9 Types of training provided to staff

	Training is provided	For those who provide training			
		Training is mndatory for all staff	Training is mandatory for some staff	Training is optional	No response on mandatory/ optional status
Emergency response	57%	63%	31%	6%	0%
First aid/CPR	64%	22%	61%	17%	0%
General health and safety	57%	31%	44%	19%	6%
Hazardous material handling	36%	20%	70%	10%	0%

D.10 Insurance types (See also insurance costs figures in first table of this section)

	Presently carry	Presently carry but considering dropping	Investigating/ planning to carry by 2005	No response
Commercial/general liability	75%	0%	0%	25%
Automobile	57%	0%	7%	36%
Collections/fine arts	36%	0%	0%	64%
Directors & Officers liability	89%	0%	0%	11%
Event cancellation	0%	0%	4%	96%
Exhibitions/loans	43%	0%	0%	57%
Transit	18%	0%	4%	79%
Terrorism	36%	0%	4%	61%
Other	18%	0%	0%	82%

D.11 Maintain a fund to offset small claims/deductibles

	Yes	Median fund size	N for median	No	No response
	0%		0	100%	0%

Seven percent of respondents report being self-insured.

D.12 Meaning of self-insured

	Set aside and manage a designated fund with internal loss assessment/ payment	Replace/repairs out of general fund budget	Does not replace value of losses	Other	No response
	0%	100%	50%	0%	0%

D.13 Policies/plans

	Have	Do not have	In development	No response
Facilities use policy	61%	21%	11%	7%
Building rental policy	68%	21%	7%	4%
Special events policy for outside groups	50%	32%	7%	11%
Special events policy for museum-sponsored events	36%	46%	7%	11%
Filming policy	39%	43%	11%	7%
Filming agreement	29%	54%	7%	11%
Policy on use of funds resulting from insurance claims on losses to collections	11%	64%	7%	18%
Cyclical maintenance plan	50%	21%	14%	14%
Emergency preparedness/disaster plan	75%	14%	7%	4%
Historic structure master plan	7%	57%	7%	29%
Integrated pest management plan	32%	43%	7%	18%

American Association of Museums

Section E: General Museums

Total responses = 118

A general museum is one that addresses two or more disciplines to a significant extent, for example a museum that interprets both art and history, or history and science. Fifty-two percent of these institutions have a parent organization.

E.1

	10th percentile	25th percentile	50th percentile	75th percentile	90th percentile	Number of responses
Operating income	$40,000	$89,079	$550,000	$2,004,476	$6,346,954	97
Operating expense	$40,060	$101,250	$769,500	$1,991,670	$8,120,545	100
Attendance	2,860	10,000	45,556	109,251	236,846	105
Full-time staff	0	1	5.5	19	69.1	116
Part-time staff	0	1	4	12	32.4	115
Maintenance staff full-time	0.0	0.0	1.0	3.0	8.0	104
Maintenance staff part-time	0.0	0.0	0.0	1.0	3.0	102
Total interior square footage	5,900	13,500	30,000	77,500	172,857	95
Insurance costs paid by institution	$1,510	$3,581	$14,000	$54,000	$124,240	71
Insurance costs paid by parent	$462	$1,425	$5,487	$25,875	$37,375	12
Total insurance costs paid	$1,333	$3,016	$13,750	$39,998	$119,487	80

E.2 Space—presence and allocation as a percentage of total space

	Present in institution (n=28)		10th percentile	25th percentile	50th percentile	75th percentile	90th percentile	Number of responses
	Yes*	No						
Exhibitions	92%	0%	14.2%	26.9%	38.4%	60.0%	76.8%	76
Collections storage	86%	3%	2.9%	6.6%	11.9%	20.4%	34.9%	73
Non-collections storage	75%	8%	1.1%	2.0%	3.6%	6.6%	14.7%	62
Offices	90%	2%	1.5%	2.5%	5.7%	8.8%	13.4%	74
Education (classrooms)	51%	34%	0.8%	1.7%	4.3%	7.5%	12.2%	45
Library/research	67%	18%	0.4%	0.9%	2.0%	3.8%	7.6%	52
Museum store	75%	11%	0.3%	0.9%	1.9%	2.9%	4.9%	62
Public space/ public functions	70%	16%	1.6%	2.7%	5.9%	15.2%	22.5%	56
Food service	36%	44%	0.4%	0.9%	1.4%	2.2%	3.9%	32
Auditorium/ theaters	36%	44%	1.1%	1.6%	3.0%	7.0%	19.4%	31
Maintenance	71%	13%	0.7%	1.1%	3.2%	5.7%	13.8%	59
Conservation/ collections prep	60%	19%	0.4%	0.8%	2.0%	4.2%	5.8%	53

(*Percentages for yes and no often do not add to 100 percent—the remainder did not answer the question.)

E.3 Space allocation in square feet

	10th percentile	25th percentile	50th percentile	75th percentile	90th percentile	Number of responses
Exhibitions	2,250	4,405	14,967	30,000	60,476	84
Collections storage	432	1,300	4,500	15,000	23,500	79
Non-collections storage	170	600	1,500	4,125	7,217	66
Offices	184	500	1,800	5,373	13,338	81
Education (classrooms)	590	850	2,000	3,831	10,263	48
Library/research	150	400	900	2,850	5,534	56
Museum store	143	225	545	1,675	3,040	68
Public space/ public functions	386	1,000	2,000	8,635	17,000	61
Food service	141	247	1,112	3,100	6,629	34
Auditorium/ theaters	975	1,500	2,750	4,727	11,960	32
Maintenance	100	361	1,550	4,199	11,710	62
Conservation/ collections prep	131	374	835	2,831	5,374	56

E.4 What is allowed in building by policy

	Collection areas	Exhibit areas	Staff offices	Public spaces	Grounds
Open flames	3%	7%	3%	12%	24%
Food	4%	24%	65%	62%	66%
Beverages (other than water)	4%	20%	71%	63%	68%
Live plants	9%	22%	59%	50%	68%
Fresh flowers	9%	29%	60%	59%	62%
Dried plant material	15%	40%	48%	52%	47%
Personal artwork	8%	17%	66%	18%	13%
Filming	24%	63%	31%	61%	68%
Photography	27%	71%	37%	66%	73%

Sixty-eight percent of respondents indicate they rent space to outside groups. Eighty-four percent report the rental revenue goes to the institution's budget (as opposed to a parent organization or other group).

E.5 Groups space is/would be rented to

	Would rent to	Have rented to in past 5 years
Religious groups	70%	45%
Political groups	49%	29%
Private groups (weddings, parties, graduations, etc.)	79%	69%
Corporate groups	85%	68%
Non-religious nonprofit groups	94%	81%
Other	11%	10%

E.6 Have exclusive agreement with caterer(s)

	Yes, one caterer	Yes, maintain a list of accepted caterers	Median percent commission taken by institution	Average commission	N for mean/ median	No	No response
Overall	14%	16%	7.5%	6.6%	22	69%	2%

E.7 Parking offered

	Have on-site parking	Median number of spaces	N for median	Have off-site parking	Median number of spaces	N for median
	75%	50	70	18%	45	17

Practice and Implementation of the Emergency Plan

Of the 59 percent of general museums that have a disaster plan (see last table in this section) 67 percent report having practiced it.

E.8 Year emergency plan practiced

	Year not specified	Before 1996	1996-1999	2000-2002	2003	2004
	14%	6%	6%	14%	37%	22%

E.9 Types of training provided to staff

	Training is provided	For those who provide training			
		Training is mndatory for all staff	Training is mandatory for some staff	Training is optional	No response on mandatory/ optional status
Emergency response	47%	46%	44%	9%	2%
First aid/CPR	48%	14%	53%	30%	4%
General health and safety	52%	39%	41%	18%	2%
Hazardous material handling	39%	13%	67%	15%	4%

E.10 Parental involvement with insurance (for respondents with parent organizations)

Institution fully covered under parent	Covered under parent, but maintains separate riders	Not covered under parent	No response
60%	24%	1%	6%

Fifty-six percent of respondents indicate the parent organization has regulations or guidelines regarding insurance to which the museum must adhere.

E.11 Does the parent pay for insurance?

Pay all costs	Pay some costs	Not pay	No response
52%	24%	8%	16%

E.12 Insurance types (See also insurance costs figures in first table of this section)

	Presently carry	Presently carry but considering dropping	Investigating/ planning to carry by 2005	No response
Commercial/general liability	74%	0%	0%	26%
Automobile	44%	0%	0%	56%
Collections/fine arts	58%	1%	0%	42%
Directors & Officers liability	49%	0%	2%	49%
Event cancellation	3%	0%	1%	96%
Exhibitions/loans	53%	0%	0%	47%
Transit	15%	0%	0%	85%
Terrorism	15%	0%	1%	84%
Other	9%	0%	0%	92%

E.13 Maintain a fund to offset small claims/deductibles

	Yes	Median fund size	N for median	No	No response
	3%		1	86%	12%

Twenty-eight percent of respondents report being self-insured.

E.14 Meaning of self-insured

Set aside and manage a designated fund with internal loss assessment/payment	Replace/repairs out of general fund budget	Does not replace value of losses	Other	No response
30%	33%	12%	24%	15%

E.15 Policies/plans

	Have	Do not have	In development	No response
Facilities use policy	58%	25%	3%	13%
Building rental policy	62%	31%	2%	6%
Special events policy for outside groups	53%	31%	3%	14%
Special events policy for museum-sponsored events	41%	42%	3%	14%
Filming policy	33%	47%	6%	14%
Filming agreement	21%	55%	4%	19%
Policy on use of funds resulting from insurance claims on losses to collections	23%	60%	2%	15%
Cyclical maintenance plan	41%	33%	12%	14%
Emergency preparedness/disaster plan	59%	29%	8%	5%
Historic structure master plan	13%	63%	11%	14%
Integrated pest management plan	50%	37%	2%	11%

Section F: Historic Houses/Sites

Total responses = 148

Forty-nine percent of these institutions have a parent organization.

F.1

	10th percentile	25th percentile	50th percentile	75th percentile	90th percentile	Number of responses
Operating income	$27,072	$98,270	$192,836	$554,799	$1,122,933	125
Operating expense	$30,000	$102,224	$219,756	$532,897	$1,566,687	125
Attendance	2,260	5,000	14,458	35,000	89,000	131
Full-time staff	0	1	2	6	19	147
Part-time staff	0	1	3	10	30	147
Maintenance staff full-time	0.0	0.0	0.0	1.5	4.9	141
Maintenance staff part-time	0.0	0.0	1.0	1.0	2.8	141
Total interior square footage	3,400	6,016	12,000	25,699	61,000	109
Insurance costs paid by institution	$1,040	$4,523	$10,492	$20,250	$59,049	86
Insurance costs paid by parent	$670	$2,086	$9,081	$27,493	$69,058	24
Total insurance costs paid	$1,380	$4,000	$10,159	$23,113	$62,600	107

F.2 Space—presence and allocation as a percentage of total space

	Present in institution (n=28)		10th percentile	25th percentile	50th percentile	75th percentile	90th percentile	Number of responses
	Yes*	No						
Exhibitions	87%	3%	4.4%	13.3%	38.1%	56.7%	75.0%	86
Collections storage	78%	9%	1.8%	3.6%	7.2%	14.0%	25.4%	81
Non-collections storage	79%	7%	1.0%	2.4%	4.5%	8.8%	15.6%	80
Offices	85%	4%	1.4%	3.1%	6.4%	11.9%	23.5%	86
Education (classrooms)	30%	47%	1.0%	1.6%	3.5%	8.7%	12.6%	30
Library/research	57%	24%	0.5%	0.8%	1.8%	4.2%	10.9%	55
Museum store	73%	14%	0.3%	1.5%	2.8%	4.9%	8.8%	76
Public space/ public functions	62%	18%	1.6%	4.3%	12.6%	28.9%	66.7%	57
Food service	20%	57%	0.4%	0.7%	1.8%	4.5%	10.0%	21
Auditorium/ theaters	21%	57%	0.8%	1.8%	2.8%	6.5%	21.7%	21
Maintenance	59%	22%	0.4%	0.8%	2.5%	6.9%	18.1%	60
Conservation/ collections prep	32%	44%	0.3%	1.0%	1.8%	3.1%	7.0%	32

(*Percentages for yes and no often do not add to 100 percent—the remainder did not answer the question.)

F.3 Space allocation in square feet

	10th percentile	25th percentile	50th percentile	75th percentile	90th percentile	Number of responses
Exhibitions	490	1,200	4,253	8,455	18,421	98
Collections storage	200	390	1,000	2,000	9,000	89
Non-collections storage	100	200	500	1,000	3,230	88
Offices	136	300	850	1,450	5,000	96
Education (classrooms)	260	437	900	2,021	3,250	34
Library/research	100	150	300	600	1,000	62
Museum store	100	185	317	600	1,200	85
Public space/ public functions	380	1,000	2,000	4,806	20,000	65
Food service	86	267	575	1,000	7,010	22
Auditorium/ theaters	188	400	1,000	2,800	13,000	23
Maintenance	50	110	500	1,550	10,000	69
Conservation/ collections prep	100	237	462	900	3,000	34

F.4 What is allowed in building by policy

	Collection areas	Exhibit areas	Staff offices	Public spaces	Grounds
Open flames	1%	8%	3%	9%	28%
Food	6%	16%	71%	55%	81%
Beverages (other than water)	5%	14%	73%	55%	80%
Live plants	7%	23%	55%	45%	76%
Fresh flowers	11%	32%	67%	53%	70%
Dried plant material	15%	40%	44%	44%	48%
Personal artwork	6%	12%	51%	12%	16%
Filming	25%	55%	30%	60%	77%
Photography	23%	57%	37%	63%	84%

Seventy-two of respondents indicate they rent space to outside groups. Seventy-nine percent report the rental revenue goes to the institution's budget (as opposed to a parent organization or other group).

F.5 Groups space is/would be rented to

	Would rent to	Have rented to in past 5 years
Religious groups	63%	36%
Political groups	44%	25%
Private groups (weddings, parties, graduations, etc.)	91%	81%
Corporate groups	88%	73%
Non-religious nonprofit groups	88%	76%
Other	12%	11%

F.6 Have exclusive agreement with caterer(s)

	Yes, one caterer	Yes, maintain a list of accepted caterers	Median percent commission taken by institution	Average commission	N for mean/ median	No	No response
Overall	3%	17%	0.0%	5.1%	26	75%	5%

F.7 Parking offered

	Have on-site parking	Median number of spaces	N for median	Have off-site parking	Median number of spaces	N for median
	74%	35	90	11%	20	13

Practice and Implementation of the Emergency Plan

Of the 55 percent of historic house/sites that have a disaster plan (see last table in this section) 42 percent report having practiced it.

F.8 Year emergency plan practiced

Year not specified	Before 1996	1996-1999	2000-2002	2003	2004
0%	0%	3%	16%	68%	13%

F.9 Types of training provided to staff

	Training is provided	For those who provide training			
		Training is mndatory for all staff	Training is mandatory for some staff	Training is optional	No response on mandatory/ optional status
Emergency response	42%	55%	31%	5%	10%
First aid/CPR	31%	22%	50%	22%	7%
General health and safety	41%	57%	28%	8%	7%
Hazardous material handling	28%	34%	54%	7%	5%

F.10 Parental involvement with insurance (for respondents with parent organizations)

Institution fully covered under parent	Covered under parent, but maintains separate riders	Not covered under parent	No response
58%	16%	16%	10%

Sixty percent of respondents indicate the parent organization has regulations or guidelines regarding insurance to which the museum must adhere.

E.11 Does the parent pay for insurance?

Pay all costs	Pay some costs	Not pay	No response
62%	11%	16%	11%

F.12 Insurance types (See also insurance costs figures in first table of this section)

	Presently carry	Presently carry but considering dropping	Investigating/ planning to carry by 2005	No response
Commercial/general liability	78%	0%	0%	22%
Automobile	33%	0%	1%	66%
Collections/fine arts	66%	0%	1%	33%
Directors & Officers liability	58%	0%	3%	39%
Event cancellation	3%	0%	2%	95%
Exhibitions/loans	35%	0%	1%	65%
Transit	12%	0%	0%	88%
Terrorism	14%	0%	2%	84%
Other	12%	0%	0%	89%

F.13 Maintain a fund to offset small claims/deductibles

Yes	Median fund size	N for median	No	No response
8%	$1,500	6	78%	14%

Twenty percent of respondents report being self-insured.

F.14 Meaning of self-insured

Set aside and manage a designated fund with internal loss assessment/ payment	Replace/repairs out of general fund budget	Does not replace value of losses	Other	No response
24%	41%	10%	10%	17%

F.15 Policies/plans

	Have	Do not have	In development	No response
Facilities use policy	58%	24%	7%	11%
Building rental policy	61%	24%	7%	8%
Special events policy for outside groups	56%	29%	5%	10%
Special events policy for museum-sponsored events	30%	47%	7%	16%
Filming policy	45%	39%	4%	11%
Filming agreement	34%	47%	5%	14%
Policy on use of funds resulting from insurance claims on losses to collections	13%	67%	4%	16%
Cyclical maintenance plan	43%	37%	9%	11%
Emergency preparedness/disaster plan	55%	25%	11%	9%
Historic structure master plan	43%	34%	13%	9%
Integrated pest management plan	37%	44%	8%	11%

Section G: History Museums/Historical Societies

Total responses = 352

Thirty-two percent of these institutions have a parent organization.

G.1

	10th percentile	25th percentile	50th percentile	75th percentile	90th percentile	Number of responses
Operating income	$22,648	$65,339	$165,836	$453,707	$1,668,012	294
Operating expense	$23,893	$64,312	$167,592	$457,750	$1,710,000	298
Attendance	1,182	3,000	8,500	25,000	71,035	301
Full-time staff	0	.25	2	5	15	348
Part-time staff	0	1	2	5	10.4	345
Maintenance staff full-time	0.0	0.0	0.0	1.0	2.0	322
Maintenance staff part-time	0.0	0.0	0.0	1.0	2.0	324
Total interior square footage	3,454	6,092	14,000	31,000	78,000	283
Insurance costs paid by institution	$1,022	$2,182	$5,268	$12,685	$31,648	239
Insurance costs paid by parent	$605	$1,066	$3,000	$6,505	$17,109	40
Total insurance costs paid	$1,000	$2,094	$5,000	$11,784	$30,209	270

G.2 Space—presence and allocation as a percentage of total space

	Present in institution (n=28)		10th percentile	25th percentile	50th percentile	75th percentile	90th percentile	Number of responses
	Yes*	No						
Exhibitions	88%	2%	12.1%	26.6%	40.9%	57.9%	77.0%	213
Collections storage	86%	3%	3.2%	7.3%	15.9%	24.1%	35.7%	210
Non-collections storage	75%	7%	0.8%	2.1%	4.0%	7.9%	16.3%	185
Offices	83%	5%	1.2%	3.1%	5.0%	9.2%	15.1%	199
Education (classrooms)	29%	39%	0.6%	1.7%	3.4%	7.1%	11.7%	71
Library/research	71%	13%	0.7%	1.4%	3.5%	6.6%	11.8%	170
Museum store	71%	11%	0.3%	0.8%	1.7%	3.6%	5.6%	178
Public space/ public functions	58%	20%	1.8%	3.3%	6.8%	14.9%	29.0%	130
Food service	21%	52%	0.4%	0.9%	1.6%	2.6%	5.0%	54
Auditorium/ theaters	26%	47%	0.6%	2.3%	6.3%	11.1%	16.7%	61
Maintenance	55%	20%	0.3%	0.8%	1.9%	3.8%	5.7%	127
Conservation/ collections prep	45%	29%	0.6%	1.0%	2.0%	4.5%	6.9%	104

(*Percentages for yes and no often do not add to 100 percent—the remainder did not answer the question.)

G.3 Space allocation in square feet

	10th percentile	25th percentile	50th percentile	75th percentile	90th percentile	Number of responses
Exhibitions	1,022	2,500	6,000	12,000	30,552	233
Collections storage	318	860	2,000	4,745	15,000	225
Non-collections storage	100	250	592	1,800	5,000	195
Offices	150	380	750	2,000	4,826	213
Education (classrooms)	400	556	1,000	2,442	5,120	76
Library/research	100	200	500	1,296	3,180	180
Museum store	50	150	400	800	1,580	191
Public space/ public functions	303	600	1,500	4,050	11,000	142
Food service	49	142	428	1,488	3,026	58
Auditorium/ theaters	394	803	1,500	3,425	7,125	66
Maintenance	50	100	400	1,000	3,000	134
Conservation/ collections prep	100	205	500	1,000	4,949	112

G.4 What is allowed in building by policy

	Collection areas	Exhibit areas	Staff offices	Public spaces	Grounds
Open flames	1%	2%	2%	8%	21%
Food	4%	14%	65%	61%	67%
Beverages (other than water)	4%	15%	70%	61%	69%
Live plants	3%	13%	44%	43%	58%
Fresh flowers	4%	16%	51%	52%	52%
Dried plant material	8%	24%	31%	36%	37%
Personal artwork	8%	14%	51%	16%	15%
Filming	21%	56%	31%	62%	65%
Photography	28%	63%	39%	65%	70%

Sixty-eight percent of respondents indicate they rent space to outside groups. Eighty percent report the rental revenue goes to the institution's budget (as opposed to a parent organization or other group).

G.5 Groups space is/would be rented to

	Would rent to	Have rented to in past 5 years
Religious groups	63%	33%
Political groups	52%	33%
Private groups (weddings, parties, graduations, etc.)	84%	63%
Corporate groups	82%	57%
Non-religious nonprofit groups	90%	70%
Other	11%	8%

G.6 Have exclusive agreement with caterer(s)

	Yes, one caterer	Yes, maintain a list of accepted caterers	Median percent commission taken by institution	Average commission	N for mean/ median	No	No response
Overall	3%	12%	0.0%	4.4%	32	82%	3%

G.7 Parking offered

	Have on-site parking	Median number of spaces	N for median	Have off-site parking	Median number of spaces	N for median
	65%	25	197	13%	50	38

Practice and Implementation of the Emergency Plan

Of the 48 percent of history museums that have a disaster plan (see last table in this section) 47 percent report having practiced it.

G.8 Year emergency plan practiced

	Year not specified	Before 1996	1996-1999	2000-2002	2003	2004
	4%	0%	4%	23%	48%	22%

G.9 Types of training provided to staff

	Training is provided	For those who provide training			
		Training is mndatory for all staff	Training is mandatory for some staff	Training is optional	No response on mandatory/ optional status
Emergency response	36%	44%	34%	18%	5%
First aid/CPR	27%	28%	44%	25%	4%
General health and safety	38%	53%	24%	15%	8%
Hazardous material handling	21%	19%	67%	11%	3%

G.10 Parental involvement with insurance (for respondents with parent organizations)

Institution fully covered under parent	Covered under parent, but maintains separate riders	Not covered under parent	No response
67%	16%	9%	8%

Fifty-four percent of respondents indicate the parent organization has regulations or guidelines regarding insurance to which the museum must adhere.

G.11 Does the parent pay for insurance?

Pay all costs	Pay some costs	Not pay	No response
59%	14%	14%	14%

G.12 Insurance types (See also insurance costs figures in first table of this section)

	Presently carry	Presently carry but considering dropping	Investigating/ planning to carry by 2005	No response
Commercial/general liability	73%	0%	1%	26%
Automobile	32%	0%	1%	67%
Collections/fine arts	52%	1%	4%	44%
Directors & Officers liability	53%	0%	6%	41%
Event cancellation	2%	0%	3%	95%
Exhibitions/loans	40%	0%	2%	58%
Transit	11%	0%	1%	88%
Terrorism	11%	0%	2%	87%
Other	12%	0%	0%	88%

G.13 Maintain a fund to offset small claims/deductibles

	Yes	Median fund size	N for median	No	No response
	5%	$52,500	8	85%	9%

Eighteen percent of respondents report being self-insured.

G.14 Meaning of self-insured

	Set aside and manage a designated fund with internal loss assessment/ payment	Replace/repairs out of general fund budget	Does not replace value of losses	Other	No response
	22%	48%	13%	16%	13%

G.15 Policies/plans

	Have	Do not have	In development	No response
Facilities use policy	53%	32%	6%	10%
Building rental policy	51%	36%	6%	8%
Special events policy for outside groups	43%	42%	8%	8%
Special events policy for museum-sponsored events	31%	53%	7%	9%
Filming policy	34%	49%	7%	10%
Filming agreement	21%	60%	7%	13%
Policy on use of funds resulting from insurance claims on losses to collections	17%	67%	4%	13%
Cyclical maintenance plan	30%	46%	12%	12%
Emergency preparedness/disaster plan	48%	34%	11%	8%
Historic structure master plan	24%	55%	10%	10%
Integrated pest management plan	30%	53%	7%	10%

Section H: Natural History/Anthropology Museums

Total responses = 46

Sixty-five percent of these institutions have a parent organization.

H.1

	10th percentile	25th percentile	50th percentile	75th percentile	90th percentile	Number of responses
Operating income	$66,750	$150,000	$1,016,016	$6,450,000	$13,800,000	43
Operating expense	$90,000	$137,250	$937,300	$4,430,000	$13,500,000	44
Attendance	3,113	15,000	60,000	189,000	330,189	43
Full-time staff	1	2	8	51.5	138.8	45
Part-time staff	.6	1.5	5	29.5	50	45
Maintenance staff full-time	0.0	0.0	1.0	3.0	6.8	41
Maintenance staff part-time	0.0	0.0	0.0	1.0	2.0	40
Total interior square footage	3,518	8,500	45,705	150,000	222,647	39
Insurance costs paid by institution	$1,000	$1,750	$8,534	$70,887	$201,005	25
Insurance costs paid by parent			$43,555			3
Total insurance costs paid	$1,000	$1,800	$9,216	$79,025	$239,330	27

H.2 Space—presence and allocation as a percentage of total space

	Present in institution (n=28)		10th percentile	25th percentile	50th percentile	75th percentile	90th percentile	Number of responses
	Yes*	No						
Exhibitions	94%	2%	18.3%	22.2%	32.1%	53.1%	60.4%	33
Collections storage	96%	0%	2.6%	6.7%	13.2%	26.9%	41.3%	35
Non-collections storage	87%	2%	0.5%	1.7%	3.0%	5.6%	22.6%	29
Offices	96%	0%	2.3%	3.9%	8.0%	10.6%	19.7%	32
Education (classrooms)	67%	24%	0.5%	1.5%	2.9%	5.6%	18.1%	21
Library/research	67%	22%	0.4%	0.9%	2.0%	4.6%	8.4%	25
Museum store	83%	11%	0.3%	0.8%	1.3%	2.5%	5.7%	31
Public space/ public functions	70%	20%	1.7%	2.6%	10.0%	13.0%	23.9%	21
Food service	35%	50%	0.3%	0.5%	1.4%	1.7%	3.3%	11
Auditorium/ theaters	41%	43%	1.0%	1.9%	3.1%	7.5%	12.5%	11
Maintenance	67%	20%	0.3%	1.0%	2.2%	6.2%	15.4%	22
Conservation/ collections prep	78%	9%	1.0%	1.6%	2.7%	6.4%	14.8%	24

(*Percentages for yes and no often do not add to 100 percent—the remainder did not answer the question.)

H.3 Space allocation in square feet

	10th percentile	25th percentile	50th percentile	75th percentile	90th percentile	Number of responses
Exhibitions	1,475	3,000	8,077	34,500	61,600	37
Collections storage	310	1,219	5,000	18,317	47,765	40
Non-collections storage	65	500	900	2,000	10,333	32
Offices	150	512	1,750	6,854	28,956	36
Education (classrooms)	242	451	1,012	2,500	7,158	23
Library/research	94	248	1,000	3,400	9,968	27
Museum store	57	150	600	1,644	3,456	32
Public space/ public functions	202	1,000	4,000	28,817	70,853	23
Food service	99	350	1,091	1,896	6,735	12
Auditorium/ theaters	1,043	1,961	4,000	7,500	14,800	11
Maintenance	105	233	1,080	7,875	15,800	25
Conservation/ collections prep	192	500	1,478	3,700	5,430	27

H.4 What is allowed in building by policy

	Collection areas	Exhibit areas	Staff offices	Public spaces	Grounds
Open flames	0%	2%	2%	4%	11%
Food	7%	24%	63%	63%	76%
Beverages (other than water)	11%	22%	76%	65%	80%
Live plants	7%	28%	54%	46%	74%
Fresh flowers	7%	28%	61%	48%	65%
Dried plant material	28%	37%	41%	35%	44%
Personal artwork	11%	11%	61%	11%	11%
Filming	48%	72%	52%	70%	67%
Photography	54%	80%	61%	78%	78%

Sixty-three percent of respondents indicate they rent space to outside groups. Seventy-nine percent report the rental revenue goes to the institution's budget (as opposed to a parent organization or other group).

H.5 Groups space is/would be rented to

	Would rent to	Have rented to in past 5 years
Religious groups	69%	41%
Political groups	52%	24%
Private groups (weddings, parties, graduations, etc.)	83%	59%
Corporate groups	97%	76%
Non-religious nonprofit groups	93%	70%
Other	21%	17%

H.6 Have exclusive agreement with caterer(s)

	Yes, one caterer	Yes, maintain a list of accepted caterers	Median percent commission taken by institution	Average commission	N for mean/median	No	No response
Overall	11%	22%	0.0%	2.3%	12	67%	0%

H.7 Parking offered

	Have on-site parking	Median number of spaces	N for median	Have off-site parking	Median number of spaces	N for median
	78%	50	29	11%		2

Practice and Implementation of the Emergency Plan

Of the 76 percent of natural history/anthropology museums that have a disaster plan (see last table in this section) 51 percent report having practiced it.

H.8 Year emergency plan practiced

	Year not specified	Before 1996	1996-1999	2000-2002	2003	2004
	5%	5%	0%	10%	68%	11%

H.9 Types of training provided to staff

	Training is provided	For those who provide training			
		Training is mndatory for all staff	Training is mandatory for some staff	Training is optional	No response on mandatory/ optional status
Emergency response	48%	18%	68%	14%	0%
First aid/CPR	61%	14%	50%	36%	0%
General health and safety	59%	30%	44%	22%	4%
Hazardous material handling	46%	19%	71%	10%	0%

H.10 Parental involvement with insurance (for respondents with parent organizations)

Institution fully covered under parent	Covered under parent, but maintains separate riders	Not covered under parent	No response
67%	27%	3%	3%

Seventy-seven percent of respondents indicate the parent organization has regulations or guidelines regarding insurance to which the museum must adhere.

H.11 Does the parent pay for insurance?

Pay all costs	Pay some costs	Not pay	No response
53%	13%	23%	10%

H.12 Insurance types (See also insurance costs figures in first table of this section)

	Presently carry	Presently carry but considering dropping	Investigating/ planning to carry by 2005	No response
Commercial/general liability	70%	2%	0%	28%
Automobile	44%	2%	0%	54%
Collections/fine arts	57%	2%	2%	39%
Directors & Officers liability	52%	2%	4%	41%
Event cancellation	2%	2%	2%	93%
Exhibitions/loans	63%	0%	0%	37%
Transit	26%	2%	0%	72%
Terrorism	15%	2%	4%	78%
Other	11%	0%	0%	89%

H.13 Maintain a fund to offset small claims/deductibles

Yes	Median fund size	N for median	No	No response
7%		1	85%	9%

Thirty-three percent of respondents report being self-insured.

H.14 Meaning of self-insured

Set aside and manage a designated fund with internal loss assessment/ payment	Replace/repairs out of general fund budget	Does not replace value of losses	Other	No response
20%	40%	33%	27%	7%

H.15 Policies/plans

	Have	Do not have	In development	No response
Facilities use policy	70%	13%	9%	9%
Building rental policy	61%	24%	9%	7%
Special events policy for outside groups	52%	30%	2%	15%
Special events policy for museum-sponsored events	48%	33%	9%	11%
Filming policy	41%	43%	7%	9%
Filming agreement	30%	46%	11%	13%
Policy on use of funds resulting from insurance claims on losses to collections	17%	54%	4%	24%
Cyclical maintenance plan	50%	33%	7%	11%
Emergency preparedness/disaster plan	76%	15%	4%	4%
Historic structure master plan	22%	63%	9%	7%
Integrated pest management plan	61%	24%	4%	11%

Section I: Nature Centers

Total responses = 17

Thirty-five percent of these institutions have a parent organization.

I.1

	10th percentile	25th percentile	50th percentile	75th percentile	90th percentile	Number of responses
Operating income	$78,331	$150,000	$327,262	$555,679	$1,013,874	15
Operating expense	$72,360	$167,672	$336,000	$716,292	$1,172,068	15
Attendance	9,000	13,524	36,000	52,225	235,400	16
Full-time staff	1	2	4.5	6	13.2	16
Part-time staff	2	3	6	9	25.2	17
Maintenance staff full-time	0.0	0.0	0.0	0.8	1.9	16
Maintenance staff part-time	0.0	0.0	1.0	2.0	6.6	16
Total interior square footage	2,250	4,681	6,300	15,750	29,315	14
Insurance costs paid by institution	$4,275	$6,460	$10,800	$14,337	$20,735	12
Insurance costs paid by parent			0			0
Total insurance costs paid	$4,275	$6,460	$10,800	$14,337	$20,735	12

I.2 Space—presence and allocation as a percentage of total space

	Present in institution (n=28)		10th percentile	25th percentile	50th percentile	75th percentile	90th percentile	Number of responses
	Yes*	No						
Exhibitions	94%	6%		11.1%	30.0%	38.4%		8
Collections storage	77%	12%		1.1%	3.3%	7.6%		7
Non-collections storage	94%	6%		5.2%	7.7%	24.1%		9
Offices	100%	0%	1.4%	4.5%	7.7%	10.7%	19.8%	10
Education (classrooms)	88%	12%		11.5%	18.8%	32.3%		9
Library/research	65%	35%		1.6%	2.0%	6.0%		6
Museum store	82%	6%		1.5%	3.1%	5.4%		8
Public space/ public functions	77%	12%		2.1%	8.2%	25.7%		5
Food service	35%	35%			2.7%			4
Auditorium/ theaters	59%	24%		5.4%	8.5%	16.2%		6
Maintenance	88%	12%		1.9%	3.1%	5.2%		9
Conservation/ collections prep	41%	41%		2.1%	2.2%	7.5%		5

(*Percentages for yes and no often do not add to 100 percent—the remainder did not answer the question.)

I.3 Space allocation in square feet

	10th percentile	25th percentile	50th percentile	75th percentile	90th percentile	Number of responses
Exhibitions	264	400	1,200	9,800	32,040	11
Collections storage		73	200	520		8
Non-collections storage	123	200	750	1,742	2,557	10
Offices	136	295	550	1,008	2,198	11
Education (classrooms)	222	717	1,495	2,868	3,533	10
Library/research		100	200	395		7
Museum store	23	195	325	519	1,137	10
Public space/ public functions		550	1,184	4,972		8
Food service		155	250	652		5
Auditorium/ theaters		930	1,000	1,980		7
Maintenance	51	90	176	932	2,387	10
Conservation/ collections prep		133	202	1,107		6

I.4 What is allowed in building by policy

	Collection areas	Exhibit areas	Staff offices	Public spaces	Grounds
Open flames	0%	0%	0%	18%	53%
Food	6%	24%	82%	71%	88%
Beverages (other than water)	6%	24%	82%	71%	88%
Live plants	41%	65%	82%	71%	77%
Fresh flowers	35%	47%	71%	59%	59%
Dried plant material	41%	53%	53%	47%	47%
Personal artwork	29%	29%	77%	35%	24%
Filming	41%	77%	53%	82%	82%
Photography	53%	82%	65%	88%	88%

Seventy-seven percent of respondents indicate they rent space to outside groups. Eighty-five percent report the rental revenue goes to the institution's budget (as opposed to a parent organization or other group).

I.5 Groups space is/would be rented to

	Would rent to	Have rented to in past 5 years
Religious groups	77%	76%
Political groups	54%	23%
Private groups (weddings, parties, graduations, etc.)	92%	69%
Corporate groups	100%	77%
Non-religious nonprofit groups	92%	69%
Other	8%	8%

I.6 Have exclusive agreement with caterer(s)

	Yes, one caterer	Yes, maintain a list of accepted caterers	Median percent commission taken by institution	Average commission	N for mean/median	No	No response
Overall	10%	18%			1	82%	0%

I.7 Parking offered

	Have on-site parking	Median number of spaces	N for median	Have off-site parking	Median number of spaces	N for median
	100%	60	15	18%	75	3

Practice and Implementation of the Emergency Plan

Of the 71 percent of nature centers that have a disaster plan (see last table in this section) 62 percent report having practiced it.

I.8 Year emergency plan practiced

	Year not specified	Before 1996	1996-1999	2000-2002	2003	2004
	12%	0%	0%	13%	63%	13%

I.9 Types of training provided to staff

	Training is provided	For those who provide training			
		Training is mndatory for all staff	Training is mandatory for some staff	Training is optional	No response on mandatory/ optional status
Emergency response	35%	33%	67%	0%	0%
First aid/CPR	82%	36%	50%	7%	7%
General health and safety	59%	30%	30%	20%	20%
Hazardous material handling	29%	40%	40%	0%	20%

I.10 Parental involvement with insurance (for respondents with parent organizations)

Institution fully covered under parent	Covered under parent, but maintains separate riders	Not covered under parent	No response
83%	0%	0%	17%

Thirty-three percent of respondents indicate the parent organization has regulations or guidelines regarding insurance to which the museum must adhere.

I.11 Does the parent pay for insurance?

Pay all costs	Pay some costs	Not pay	No response
50%	0%	33%	17%

I.12 Insurance types (See also insurance costs figures in first table of this section)

	Presently carry	Presently carry but considering dropping	Investigating/ planning to carry by 2005	No response
Commercial/general liability	88%	0%	0%	12%
Automobile	71%	0%	0%	29%
Collections/fine arts	24%	0%	0%	77%
Directors & Officers liability	65%	0%	0%	35%
Event cancellation	6%	0%	0%	94%
Exhibitions/loans	12%	0%	0%	88%
Transit	0%	0%	0%	100%
Terrorism	12%	0%	0%	88%
Other	12%	0%	0%	88%

I.13 Maintain a fund to offset small claims/deductibles

	Yes	Median fund size	N for median	No	No response
	12%		1	82%	6%

Eighteen percent of respondents report being self-insured.

I.14 Meaning of self-insured

	Set aside and manage a designated fund with internal loss assessment/ payment	Replace/repairs out of general fund budget	Does not replace value of losses	Other	No response
	0%	67%	0%	33%	0%

I.15 Policies/plans

	Have	Do not have	In development	No response
Facilities use policy	41%	47%	0%	12%
Building rental policy	65%	35%	0%	0%
Special events policy for outside groups	53%	41%	0%	6%
Special events policy for museum-sponsored events	35%	53%	0%	12%
Filming policy	24%	71%	0%	6%
Filming agreement	12%	76%	0%	12%
Policy on use of funds resulting from insurance claims on losses to collections	12%	65%	0%	24%
Cyclical maintenance plan	53%	29%	6%	12%
Emergency preparedness/disaster plan	71%	29%	0%	0%
Historic structure master plan	12%	76%	0%	12%
Integrated pest management plan	29%	71%	0%	0%

Section J: Science/Technology Center/Museum

Total responses = 40

Twenty-eight percent of these institutions have a parent organization.

J.1

	10th percentile	25th percentile	50th percentile	75th percentile	90th percentile	Number of responses
Operating income	$147,790	$504,089	$1,466,931	$6,929,711	$19,725,574	38
Operating expense	$150,000	$593,588	$1,214,604	$6,000,000	$20,500,000	39
Attendance	15,000	37,517	122,836	607,328	892,948	36
Full-time staff	2	5	13	68.75	178.7	40
Part-time staff	1	4	8	44	119	39
Maintenance staff full-time	0.0	0.0	1.0	6.0	13.1	38
Maintenance staff part-time	0.0	0.0	0.0	2.0	3.1	38
Total interior square footage	5,327	13,050	49,500	155,000	377,296	38
Insurance costs paid by institution	$2,308	$21,427	$48,335	$135,684	$400,210	28
Insurance costs paid by parent						0
Total insurance costs paid	$2,308	$21,427	$48,335	$135,684	$400,210	28

J.2 Space—presence and allocation as a percentage of total space

	Present in institution (n=28)		10th percentile	25th percentile	50th percentile	75th percentile	90th percentile	Number of responses
	Yes*	No						
Exhibitions	95%	0%	7.1%	20.2%	27.9%	42.5%	59.7%	29
Collections storage	70%	18%	0.5%	1.8%	3.4%	14.6%	51.0%	20
Non-collections storage	85%	8%	1.7%	3.0%	5.0%	12.2%	22.3%	29
Offices	93%	0%	1.8%	5.4%	8.2%	11.6%	24.8%	30
Education (classrooms)	83%	5%	1.0%	2.2%	3.3%	14.6%	30.7%	26
Library/research	48%	33%	0.3%	0.6%	2.1%	5.9%	23.4%	14
Museum store	85%	13%	0.8%	1.0%	1.7%	2.8%	7.6%	27
Public space/ public functions	75%	13%	3.9%	5.1%	8.1%	21.5%	41.5%	22
Food service	53%	33%	0.8%	0.9%	1.7%	4.1%	11.0%	18
Auditorium/ theaters	73%	10%	1.1%	3.8%	9.1%	15.5%	35.3%	24
Maintenance	75%	8%	0.3%	1.0%	3.9%	14.1%	29.0%	24
Conservation/ collections prep	43%	35%	0.6%	0.8%	3.4%	5.2%	16.8%	13

(*Percentages for yes and no often do not add to 100 percent—the remainder did not answer the question.)

J.3 Space allocation in square feet

	10th percentile	25th percentile	50th percentile	75th percentile	90th percentile	Number of responses
Exhibitions	1,650	6,400	12,710	48,750	75,500	32
Collections storage	330	600	1,942	5,000	14,100	22
Non-collections storage	200	1,000	3,000	8,000	19,412	29
Offices	500	850	4,500	16,003	34,760	31
Education (classrooms)	640	1,000	2,500	8,000	15,300	27
Library/research	129	400	890	3,000	15,442	15
Museum store	150	435	1,500	3,000	4,285	29
Public space/ public functions	1,000	1,524	7,353	26,250	69,492	24
Food service	200	800	3,200	8,542	12,000	19
Auditorium/ theaters	820	1,842	5,000	15,500	31,080	25
Maintenance	50	300	2,154	13,988	48,421	25
Conservation/ collections prep	200	344	500	7,700	9,180	13

J.4 What is allowed in building by policy

	Collection areas	Exhibit areas	Staff offices	Public spaces	Grounds
Open flames	0%	5%	0%	13%	13%
Food	8%	35%	83%	70%	73%
Beverages (other than water)	8%	35%	85%	78%	70%
Live plants	10%	45%	80%	70%	73%
Fresh flowers	5%	33%	75%	63%	63%
Dried plant material	23%	45%	53%	43%	45%
Personal artwork	10%	30%	78%	30%	23%
Filming	28%	80%	58%	83%	80%
Photography	30%	83%	60%	85%	85%

Eighty-five percent of respondents indicate they rent space to outside groups. Eighty-eight percent report the rental revenue goes to the institution's budget (as opposed to a parent organization or other group).

J.5 Groups space is/would be rented to

	Would rent to	Have rented to in past 5 years
Religious groups	68%	44%
Political groups	56%	32%
Private groups (weddings, parties, graduations, etc.)	94%	85%
Corporate groups	91%	88%
Non-religious nonprofit groups	97%	88%
Other	12%	12%

J.6 Have exclusive agreement with caterer(s)

	Yes, one caterer	Yes, maintain a list of accepted caterers	Median percent commission taken by institution	Average commission	N for mean/ median	No	No response
Overall	25%	15%	12.5%	14.9%	9	60%	0%

J.7 Parking offered

	Have on-site parking	Median number of spaces	N for median	Have off-site parking	Median number of spaces	N for median
	75%	113	28	8%	200	3

Practice and Implementation of the Emergency Plan

Of the 78 percent of science/ technology centers/museums that have a disaster plan (see last table in this section) 67 percent report having practiced it.

J.8 Year emergency plan practiced

	Year not specified	Before 1996	1996-1999	2000-2002	2003	2004
	8%	0%	0%	13%%	50%	29%

J.9 Types of training provided to staff

	Training is provided	For those who provide training			
		Training is mndatory for all staff	Training is mandatory for some staff	Training is optional	No response on mandatory/ optional status
Emergency response	65%	27%	65%	4%	4%
First aid/CPR	73%	10%	79%	10%	0%
General health and safety	65%	35%	50%	12%	4%
Hazardous material handling	48%	5%	84%	11%	0%

J.10 Parental involvement with insurance (for respondents with parent organizations)

Institution fully covered under parent	Covered under parent, but maintains separate riders	Not covered under parent	No response
91%	0%	0%	9%

Seventy-three percent of respondents indicate the parent organization has regulations or guidelines regarding insurance to which the museum must adhere.

J.11 Does the parent pay for insurance?

Pay all costs	Pay some costs	Not pay	No response
73%	0%	9%	18%

J.12 Insurance types (See also insurance costs figures in first table of this section)

	Presently carry	Presently carry but considering dropping	Investigating/ planning to carry by 2005	No response
Commercial/general liability	88%	0%	0%	12%
Automobile	75%	0%	0%	25%
Collections/fine arts	43%	0%	0%	58%
Directors & Officers liability	75%	0%	3%	23%
Event cancellation	5%	0%	3%	93%
Exhibitions/loans	58%	0%	0%	43%
Transit	25%	0%	0%	75%
Terrorism	25%	0%	0%	75%
Other	20%	0%	0%	80%

J.13 Maintain a fund to offset small claims/deductibles

Yes	Median fund size	N for median	No	No response
10%		2	83%	8%

Thirteen percent of respondents report being self-insured.

J.14 Meaning of self-insured

Set aside and manage a designated fund with internal loss assessment/ payment	Replace/repairs out of general fund budget	Does not replace value of losses	Other	No response
40%	60%	0%	0%	0%

J.15 Policies/plans

	Have	Do not have	In development	No response
Facilities use policy	68%	18%	5%	10%
Building rental policy	75%	15%	3%	8%
Special events policy for outside groups	73%	18%	0%	10%
Special events policy for museum-sponsored events	53%	35%	0%	13%
Filming policy	38%	48%	3%	13%
Filming agreement	20%	55%	5%	20%
Policy on use of funds resulting from insurance claims on losses to collections	13%	63%	0%	25%
Cyclical maintenance plan	55%	23%	8%	15%
Emergency preparedness/disaster plan	78%	10%	8%	5%
Historic structure master plan	15%	70%	0%	15%
Integrated pest management plan	40%	43%	3%	15%

Section K: Specialized Museums

Total responses = 156

A specialized museum is one that does not fall into or combine any of the other discipline areas listed as a choice in the survey (e.g, art, history, natural history/anthropology, etc.).This category is often chosen, for example, by ethnically or culturally specific organizations, or museums focusing on one type of object such as clocks, quilts, stamps, etc. See appendix I for a complete list of respondents that identified themselves as "specialized museums".

Forty percent of these institutions have a parent organization.

K.1

	10th percentile	25th percentile	50th percentile	75th percentile	90th percentile	Number of responses
Operating income	$22,558	$74,177	$268,000	$862,136	$2,670,063	132
Operating expense	$21,746	$90,000	$265,000	$904,417	$2,915,694	135
Attendance	1,818	5,000	20,000	65,057	168,590	132
Full-time staff	0	1	2	6.5	26.6	153
Part-time staff	0	0	2	6	14.7	152
Maintenance staff full-time	0.0	0.0	0.0	1.0	4.0	143
Maintenance staff part-time	0.0	0.0	0.0	1.0	3.0	140
Total interior square footage	2,500	5,000	16,000	43,000	112,180	135
Insurance costs paid by institution	$1,460	$3,857	$10,900	$30,000	$83,983	91
Insurance costs paid by parent	$2,920	$6,180	$21,193	$72,000	$1,155,720	13
Total insurance costs paid	$1,831	$3,981	$12,500	$31,800	$83,983	101

K.2 Space—presence and allocation as a percentage of total space

	Present in institution (n=28)		10th percentile	25th percentile	50th percentile	75th percentile	90th percentile	Number of responses
	Yes*	No						
Exhibitions	88%	2%	9.6	22.2	46.3	60.5	75.0	102
Collections storage	84%	6%	1.2	3.8	9.1	21.8	40.2	98
Non-collections storage	70%	13%	1.1	2.3	3.6	8.6	15.6	77
Offices	88%	1%	1.3	2.7	5.0	10.1	17.3	100
Education (classrooms)	40%	36%	1.0	1.7	3.9	8.0	21.8	48
Library/research	62%	22%	0.5	1.5	2.5	4.9	10.2	65
Museum store	76%	10%	0.7	1.3	2.1	4.7	10.0	85
Public space/ public functions	58%	20%	2.3	4.2	10.0	21.0	42.5	54
Food service	24%	52%	0.4	0.7	1.6	3.6	7.0	26
Auditorium/ theaters	33%	43%	0.5	1.5	3.8	6.4	9.7	35
Maintenance	50%	29%	0.3	0.5	1.5	6.6	14.2	55
Conservation/ collections prep	42%	32%	0.1	0.5	2.0	5.5	11.2	41

(*Percentages for yes and no often do not add to 100 percent—the remainder did not answer the question.)

K.3 Space allocation in square feet

	10th percentile	25th percentile	50th percentile	75th percentile	90th percentile	Number of responses
Exhibitions	1,000	2,200	5,000	15,472	48,300	108
Collections storage	140	500	1,297	5,000	14,100	104
Non-collections storage	100	300	1,000	3,177	9,800	80
Offices	117	300	800	2,653	8,659	106
Education (classrooms)	250	500	1,400	2,744	8,000	51
Library/research	100	200	556	1,765	7,908	68
Museum store	100	231	500	1,200	2,391	88
Public space/ public functions	200	1,000	3,300	7,411	23,600	56
Food service	100	200	672	2,000	5,050	27
Auditorium/ theaters	144	462	1,200	3,156	7,900	37
Maintenance	58	112	500	1,800	8,294	57
Conservation/ collections prep	100	200	533	1,275	5,320	46

K.4 What is allowed in building by policy

	Collection areas	Exhibit areas	Staff offices	Public spaces	Grounds
Open flames	3%	3%	5%	8%	21%
Food	4%	23%	68%	60%	65%
Beverages (other than water)	3%	25%	72%	60%	65%
Live plants	6%	17%	53%	42%	55%
Fresh flowers	6%	20%	58%	47%	51%
Dried plant material	6%	21%	35%	32%	30%
Personal artwork	6%	14%	58%	12%	8%
Filming	29%	71%	39%	68%	69%
Photography	32%	72%	42%	71%	72%

Sixty percent of respondents indicate they rent space to outside groups. Eighty-four percent report the rental revenue goes to the institution's budget (as opposed to a parent organization or other group).

K.5 Groups space is/would be rented to

	Would rent to	Have rented to in past 5 years
Religious groups	65%	37%
Political groups	57%	41%
Private groups (weddings, parties, graduations, etc.)	84%	67%
Corporate groups	89%	63%
Non-religious nonprofit groups	97%	74%
Other	16%	12%

K.6 Have exclusive agreement with caterer(s)

	Yes, one caterer	Yes, maintain a list of accepted caterers	Median percent commission taken by institution	Average commission	N for mean/ median	No	No response
Overall	10%	14%	0.0%	4.2%	26	73%	3%

K.7 Parking offered

	Have on-site parking	Median number of spaces	N for median	Have off-site parking	Median number of spaces	N for median
	73%	50	99	12%	200	13

Practice and Implementation of the Emergency Plan

Of the 55 percent of specialized museums that have a disaster plan (see last table in this section) 63 percent report having practiced it.

K.8 Year emergency plan practiced

	Year not specified	Before 1996	1996-1999	2000-2002	2003	2004
	8%	0%	2%	16%	57%	18%

K.9 Types of training provided to staff

	Training is provided	For those who provide training			
		Training is mndatory for all staff	Training is mandatory for some staff	Training is optional	No response on mandatory/ optional status
Emergency response	46%	44%	37%	16%	4%
First aid/CPR	37%	19%	53%	25%	4%
General health and safety	46%	42%	34%	16%	9%
Hazardous material handling	31%	18%	65%	14%	2%

K.10 Parental involvement with insurance (for respondents with parent organizations)

Institution fully covered under parent	Covered under parent, but maintains separate riders	Not covered under parent	No response
78%	8%	6%	8%

Fifty-seven percent of respondents indicate the parent organization has regulations or guidelines regarding insurance to which the museum must adhere.

K.11 Does the parent pay for insurance?

Pay all costs	Pay some costs	Not pay	No response
65%	10%	11%	14%

K.12 Insurance types (See also insurance costs figures in first table of this section)

	Presently carry	Presently carry but considering dropping	Investigating/ planning to carry by 2005	No response
Commercial/general liability	70%	0%	0%	30%
Automobile	36%	0%	1%	63%
Collections/fine arts	60%	0%	3%	37%
Directors & Officers liability	53%	0%	6%	41%
Event cancellation	6%	0%	2%	92%
Exhibitions/loans	44%	0%	2%	55%
Transit	17%	0%	2%	81%
Terrorism	24%	1%	1%	75%
Other	12%	1%	0%	87%

K.13 Maintain a fund to offset small claims/deductibles

	Yes	Median fund size	N for median	No	No response
	6%	$5,000	5	83%	12%

Twenty-three percent of respondents report being self-insured

K.14 Meaning of self-insured

Set aside and manage a designated fund with internal loss assessment/ payment	Replace/repairs out of general fund budget	Does not replace value of losses	Other	No response
11%	61%	6%	17%	11%

K.15 Policies/plans

	Have	Do not have	In development	No response
Facilities use policy	44%	33%	13%	10%
Building rental policy	40%	41%	10%	9%
Special events policy for outside groups	39%	44%	8%	10%
Special events policy for museum-sponsored events	31%	49%	8%	12%
Filming policy	35%	49%	8%	8%
Filming agreement	24%	61%	7%	8%
Policy on use of funds resulting from insurance claims on losses to collections	14%	67%	7%	12%
Cyclical maintenance plan	30%	41%	13%	16%
Emergency preparedness/disaster plan	55%	29%	8%	8%
Historic structure master plan	14%	67%	6%	14%
Integrated pest management plan	33%	51%	6%	10%

Section L: Museums with Municipal or County Governance

Total responses = 124

These respondents identified themselves as being governed by municipalities or counties. Seventy-six percent consider the municipal or county government to be their parent organization. Thirteen percent are part of a museum system.

L.1 Discipline

	Percentage of sample	Number of responses
Aquarium	1.6%	2
Arboretum/botanic garden	2%	3
Art museum	9.7%	12
Children's/youth museum	0.8%	1
General museum	16.1%	20
Historic house/site	12.9%	16
History museum/historical society	35.5%	44
Natural history/anthropology museum	5.6%	7
Nature center	1.6%	2
Science/technology center/museum	2.4%	3
Specialized museum	4.0%	5
Zoo	7.3%	9
Other	0%	0

L.2

	10th percentile	25th percentile	50th percentile	75th percentile	90th percentile	Number of responses
Operating income	$36,411	$100,000	$299,621	$1,100,000	$5,739,685	87
Operating expense	$40,397	$101,641	$382,641	$1,188,750	$5,157,918	94
Attendance	2,461	6,750	21,000	86,517	340,632	101
Full-time staff	0	1	3	10.5	39	122
Part-time staff	0	1	3	7	23	121
Maintenance staff full-time	0	0	0	2	5	120
Maintenance staff part-time	0	0	0	1	3	120
Total interior square footage	4,790	8,764	23,253	46,659	97,747	96
Insurance costs paid by institution	$500	$1,896	$9,500	$19,561	$101,487	38
Insurance costs paid by parent	$522	$1,049	$4,214	$15,592	$169,586	18
Total insurance costs paid	$504	$1,183	$7,000	$17,746	$95,174	50

L.3 Space—presence and allocation as a percentage of total space

	Present in institution (n=28)		10th percentile	25th percentile	50th percentile	75th percentile	90th percentile	Number of responses
	Yes*	No						
Exhibitions	88%	2%	12.3%	23.5%	42.2%	56.1%	76.0%	73
Collections storage	82%	6%	1.7%	3.5%	11.4%	20.6%	35.3%	68
Non-collections storage	76%	9%	1.1%	2.1%	5.6%	9.1%	24.4%	65
Offices	85%	5%	1.5%	2.5%	4.3%	7.9%	10.5%	70
Education (classrooms)	44%	31%	1.1%	2.1%	6.0%	10.0%	15.2%	41
Library/research	64%	18%	0.6%	1.1%	1.6%	4.9%	7.5%	53
Museum store	65%	19%	0.4%	0.9%	1.8%	2.9%	5.2%	54
Public space/ public functions	57%	20%	1.8%	3.4%	8.4%	21.1%	31.1%	38
Food service	28%	44%	0.5%	0.9%	2.0%	4.3%	12.8%	25
Auditorium/ theaters	29%	44%	1.2%	2.7%	5.0%	10.4%	15.0%	26
Maintenance	61%	17%	0.6%	1.0%	2.2%	4.4%	6.5%	53
Conservation/ collections prep	44%	32%	0.6%	1.2%	2.4%	4.3%	7.5%	37

(*Percentages for yes and no often do not add to 100 percent—the remainder did not answer the question.)

American Association of Museums

L.4 Space allocation in square feet

	10th percentile	25th percentile	50th percentile	75th percentile	90th percentile	Number of responses
Exhibitions	1,360	3,000	6,526	18,000	51,326	83
Collections storage	181	620	1,621	6,224	12,372	75
Non-collections storage	101	287	1,000	2,125	9,015	70
Offices	195	300	1,000	2,000	5,019	78
Education (classrooms)	371	710	1,780	3,036	6,552	45
Library/research	125	249	561	1,422	2,100	57
Museum store	84	184	500	1,100	2,268	61
Public space/ public functions	475	1,170	2,500	8,772	19,378	44
Food service	94	290	500	2,850	7,100	27
Auditorium/ theaters	591	1,725	2,450	5,275	8,914	26
Maintenance	96	197	500	2,000	3,997	57
Conservation/ collections prep	200	270	500	2,030	5,180	39

L.5 What is allowed in building by policy

	Collection areas	Exhibit areas	Staff offices	Public spaces	Grounds
Open flames	2%	4%	4%	10%	26%
Food	5%	23%	66%	60%	69%
Beverages (other than water)	4%	21%	72%	62%	70%
Live plants	7%	26%	52%	51%	66%
Fresh flowers	10%	26%	57%	52%	56%
Dried plant material	19%	37%	41%	46%	41%
Personal artwork	5%	13%	56%	12%	6%
Filming	23%	56%	32%	60%	68%
Photography	27%	65%	36%	65%	73%

Sixty-nine percent of respondents indicate they rent space to outside groups. Fifty-six percent report the rental revenue goes to the institution's budget (as opposed to a parent organization or other group).

L.6 Groups space is/would be rented to

	Would rent to	Have rented to in past 5 years
Religious groups	76%	45%
Political groups	59%	34%
Private groups (weddings, parties, graduations, etc.)	88%	68%
Corporate groups	85%	62%
Non-religious nonprofit groups	93%	72%
Other	14%	12%

L.7 Have exclusive agreement with caterer(s)

	Yes, one caterer	Yes, maintain a list of accepted caterers	Median percent commission taken by institution	Average commission	N for mean/ median	No	No response
Overall	9%	11%	9.0%	8.4%	18	79%	1%

L.8 Parking offered

	Have on-site parking	Median number of spaces	N for median	Have off-site parking	Median number of spaces	N for median
	73%	50	76	15%	25	18

Practice and Implementation of the Emergency Plan

Of the 67 percent of county/ municipal museums that have a disaster plan (see last table in this section) 61 percent report having practiced it.

L.9 Year emergency plan practiced

	Year not specified	Before 1996	1996-1999	2000-2002	2003	2004
	15%	2%	2%	13%	50%	17%

L.10 Types of training provided to staff

	Training is provided	For those who provide training			
		Training is mndatory for all staff	Training is mandatory for some staff	Training is optional	No response on mandatory/ optional status
Emergency response	53%	41%	39%	15%	5%
First aid/CPR	60%	20%	45%	28%	7%
General health and safety	65%	46%	26%	20%	8%
Hazardous material handling	45%	25%	54%	14%	7%

L.11 Parental involvement with insurance (for respondents with parent organizations)

Institution fully covered under parent	Covered under parent, but maintains separate riders	Not covered under parent	No response
69%	16%	6%	9%

Sixty-six percent of respondents indicate the parent organization has regulations or guidelines regarding insurance to which the museum must adhere.

L.12 Does the parent pay for insurance?

Pay all costs	Pay some costs	Not pay	No response
65%	16%	7%	12%

L.13 Insurance types (See also insurance costs figures in first table of this section)

	Presently carry	Presently carry but considering dropping	Investigating/ planning to carry by 2005	No response
Commercial/general liability	66%	0%	0%	34%
Automobile	42%	0%	0%	58%
Collections/fine arts	59%	0%	1%	40%
Directors & Officers liability	36%	0%	5%	59%
Event cancellation	4%	0%	2%	94%
Exhibitions/loans	48%	0%	0%	52%
Transit	15%	0%	0%	86%
Terrorism	12%	0%	1%	87%
Other	4%	0%	0%	96%

L.14 Maintain a fund to offset small claims/deductibles

	Yes	Median fund size	N for median	No	No response
	15%	$20,000	7	69%	17%

Forty-three percent of respondents report being self-insured.

L.15 Meaning of self-insured

	Set aside and manage a designated fund with internal loss assessment/ payment	Replace/repairs out of general fund budget	Does not replace value of losses	Other	No response
	40%	42%	8%	15%	9%

L.16 Policies/plans

	Have	Do not have	In development	No response
Facilities use policy	60%	27%	6%	6%
Building rental policy	62%	30%	3%	5%
Special events policy for outside groups	51%	40%	2%	6%
Special events policy for museum-sponsored events	39%	48%	4%	9%
Filming policy	38%	50%	4%	8%
Filming agreement	18%	65%	5%	13%
Policy on use of funds resulting from insurance claims on losses to collections	14%	69%	4%	13%
Cyclical maintenance plan	44%	39%	5%	12%
Emergency preparedness/disaster plan	67%	24%	5%	4%
Historic structure master plan	23%	60%	8%	10%
Integrated pest management plan	52%	36%	6%	6%

Section M: Museums with State Governance

Total responses = 126

These respondents identified themselves as being state-governed. Interestingly, 12 do not consider the state to be a parent organization, perhaps because they are independently chartered. Fifty-three percent of these museums are part of a state college or university, and 18 percent are part of a state museum system.

M.1 Discipline

	Percentage of sample	Number of responses
Aquarium	0.8%	1
Arboretum/botanic garden	0%	0
Art museum	31.0%	39
Children's/youth museum	0.0%	0
General museum	12.7%	16
Historic house/site	14.3%	18
History museum/historical society	16.7%	21
Natural history/anthropology museum	10.3%	13
Nature center	0.0%	0
Science/technology center/museum	0.8%	1
Specialized museum	12.7%	16
Zoo	0.8%	1
Other	0%	0

M.2

	10th percentile	25th percentile	50th percentile	75th percentile	90th percentile	Number of responses
Operating income	$43,382	$148,850	$502,585	$2,104,343	$7,412,623	104
Operating expense	$38,649	$150,500	$502,585	$2,100,811	$7,744,360	104
Attendance	2,542	14,931	35,000	85,000	239,596	111
Full-time staff	1	2	4	17.5	70	125
Part-time staff	0	1	4	11.5	28	125
Maintenance staff full-time	0	0	1	2	7	116
Maintenance staff part-time	0	0	0	1	3	114
Total interior square footage	3,585	7,900	22,150	70,213	190,027	106
Insurance costs paid by institution	$768	$1,800	$4,803	$19,778	$67,019	46
Insurance costs paid by parent	$1,780	$3,952	$8,000	$35,640	$86,493	21
Total insurance costs paid	$1,278	$2,398	$5,687	$25,167	$84,855	62

M.3 Space—presence and allocation as a percentage of total space

	Present in institution (n=28)		10th percentile	25th percentile	50th percentile	75th percentile	90th percentile	Number of responses
	Yes*	No						
Exhibitions	90%	2%	17.9%	28.4%	36.2%	56.1%	72.4%	86
Collections storage	90%	3%	3.2%	6.4%	14.1%	22.4%	34.5%	83
Non-collections storage	82%	6%	0.7%	1.4%	4.0%	8.5%	16.5%	71
Offices	90%	2%	1.7%	4.0%	8.3%	12.9%	18.8%	82
Education (classrooms)	48%	36%	0.4%	1.1%	2.4%	6.1%	10.9%	44
Library/research	52%	31%	0.3%	0.6%	1.4%	3.3%	7.8%	47
Museum store	64%	20%	0.3%	0.8%	1.5%	2.6%	3.5%	61
Public space/ public functions	61%	19%	1.1%	1.8%	5.4%	17.6%	39.7%	56
Food service	23%	56%	0.5%	1.0%	1.5%	2.3%	4.0%	20
Auditorium/ theaters	40%	42%	0.8%	2.1%	3.8%	9.0%	13.8%	36
Maintenance	57%	25%	0.3%	0.6%	1.7%	6.8%	18.3%	48
Conservation/ collections prep	61%	21%	0.6%	1.3%	3.1%	6.0%	12.9%	55

(*Percentages for yes and no often do not add to 100 percent—the remainder did not answer the question.)

M.4 Space allocation in square feet

	10th percentile	25th percentile	50th percentile	75th percentile	90th percentile	Number of responses
Exhibitions	1,132	3,000	10,000	24,111	61,800	90
Collections storage	400	1,000	3,871	10,337	38,000	89
Non-collections storage	100	400	1,000	3,500	7,964	75
Offices	300	500	1,800	5,200	17,340	87
Education (classrooms)	425	637	1,000	3,585	8,880	46
Library/research	100	200	500	2,745	10,000	49
Museum store	100	285	600	1,200	3,000	63
Public space/ public functions	362	646	2,200	10,318	25,000	57
Food service	100	175	1,100	4,813	7,751	21
Auditorium/ theaters	400	915	2,400	4,388	12,400	37
Maintenance	91	200	747	3,145	24,900	50
Conservation/ collections prep	250	500	1,000	3,000	6,432	59

M.5 What is allowed in building by policy

	Collection areas	Exhibit areas	Staff offices	Public spaces	Grounds
Open flames	2%	2%	5%	6%	20%
Food	5%	23%	69%	67%	78%
Beverages (other than water)	5%	21%	76%	63%	75%
Live plants	6%	13%	55%	44%	67%
Fresh flowers	8%	23%	66%	60%	60%
Dried plant material	12%	25%	40%	40%	37%
Personal artwork	6%	10%	69%	16%	13%
Filming	29%	63%	37%	69%	67%
Photography	37%	71%	46%	72%	75%

Sixty-four percent of respondents indicate they rent space to outside groups. Seventy-three percent report the rental revenue goes to the institution's budget (as opposed to a parent organization or other group).

M.6 Groups space is/would be rented to

	Would rent to	Have rented to in past 5 years
Religious groups	51%	31%
Political groups	47%	30%
Private groups (weddings, parties, graduations, etc.)	75%	63%
Corporate groups	86%	70%
Non-religious nonprofit groups	90%	80%
Other	37%	36%

M.7 Have exclusive agreement with caterer(s)

	Yes, one caterer	Yes, maintain a list of accepted caterers	Median percent commission taken by institution	Average commission	N for mean/ median	No	No response
Overall	17%	14%	0%	2.5%	29	67%	2%

M.8 Parking offered

	Have on-site parking	Median number of spaces	N for median	Have off-site parking	Median number of spaces	N for median
	67%	55	70	10%	42.5	6

Practice and Implementation of the Emergency Plan

Of the 78 percent of state museums that have a disaster plan (see last table in this section) 58 percent report having practiced it.

M.9 Year emergency plan practiced

	Year not specified	Before 1996	1996-1999	2000-2002	2003	2004
	3%	2%	0%	12%	58%	25%

M.10 Types of training provided to staff

	Training is provided	For those who provide training			
		Training is mndatory for all staff	Training is mandatory for some staff	Training is optional	No response on mandatory/ optional status
Emergency response	62%	46%	41%	10%	3%
First aid/CPR	54%	18%	50%	29%	3%
General health and safety	56%	40%	39%	19%	3%
Hazardous material handling	48%	20%	66%	15%	0%

M.11 Parental involvement with insurance (for respondents with parent organizations)

Institution fully covered under parent	Covered under parent, but maintains separate riders	Not covered under parent	No response
57%	29%	7%	7%

Sixty-nine percent of respondents indicate the parent organization has regulations or guidelines regarding insurance to which the museum must adhere.

M.12 Does the parent pay for insurance?

Pay all costs	Pay some costs	Not pay	No response
58%	20%	9%	13%

M.13 Insurance types (See also insurance costs figures in first table of this section)

	Presently carry	Presently carry but considering dropping	Investigating/ planning to carry by 2005	No response
Commercial/general liability	59%	1%	0%	41%
Automobile	48%	1%	1%	50%
Collections/fine arts	66%	1%	0%	33%
Directors & Officers liability	37%	1%	1%	62%
Event cancellation	6%	1%	1%	93%
Exhibitions/loans	58%	0%	0%	42%
Transit	31%	1%	0%	68%
Terrorism	15%	1%	1%	83%
Other	5%	0%	0%	95%

I speculate that a large number of respondents were unable to identify their insurance coverage because it is provided through the state, and they are unacquainted with the specifics.

M.14 Maintain a fund to offset small claims/deductibles

	Yes	Median fund size	N for median	No	No response
	10%	$1,000	7	68%	21%

Fifty-eight percent of respondents report being self-insured.

M.15 Meaning of self-insured

	Set aside and manage a designated fund with internal loss assessment/ payment	Replace/repairs out of general fund budget	Does not replace value of losses	Other	No response
	36%	38%	10%	14%	15%

M.16 Policies/plans

	Have	Do not have	In development	No response
Facilities use policy	69%	17%	4%	10%
Building rental policy	54%	28%	7%	11%
Special events policy for outside groups	63%	22%	4%	10%
Special events policy for museum-sponsored events	48%	30%	7%	14%
Filming policy	50%	29%	10%	11%
Filming agreement	36%	40%	10%	15%
Policy on use of funds resulting from insurance claims on losses to collections	28%	47%	4%	21%
Cyclical maintenance plan	48%	30%	8%	13%
Emergency preparedness/disaster plan	78%	9%	7%	6%
Historic structure master plan	17%	60%	5%	18%
Integrated pest management plan	52%	32%	4%	12%

Section N: Museums that Have a Museum Parent Organization or Are Part of a Museum System

Total responses = 113

A museum system is an arrangement in which two or more museums or museums facilities share a common parent organization. The components of a museum system may be museums operating independently or quasi-independently with distinct budgets and governing authorities, or separate, distinguishable sites all managed by the same organization. Systems represented among the survey respondents include the U.S. Army museums, the Smithsonian Institution, the Carnegie Museums, the Museum of New Mexico, and the Pennsylvania Historical and Museums Commission. Of these respondents, 44 percent have private nonprofit governance, 20 percent state, 12 percent federal, 9 percent municipal, 5 percent county, 10 percent dual, and one organization is for-profit.

N.1 Discipline

	Percentage of sample	Number of responses
Aquarium	0.9%	1
Arboretum/botanic garden	0%	0
Art museum	8.0%	9
Children's/youth museum	0.9%	1
General museum	11.5%	13
Historic house/site	20.4%	23
History museum/historical society	36.3%	41
Natural history/anthropology museum	5.3%	6
Nature center	0.9%	1
Science/technology center/museum	0.9%	1
Specialized museum	14.2%	16
Zoo	0.9%	1
Other	0%	0

N.2

	10th percentile	25th percentile	50th percentile	75th percentile	90th percentile	Number of responses
Operating income	$14,900	$63,961	$286,340	$1,366,500	$5,553,055	97
Operating expense	$24,473	$81,095	$280,000	$1,712,919	$5,348,280	97
Attendance	2,000	6,700	22,537	76,592	309,000	103
Full-time staff	0	1	3	16	46	111
Part-time staff	0	1	3	7.25	24	110
Maintenance staff full-time	0	0	0	2	7	107
Maintenance staff part-time	0	0	1	1	5	105
Total interior square footage	3,740	8,700	22,650	67,493	174,378	96
Insurance costs paid by institution	$1,000	$1,965	$7,000	$19,705	$79,025	39
Insurance costs paid by parent	$873	$1,500	$4,000	$29,629	$83,167	35
Total insurance costs paid	$997	$1,981	$6,713	$26,750	$79,098	68

N.3 Space—presence and allocation as a percentage of total space

	Present in institution (n=28)		10th percentile	25th percentile	50th percentile	75th percentile	90th percentile	Number of responses
	Yes*	No						
Exhibitions	89%	3%	17.1%	27.0%	42.9%	61.6%	76.3%	82
Collections storage	78%	10%	1.9%	4.6%	11.5%	16.7%	24.8%	71
Non-collections storage	79%	6%	0.6%	2.7%	5.3%	9.5%	17.1%	67
Offices	86%	5%	1.1%	2.4%	4.8%	8.9%	13.4%	75
Education (classrooms)	42%	37%	0.1%	1.7%	2.8%	7.3%	10.5%	39
Library/research	67%	20%	0.3%	0.9%	1.7%	4.0%	5.6%	59
Museum store	78%	9%	0.6%	1.0%	1.9%	2.9%	4.3%	75
Public space/ public functions	63%	17%	2.0%	4.3%	8.3%	14.0%	25.6%	52
Food service	29%	51%	0.5%	0.7%	1.5%	2.4%	5.4%	27
Auditorium/ theaters	33%	44%	0.7%	1.7%	2.5%	6.2%	12.5%	30
Maintenance	65%	17%	0.3%	0.8%	2.3%	5.1%	9.0%	52
Conservation/ collections prep	46%	31%	0.3%	0.9%	2.2%	3.3%	11.6%	40

(*Percentages for yes and no often do not add to 100 percent—the remainder did not answer the question.)

N.4 Space allocation in square feet

	10th percentile	25th percentile	50th percentile	75th percentile	90th percentile	Number of responses
Exhibitions	1,500	3,350	10,000	28,750	60,398	88
Collections storage	300	720	2,500	9,186	22,740	76
Non-collections storage	108	500	1,000	4,050	10,000	70
Offices	106	400	1,000	4,000	11,400	82
Education (classrooms)	336	809	1,400	3,250	7,720	41
Library/research	100	200	500	1,916	2,398	64
Museum store	100	214	475	1,200	2,500	80
Public space/ public functions	430	1,000	2,500	9,533	30,200	55
Food service	95	325	900	1,563	5,325	28
Auditorium/ theaters	138	575	2,000	3,500	7,990	30
Maintenance	100	100	500	2,000	14,971	55
Conservation/ collections prep	100	367	625	1,967	5,059	44

N.5 What is allowed in building by policy

	Collection areas	Exhibit areas	Staff offices	Public spaces	Grounds
Open flames	1%	3%	4%	7%	26%
Food	5%	17%	65%	56%	72%
Beverages (other than water)	5%	17%	69%	52%	74%
Live plants	12%	24%	54%	40%	70%
Fresh flowers	9%	23%	58%	52%	65%
Dried plant material	16%	35%	37%	37%	46%
Personal artwork	11%	17%	61%	11%	11%
Filming	29%	71%	35%	68%	77%
Photography	33%	73%	40%	69%	77%

Seventy-one percent of respondents indicate they rent space to outside groups. Sixty-one percent report the rental revenue goes to the institution's budget (as opposed to a parent organization or other group).

N.6 Groups space is/would be rented to

	Would rent to	Have rented to in past 5 years
Religious groups	66%	40%
Political groups	53%	34%
Private groups (weddings, parties, graduations, etc.)	79%	64%
Corporate groups	86%	61%
Non-religious nonprofit groups	91%	73%
Other	13%	11%

N.7 Have exclusive agreement with caterer(s)

	Yes, one caterer	Yes, maintain a list of accepted caterers	Median percent commission taken by institution	Average commission	N for mean/ median	No	No response
Overall	5%	14%	4.5%	7.1%	16	80%	1%

N.8 Parking offered

	Have on-site parking	Median number of spaces	N for median	Have off-site parking	Median number of spaces	N for median
	73%	55.5	72	15%	50	13

Practice and Implementation of the Emergency Plan

Of the 58 percent of museums in museum systems that have a disaster plan (see last table in this section) 53 percent report having practiced it.

N.9 Year emergency plan practiced

	Year not specified	Before 1996	1996-1999	2000-2002	2003	2004
	13%	0%	0%	18%	53%	18%

N.10 Types of training provided to staff

	Training is provided	For those who provide training			
		Training is mndatory for all staff	Training is mandatory for some staff	Training is optional	No response on mandatory/ optional status
Emergency response	50%	46%	32%	18%	5%
First aid/CPR	46%	19%	50%	27%	4%
General health and safety	58%	52%	35%	11%	3%
Hazardous material handling	45%	18%	69%	12%	2%

N.11 Parental involvement with insurance (for respondents with parent organizations)

Institution fully covered under parent	Covered under parent, but maintains separate riders	Not covered under parent	No response
67%	15%	11%	7%

Fifty-five percent of respondents indicate the parent organization has regulations or guidelines regarding insurance to which the museum must adhere.

N.12 Does the parent pay for insurance?

Pay all costs	Pay some costs	Not pay	No response
57%	18%	13%	12%

N.13 Insurance types (See also insurance costs figures in first table of this section)

	Presently carry	Presently carry but considering dropping	Investigating/ planning to carry by 2005	No response
Commercial/general liability	66%	0%	2%	33%
Automobile	45%	0%	3%	52%
Collections/fine arts	53%	0%	4%	43%
Directors & Officers liability	48%	0%	7%	45%
Event cancellation	4%	0%	5%	91%
Exhibitions/loans	47%	0%	3%	50%
Transit	16%	0%	1%	83%
Terrorism	15%	0%	2%	83%
Other	4%	0%	0%	97%

N.14 Maintain a fund to offset small claims/deductibles

	Yes	Median fund size	N for median	No	No response
	7%	$10,000	7	78%	15%

Thirty-four percent of respondents report being self-insured.

N.15 Meaning of self-insured

Set aside and manage a designated fund with internal loss assessment/ payment	Replace/repairs out of general fund budget	Does not replace value of losses	Other	No response
34%	42%	11%	18%	5%

N.16 Policies/plans

	Have	Do not have	In development	No response
Facilities use policy	59%	22%	8%	11%
Building rental policy	54%	27%	9%	10%
Special events policy for outside groups	51%	30%	7%	12%
Special events policy for museum-sponsored events	40%	36%	11%	13%
Filming policy	37%	38%	10%	15%
Filming agreement	27%	48%	9%	16%
Policy on use of funds resulting from insurance claims on losses to collections	19%	55%	7%	19%
Cyclical maintenance plan	39%	35%	11%	16%
Emergency preparedness/disaster plan	58%	20%	10%	12%
Historic structure master plan	20%	46%	17%	17%
Integrated pest management plan	42%	35%	7%	15%

Section O: Museums with a University Parent

Total responses = 125

This appendix presents data for responding museums that have colleges or universities as parent organizations. Sixty-seven are state governed, 51 are private nonprofit, six have dual governance (usually state/private nonprofit), and one is municipal.

O.1 Discipline

	Percentage of sample	Number of responses
Aquarium	0%	0
Arboretum/botanic garden	0.8%	1
Art museum	59.2	74
Children's/youth museum	0%	0
General museum	6.4%	8
Historic house/site	1.6%	2
History museum/historical society	4.0%	5
Natural history/anthropology museum	12.8%	16
Nature center	0%	0
Science/technology center/museum	3.2%	4
Specialized museum	12.0%	15
Zoo	0%	0
Other	0%	0

O.2

	10th percentile	25th percentile	50th percentile	75th percentile	90th percentile	Number of responses
Operating income	$44,764	$133,000	$400,000	$1,652,342	$3,318,079	99
Operating expense	$37,170	$116,250	$317,688	$1,401,938	$3,356,456	105
Attendance	2,915	9,829	24,500	60,000	130,450	108
Full-time staff	1	2	4	11	28	123
Part-time staff	0	1	4	10	23	123
Maintenance staff FT	0	0	0	1	4	111
Maintenance staff PT	0	0	0	1	2	110
Total interior square footage	3,090	5,262	17,966	41,197	107,849	108
Insurance costs paid by institution	$950	$2,000	$4,806	$14,850	$20,000	39
Insurance costs paid by parent	$1,980	$5,322	$29,034	$84,365	$3,325,898	26
Total insurance costs paid	$1,480	$2,500	$6,600	$29,084	$130,000	57

0.3 Space—presence and allocation as a percentage of total space

	Present in institution (n=28)		10th percentile	25th percentile	50th percentile	75th percentile	90th percentile	Number of responses
	Yes*	No						
Exhibitions	94%	2%	21.7%	29.3%	40.0%	58.1%	78.8%	92
Collections storage	94%	3%	4.3%	7.2%	15.3%	25.2%	37.4%	88
Offices	82%	9%	0.7%	1.7%	3.4%	7.5%	17.8%	74
Education (classrooms)	92%	2%	2.3%	5.0%	9.3%	13.2%	18.7%	84
Library/research	46%	36%	0.6%	2.2%	4.3%	8.9%	17.0%	46
Museum store	46%	37%	0.3%	0.6%	1.8%	4.0%	8.7%	41
Public space/ public functions	57%	27%	1.4%	2.9%	6.2%	15.4%	32.3%	49
Food service	21%	62%	0.7%	1.0%	1.7%	2.0%	3.9%	16
Auditorium/ theaters	29%	52%	1.9%	2.3%	5.2%	10.2%	23.9%	25
Maintenance	44%	38%	0.3%	0.7%	1.8%	4.1%	13.8%	35
Conservation/ collections prep	62%	22%	0.9%	1.6%	4.4%	7.1%	12.9%	55

(*Percentages for yes and no often do not add to 100 percent—the remainder did not answer the question.)

0.4 Space allocation in square feet

	10th percentile	25th percentile	50th percentile	75th percentile	90th percentile	Number of responses
Exhibitions	1,399	2,635	6,000	13,515	28,296	101
Collections storage	249	1,000	3,000	5,822	16,550	98
Non-collections storage	100	227	895	1,215	4,369	80
Offices	280	445	1,025	3,000	9,993	94
Education (classrooms)	324	500	900	1,950	8,000	49
Library/research	61	158	478	1,000	6,500	44
Museum store	83	200	500	915	2,000	46
Public space/ public functions	264	685	2,000	3,967	13,330	52
Food service	49	163	500	2,000	2,550	18
Auditorium/ theaters	400	950	2,000	3,186	4,446	25
Maintenance	48	200	600	1,505	11,000	39
Conservation/ collections prep	120	400	868	1,545	3,750	62

0.5 What is allowed in building by policy

	Collection areas	Exhibit areas	Staff offices	Public spaces	Grounds
Open flames	2%	2%	2%	5%	15%
Food	2%	30%	75%	72%	81%
Beverages (other than water)	2%	26%	82%	70%	78%
Live plants	5%	17%	60%	49%	67%
Fresh flowers	7%	33%	75%	73%	64%
Dried plant material	8%	21%	46%	43%	39%
Personal artwork	3%	5%	73%	14%	11%
Filming	22%	53%	42%	62%	62%
Photography	32%	59%	50%	70%	72%

Fifty-five percent of respondents indicate they rent space to outside groups. Eighty-four percent report the rental revenue goes to the institution's budget (as opposed to a parent organization or other group).

0.6 Groups space is/would be rented to

	Would rent to	Have rented to in past 5 years
Religious groups	48%	29%
Political groups	41%	22%
Private groups (weddings, parties, graduations, etc.)	65%	52%
Corporate groups	84%	62%
Non-religious nonprofit groups	91%	75%
Other	43%	38%

0.7 Have exclusive agreement with caterer(s)

	Yes, one caterer	Yes, maintain a list of accepted caterers	Median percent commission taken by institution	Average commission	N for mean/ median	No	No response
Overall	23%	17%	0%	1.1%	33	58%	2%

0.8 Parking offered

	Have on-site parking	Median number of spaces	N for median	Have off-site parking	Median number of spaces	N for median
	56%	30	48	9%	37.5	4

Practice and Implementation of the Emergency Plan

Of the 71 percent of university museums that have a disaster plan (see last table in this section) 57 percent report having practiced it.

0.9 Year emergency plan practiced

	Year not specified	Before 1996	1996-1999	2000-2002	2003	2004
	5%	4%	2%	9%	53%	27%

O.10 Types of training provided to staff

	Training is provided	For those who provide training			
		Training is mndatory for all staff	Training is mandatory for some staff	Training is optional	No response on mandatory/ optional status
Emergency response	54%	40%	43%	15%	3%
First aid/CPR	41%	8%	49%	39%	4%
General health and safety	47%	29%	34%	31%	7%
Hazardous material handling	44%	13%	64%	22%	2%

O.11 Parental involvement with insurance (for respondents with parent organizations)

Institution fully covered under parent	Covered under parent, but maintains separate riders	Not covered under parent	No response
64%	27%	2%	6%

Seventy-three percent of respondents indicate the parent organization has regulations or guidelines regarding insurance to which the museum must adhere.

O.12 Does the parent pay for insurance?

Pay all costs	Pay some costs	Not pay	No response
64%	19%	10%	7%

O.13 Insurance types (See also insurance costs figures in first table of this section)

	Presently carry	Presently carry but considering dropping	Investigating/ planning to carry by 2005	No response
Commercial/general liability	62%	1%	0%	37%
Automobile	46%	1%	1%	52%
Collections/fine arts	74%	1%	0%	25%
Directors & Officers liability	39%	1%	0%	60%
Event cancellation	5%	1%	2%	93%
Exhibitions/loans	71%	0%	0%	29%
Transit	42%	1%	1%	57%
Terrorism	22%	1%	1%	77%
Other	6%	0%	0%	94%

0.14 Maintain a fund to offset small claims/deductibles

	Yes	Median fund size	N for median	No	No response
	14%	$2,000	7	72%	14%

Forty-two percent of respondents report being self-insured.

0.15 Meaning of self-insured

	Set aside and manage a designated fund with internal loss assessment/ payment	Replace/repairs out of general fund budget	Does not replace value of losses	Other	No response
	40%	46%	14%	8%	8%

0.16 Policies/plans

	Have	Do not have	In development	No response
Facilities use policy	58%	20%	8%	14%
Building rental policy	46%	30%	10%	14%
Special events policy for outside groups	53%	29%	6%	12%
Special events policy for museum-sponsored events	41%	35%	9%	15%
Filming policy	45%	32%	9%	14%
Filming agreement	24%	48%	10%	18%
Policy on use of funds resulting from insurance claims on losses to collections	25%	50%	6%	19%
Cyclical maintenance plan	45%	32%	6%	18%
Emergency preparedness/disaster plan	71%	13%	6%	10%
Historic structure master plan	12%	64%	3%	21%
Integrated pest management plan	46%	32%	9%	14%

Section P: Museums with Other Nongovernmental Parent Organizations

Total responses = 96

These respondents indicate they have a parent organization that is not a museum system, college/university, or government entity. Their parents include:

Airport
Arts Center
Arts Council
Aviation Association
Church
Community of Former Nuns
Corporation
Cultural Center Corporation
Daughters of The American Revolution
Family Foundation

Foundation
Friends Group
Genealogical Association
Heritage Society
Historic Preservation Organization
Historical Society
Home for The Aged
Hospital
Independent Secondary School
Institute of Fine Arts
Junior League
Library
Library & Historical Society
Motorcyclist Member Organization
National Society of the Colonial Dames of America

Nonprofit Association
Nonprofit Corporation
Nonprofit Preservation Association
Non-Profit Sports Association
Preservation Foundation
Private Foundation
Private Nonprofit Library/Museum/Cemetery
School System
Society
Supreme Council Scottish Rite Freemasons
Symphony Orchestra
Theme Park
Trust for Historic Preservation

P.1 Discipline

	Percentage of sample	Number of responses
Aquarium	0.0%	0
Arboretum/botanic garden	0%	0
Art museum	16.7%	16
Children's/youth museum	0.0%	0
General museum	7.3%	7
Historic house/site	22.9%	22
History museum/historical society	26.0%	25
Natural history/anthropology museum	1.0%	1
Nature center	1.0%	1
Science/technology center/museum	3.1%	3
Specialized museum	19.8%	19
Zoo	1.0%	1
Other	1%	1

P.2

	10th percentile	25th percentile	50th percentile	75th percentile	90th percentile	Number of responses
Operating income	$11,962	$52,250	$170,005	$613,875	$2,258,553	78
Operating expense	$17,727	$58,033	$175,000	$998,360	$2,767,547	79
Attendance	1,450	3,625	7,468	35,000	142,500	84
Full-time staff	0	0	2	6	27	96
Part-time staff	0	1	2	6	11	95
Maintenance staff full-time	0	0	0	1	4	87
Maintenance staff part-time	0	0	0	1	3	88
Total interior square footage	3,000	5,500	12,000	40,000	130,760	75
Insurance costs paid by institution	$663	$2,750	$10,248	$18,895	$46,741	26
Insurance costs paid by parent	$1,008	$3,000	$9,000	$23,113	$217,432	43
Total insurance costs paid	$820	$3,000	$10,000	$28,000	$108,365	63

P.3 Space—presence and allocation as a percentage of total space

	Present in institution (n=28)		10th percentile	25th percentile	50th percentile	75th percentile	90th percentile	Number of responses
	Yes*	No						
Exhibitions	86%	5%	9.8%	24.4%	46.3%	72.2%	86.2%	57
Collections storage	82%	5%	1.5%	4.5%	9.0%	17.1%	36.2%	58
Non-collections storage	77%	7%	1.1%	2.3%	4.9%	9.0%	16.2%	56
Offices	83%	5%	1.8%	3.3%	6.1%	10.8%	19.4%	60
Education (classrooms)	34%	42%	1.1%	1.7%	4.6%	13.5%	27.8%	21
Library/research	70%	14%	0.5%	1.3%	2.2%	7.4%	16.2%	46
Museum store	72%	17%	0.4%	1.1%	0.2%	4.4%	12.9%	53
Public space/ public functions	60%	20%	0.2%	8.3%	15.4%	35.2%	70.3%	33
Food service	29%	50%	0.2%	0.9%	1.8%	3.2%	9.2%	21
Auditorium/ theaters	28%	51%	1.4%	3.0%	8.4%	12.1%	53.2%	18
Maintenance	50%	23%	0.4%	0.5%	1.9%	6.0%	13.4%	34
Conservation/ collections prep	42%	32%	0.6%	1.6%	3.0%	5.3%	7.4%	24

(*Percentages for yes and no often do not add to 100 percent—the remainder did not answer the question.)

P.4 Space allocation in square feet

	10th percentile	25th percentile	50th percentile	75th percentile	90th percentile	Number of responses
Exhibitions	750	2,000	6,000	13,200	28,500	64
Collections storage	200	400	1,000	4,000	11,424	63
Non-collections storage	100	200	500	1,800	5,500	59
Offices	188	388	1,000	2,400	5,000	63
Education (classrooms)	369	731	900	2,758	8,000	22
Library/research	80	182	400	1,000	4,000	49
Museum store	94	150	372	912	1,790	56
Public space/ public functions	737	1,275	2,691	10,875	20,000	34
Food service	99	197	359	962	5,000	22
Auditorium/ theaters	685	1,446	4,825	9,056	11,450	18
Maintenance	36	100	800	1,900	10,000	37
Conservation/ collections prep	185	334	588	1,000	4,235	24

P.5 What is allowed in building by policy

	Collection areas	Exhibit areas	Staff offices	Public spaces	Grounds
Open flames	0%	6%	0%	16%	27%
Food	8%	20%	64%	66%	75%
Beverages (other than water)	7%	19%	71%	67%	75%
Live plants	8%	25%	54%	57%	69%
Fresh flowers	13%	25%	58%	67%	61%
Dried plant material	16%	36%	44%	50%	48%
Personal artwork	3%	13%	54%	13%	8%
Filming	26%	61%	38%	61%	68%
Photography	29%	65%	44%	68%	75%

Sixty-three percent of respondents indicate they rent space to outside groups. Sixty-five percent report the rental revenue goes to the institution's budget (as opposed to a parent organization or other group).

P.6 Groups space is/would be rented to

	Would rent to	Have rented to in past 5 years
Religious groups	60%	25%
Political groups	43%	25%
Private groups (weddings, parties, graduations, etc.)	87%	77%
Corporate groups	88%	72%
Non-religious nonprofit groups	90%	75%
Other	12%	10%

P.7 Have exclusive agreement with caterer(s)

	Yes, one caterer	Yes, maintain a list of accepted caterers	Median percent commission taken by institution	Average commission	N for mean/ median	No	No response
Overall	13%	17%	0%	4.0%	20	70%	1%

P.8 Parking offered

	Have on-site parking	Median number of spaces	N for median	Have off-site parking	Median number of spaces	N for median
	73%	36.5	54	18%	40	13

Practice and Implementation of the Emergency Plan

Of the 49 percent of museums with "other" parents that have a disaster plan (see last table in this section) 56 percent report having practiced it.

P.9 Year emergency plan practiced

	Year not specified	Before 1996	1996-1999	2000-2002	2003	2004
	6%	0%	6%	16%	45%	26%

P.10 Types of training provided to staff

	Training is provided	For those who provide training			
		Training is mndatory for all staff	Training is mandatory for some staff	Training is optional	No response on mandatory/ optional status
Emergency response	39%	35%	46%	16%	3%
First aid/CPR	44%	10%	55%	29%	7%
General health and safety	36%	51%	20%	17%	11%
Hazardous material handling	24%	17%	70%	13%	0%

P.11 Parental involvement with insurance (for respondents with parent organizations)

Institution fully covered under parent	Covered under parent, but maintains separate riders	Not covered under parent	No response
64%	15%	17%	5%

Forty-six percent of respondents indicate the parent organization has regulations or guidelines regarding insurance to which the museum must adhere.

L.12 Does the parent pay for insurance?

Pay all costs	Pay some costs	Not pay	No response
63%	10%	19%	8%

P.13 Insurance types (See also insurance costs figures in first table of this section)

	Presently carry	Presently carry but considering dropping	Investigating/ planning to carry by 2005	No response
Commercial/general liability	80%	0%	0%	20%
Automobile	34%	0%	0%	66%
Collections/fine arts	67%	1%	3%	29%
Directors & Officers liability	59%	0%	5%	35%
Event cancellation	3%	0%	3%	94%
Exhibitions/loans	49%	0%	3%	48%
Transit	20%	0%	2%	78%
Terrorism	20%	1%	3%	76%
Other	10%	0%	0%	90%

P.14 Maintain a fund to offset small claims/deductibles

	Yes	Median fund size	N for median	No	No response
	10%	$1,000	3	78%	12%

Fourteen percent of respondents report being self-insured.

P.15 Meaning of self-insured

	Set aside and manage a designated fund with internal loss assessment/payment	Replace/repairs out of general fund budget	Does not replace value of losses	Other	No response
	23%	46%	0%	15%	39%

P.16 Policies/plans

	Have	Do not have	In development	No response
Facilities use policy	43%	30%	14%	14%
Building rental policy	49%	30%	9%	11%
Special events policy for outside groups	43%	36%	7%	14%
Special events policy for museum-sponsored events	32%	48%	5%	15%
Filming policy	35%	47%	5%	13%
Filming agreement	25%	56%	4%	15%
Policy on use of funds resulting from insurance claims on losses to collections	19%	61%	3%	17%
Cyclical maintenance plan	30%	35%	15%	20%
Emergency preparedness/disaster plan	49%	31%	11%	8%
Historic structure master plan	22%	54%	8%	16%
Integrated pest management plan	34%	48%	5%	13%

Section Q: Museums with Operating Expenses over $6 million

Total responses = 110

Throughout this publication, we report on the data broken out by the size of the museum's operating expenses, using quartiles (four sections each containing one quarter of the responding museums). Because so many small museums are represented in the survey, the largest quartile lumps together all museums with operating expenses over $1,750,000. We realize that a museum with $1 million in expenses is very different from one with multi-million dollar expenses, so this section presents the data just for museums with operating expenses over $6 million (roughly the largest 10 percent of respondents). Twenty-five percent of these institutions have parent organizations.

Q.1 Discipline

	Percentage of sample	Number of responses
Aquarium	1.8%	2
Arboretum/botanic garden	3.6%	4
Art museum	37.3%	41
Children's/youth museum	1.8%	2
General museum	9.1%	10
Historic house/site	2.7%	3
History museum/historical society	10.0%	11
Natural history/anthropology museum	9.1%	10
Nature center	0%	0
Science/technology center/museum	9.1%	10
Specialized museum	5.5%	6
Zoo	10.0%	11
Other	0%	0

Q.2

	10th percentile	25th percentile	50th percentile	75th percentile	90th percentile	Number of responses
Operating income	$6,400,000	$8,179,375	$11,144,378	$18,469,542	$39,567,916	110
Operating expense	$6,598,056	$8,300,304	$11,488,030	$18,402,340	$36,594,960	110
Attendance	131,994	178,685	350,000	834,328	1,286,561	103
Full-time staff	61	74	109	199	324	108
Part-time staff	9	23	46	99	246	106
Maintenance staff full-time	3	6	9	22	48	107
Maintenance staff part-time	0	0	0	3	8	104
Total interior square footage	86,127	136,080	198,000	360,225	634,473	101
Insurance costs paid by institution	$18,410	$90,235	$175,367	$320,620	$649,136	96
Insurance costs paid by parent	$77,500	$152,500	$286,000	$500,000	$1,666,274	10
Total insurance costs paid	$40,676	$105,713	$196,000	$384,302	$705,600	97

Q.3 Space—presence and allocation as a percentage of total space

	Present in institution (n=28)		10th percentile	25th percentile	50th percentile	75th percentile	90th percentile	Number of responses
	Yes*	No						
Exhibitions	95%	1%	9.0%	17.9%	24.6%	36.1%	48.0%	89
Collections storage	93%	2%	1.6%	2.9%	7.5%	16.0%	25.0%	86
Non-collections storage	86%	5%	0.7%	1.7%	3.2%	7.3%	13.2%	78
Offices	95%	0%	3.5%	6.1%	9.3%	13.1%	19.5%	88
Education (classrooms)	85%	10%	0.5%	1.2%	2.3%	4.1%	9.0%	76
Library/research	87%	5%	0.4%	1.1%	1.9%	3.7%	6.9%	82
Museum store	92%	2%	0.4%	0.7%	1.3%	2.2%	2.9%	88
Public space/ public functions	82%	7%	2.2%	4.5%	7.6%	17.5%	33.4%	73
Food service	84%	11%	0.7%	1.1%	1.8%	3.6%	5.7%	78
Auditorium/ theaters	82%	11%	0.7%	1.4%	2.6%	4.6%	11.6%	72
Maintenance	90%	1%	0.5%	1.8%	4.9%	12.4%	21.1%	82
Conservation/ collections prep	79%	9%	0.4%	1.0%	2.3%	3.3%	6.2%	71

(*Percentages for yes and no often do not add to 100 percent—the remainder did not answer the question.)

Q.4 Space allocation in square feet

	10th percentile	25th percentile	50th percentile	75th percentile	90th percentile	Number of responses
Exhibitions	17,758	31,467	52,766	80,000	167,542	95
Collections storage	2,160	5,612	16,000	39,000	69,000	91
Non-collections storage	1,500	3,317	7.327	15,000	47,000	82
Offices	6,360	11,428	19,360	30,936	63,000	93
Education (classrooms)	1,187	2,477	4,496	9,950	21,918	80
Library/research	600	1,900	4,050	10,000	28.950	86
Museum store	761	1,597	3,000	5,000	8,541	93
Public space/ public functions	4,828	10,000	17,000	48,895	88,790	77
Food service	920	2,096	4,160	9,115	19,106	81
Auditorium/ theaters	2,070	3,219	5,168	11,359	29,955	76
Maintenance	885	4,000	12,350	22,887	50,660	86
Conservation/ collections prep	848	2,040	5,000	9,300	18,047	75

Q.5 What is allowed in building by policy

	Collection areas	Exhibit areas	Staff offices	Public spaces	Grounds
Open flames	3%	5%	1%	18%	26%
Food	12%	21%	85%	86%	85%
Beverages (other than water)	10%	20%	90%	84%	85%
Live plants	23%	42%	82%	79%	85%
Fresh flowers	24%	42%	90%	87%	79%
Dried plant material	31%	44%	74%	73%	63%
Personal artwork	5%	10%	85%	17%	15%
Filming	44%	67%	45%	81%	77%
Photography	56%	71%	61%	87%	83%

Ninety-one percent of respondents indicate they rent space to outside groups. Ninety-four percent report the rental revenue goes to the institution's budget (as opposed to a parent organization or other group).

Q.6 Groups space is/would be rented to

	Would rent to	Have rented to in past 5 years
Religious groups	68%	43%
Political groups	57%	39%
Private groups (weddings, parties, graduations, etc.)	88%	72%
Corporate groups	100%	79%
Non-religious nonprofit groups	99%	77%
Other	10%	8%

Q.7 Have exclusive agreement with caterer(s)

	Yes, one caterer	Yes, maintain a list of accepted caterers	Median percent commission taken by institution	Average commission	N for mean/ median	No	No response
Overall	34%	38%	10%	8.9%	57	27%	1%

Q.8 Parking offered

	Have on-site parking	Median number of spaces	N for median	Have off-site parking	Median number of spaces	N for median
	77%	342	77	11%	300	11

Practice and Implementation of the Emergency Plan

Of the 91 percent of museums with operating expenses over $6 million that have a disaster plan (see last table in this section) 81 percent report having practiced it.

Q.9 Year emergency plan practiced

	Year not specified	Before 1996	1996-1999	2000-2002	2003	2004
	6%	2%	0%	13%	48%	31%

Q.10 Types of training provided to staff

	Training is provided	For those who provide training			
		Training is mndatory for all staff	Training is mandatory for some staff	Training is optional	No response on mandatory/ optional status
Emergency response	85%	30%	68%	2%	0%
First aid/CPR	83%	2%	79%	18%	1%
General health and safety	80%	40%	50%	9%	1%
Hazardous material handling	75%	4%	92%	4%	1%

Q.11 Parental involvement with insurance (for respondents with parent organizations)

Institution fully covered under parent	Covered under parent, but maintains separate riders	Not covered under parent	No response
63%	19%	19%	0%%

Fifty-two percent of respondents indicate the parent organization has regulations or guidelines regarding insurance to which the museum must adhere.

Q.12 Does the parent pay for insurance?

Pay all costs	Pay some costs	Not pay	No response
33%	41%	22%	4%

Q.13 Insurance types (See also insurance costs figures in first table of this section)

	Presently carry	Presently carry but considering dropping	Investigating/ planning to carry by 2005	No response
Commercial/general liability	88%	1%	0%	11%
Automobile	86%	1%	0%	13%
Collections/fine arts	85%	1%	1%	14%
Directors & Officers liability	90%	1%	0%	9%
Event cancellation	13%	1%	1%	85%
Exhibitions/loans	80%	0%	0%	20%
Transit	42%	1%	0%	57%
Terrorism	51%	1%	3%	45%
Other	28%	0%	0%	72%

Q.14 Maintain a fund to offset small claims/deductibles

	Yes	Median fund size	N for median	No	No response
	10%	$50,000	6	87%	3%

Twenty-one percent of respondents report being self-insured.

Q.15 Meaning of self-insured

	Set aside and manage a designated fund with internal loss assessment/ payment	Replace/repairs out of general fund budget	Does not replace value of losses	Other	No response
	17%	39%	9%	39%	4%

Q.16 Policies/plans

	Have	Do not have	In development	No response
Facilities use policy	74%	13%	3%	11%
Building rental policy	75%	11%	4%	10%
Special events policy for outside groups	79%	7%	3%	11%
Special events policy for museum-sponsored events	59%	25%	5%	12%
Filming policy	65%	16%	5%	13%
Filming agreement	44%	31%	5%	21%
Policy on use of funds resulting from insurance claims on losses to collections	25%	48%	5%	22%
Cyclical maintenance plan	68%	12%	7%	13%
Emergency preparedness/disaster plan	91%	2%	1%	6%
Historic structure master plan	25%	48%	7%	20%
Integrated pest management plan	67%	20%	2%	11%

Glossary

Terms marked with an asterisk (*) were included in the survey instrument glossary.

Commercial general liability insurance*: protects against bodily injury and property damage claims. Provides separate limits of coverage for general liability, legal and fire liability, products, personal liability, and medical payments.

Confidence interval: a plus-or-minus figure that gives you the range within which the "real" answer lies.

Cyclical maintenance plan*: a plan outlining the work to be carried out on a regular basis concerning servicing and preventative maintenance to prolong the useful life of buildings and equipment, to keep facilities in working order, and to reduce the need for responsive repairs.

Dual governance*: a governance structure in which two separate legal entities share governance of the museum. This involves dividing or sharing basic governance responsibilities such as determining mission and purpose; hiring, supporting, and evaluating the director; strategic planning; obtaining and managing resources; and monitoring the organization's programs and services. For example: a museum jointly governed by a city government, which owns the collections and the building and hires the staff, and a private nonprofit, which determines museum policy and operates the museum. *Does not automatically include museums that have separately incorporated friends organizations, unless the friends organization has significant responsibility for governance of the museum.*

Earned income: money earned by providing goods or services where the amount paid is comparable to the actual value of the goods or services. Includes admission revenue, food and museum store sales, building rental, fairs and festivals, etc. The following types of revenue do not qualify as earned income: undesignated, unrestricted, or general operating grants; contributions from individuals; bequests; and sponsorships of special events.

Emergency response training*: theoretical and/or practical instruction regarding how to respond to situations that threaten visitors, staff, collections, or facilities such as flood, fire, earthquakes, severe weather, terrorism, etc.

General health and safety training*: theoretical and/or practical instruction regarding such issues as office ergonomics, safe back and lifting, blood borne and airborne pathogen safety, hazards communication, and use of Material Safety Data Sheets.

General museum*: a museum that addresses two or more disciplines to a significant extent, for example, a museum that interprets both art and history or both history and science. Synonym: multidisciplinary museum.

Governing Authority*: The body with legal and fiduciary responsibility for the museum and for approving museum policy. *Names of governing authority include but are not limited to:* advisory council, board of commissioners, board of directors, board of managers, board of regents, board of trustees, city council, commission.

Hazardous material handling training*: theoretical and/or practical instruction in identification, handling, transport, and cleanup of hazardous materials, and use of protective equipment.

Historic structure master plan*: a detailed document guiding the rehabilitation of an entire structure that uses a preservation approach. Various levels of importance are assigned to different features based on public visibility and historic architectural significance. The plan serves as a tool for the architect and is used in conjunction with an overall master plan.

Integrated pest management plan*: plan that coordinates information about pests and environmental conditions with available pest control methods to prevent unacceptable levels of pest damage while minimizing hazards to people, property, collections, and the environment. IPM programs apply a holistic approach to pest management decision-making, and consider all appropriate options, including but not limited to pesticides.

Interior square footage: the total square footage inside the museum building or buildings, including offices, collections storage, exhibit space, museum store, etc. If the museum exists within a larger, non-museum structure, only the square footage occupied by museum activities.

Museum system*: two or more museums or museum facilities that share a common *parent organization*. The component parts of a museum system may be museums operating independently or quasi-independently with distinct budgets and governing authorities, or may simply be separate, distinguishable sites all managed by the same organization.

Off-site facility*: a term used by the museum community to refer to owned or rented facilities away from the museum's main location. There is no formal definition for when a facility is "off" site as opposed to simply being one of multiple sites. Answer this question by applying the term as it is used at your institution.

Operating income or operating expenses*: income generated by or expenditures supporting the museum's general operations in a given fiscal year, including exhibitions, education, education, conservation, collections management, acquisitions, research, training, development, and administration. Includes any portion of income from the endowment that is applied to operating expenses in a given year. Does not include capital expenditures.

Parent organization*: an organization having one or more subordinate organizations under its general supervision and control. The parent has ultimate legal and fiduciary responsibility for these organizations.

Percentiles: in this survey data are divided into percentile groups. Each percentile gives the value for which the specified percentage of the survey population falls above or below that value. For example:

- The 10th percentile gives the figure at which 10 percent of museums fall at or below this point, and 90 percent fall above it.
- The 50th percentile is the **mean**, e.g., the point at which half of all responses fall above this point, half fall at or below it.
- The 90th percentile gives the figure at which 90 percent of all responses fall at or below this point, and 10 percent fall above it.

Risk management*: the overall process of identifying, controlling, and minimizing the impact of uncertain events in order to reduce the likelihood of their occurrence and/or the severity of their impact.

Specialized Museum*: a museum that does not fall into or combine any of the other discipline areas listed in question 3 of the survey. *For example, air & space, military, maritime, transportation, quilt, clock, and stamp museums.*

Support organization: a separately incorporated organization whose primary purpose is the support of the museum. This may involve providing financial support, volunteers, or expertise. May be known as an auxiliary, external support group, friends group, or affiliate organization.

Resources

General

Collective Vision: Starting and Sustaining a Children's Museum. Association of Children's Museums, 1997, 2002. This comprehensive guide for new and existing institutions features articles by 77 experts inside and outside the children's museum field. Relevant topics include building and site planning, insurance, long-range planning, and budgets. Much of the information is broadly applicable to other types of museums.

Managing Risk in Nonprofit Organizations: A Comprehensive Guide, Melanie L. Herman, George L. Head, Peggy M. Jackson, and Toni E. Fogarty. John Wiley and Sons, Inc., 2004. A comprehensive examination of risk management in nonprofits. Includes the types of risks facing nonprofits, financial management of risks, and insurance. Also presents a valuable examination of the reasons to accept some risks in the interests of mission delivery.

Storage of Natural History Collections: A Preventative Conservation Approach, Carolyn L. Rose, Catherine A. Hawks, and Hugh H. Genoways, eds. Society for the Preservation of Natural History Collections, 1995. Generally applicable to all types of museums, this book features topics relevant to facilities and risk management, including preventative conservation, security systems, fire prevention, emergency preparedness, and pest management.

Space Usage

The Manual of Museum Planning, 2nd ed., Gail Dexter Lord and Barry Lord, eds. AltaMira Press, 1999. This definitive text discusses planning for people and collections in a museum. It provides guidance for feasibility studies, functional programs, new construction and expansion, and project management and includes charts, checklists, a glossary, and bibliography.

Facilities Management

"Facilities Management" in *Museum Administration: An Introduction,* Hugh H. Genoways and Lynne M. Ireland. AltaMira Press, 2003. This chapter provides a brief overview of issues related to buildings and space usage; facility operations such as housekeeping, emergency preparedness, and health and safety; integrated pest management; security; and visitor services.

Housekeeping for Historic Homes and House Museums, Melissa M. Heaver. National Trust for Historic Preservation, 2000. This spiral-bound booklet provides advice about cleaning interior spaces and collections in historic house museums—ranging from walls, ceilings, and floors to furniture, glass, and textiles. It includes a sample cleaning schedule, a list of supplies and suppliers, and a brief bibliography. Available from the National Trust for Historic Preservation; www.nationaltrust.org.

Museum Handbook, National Parks Service. "Museum Housekeeping," chapter 13 in Part I, includes an overview of the topic, help with writing a museum housekeeping plan, a bibliography, and sample housekeeping checklists. Available in PDF from the NPS website: www.cr.nps.gov/museum/publications/handbook.html.

Integrated Pest Management

Common Sense Pest Control, William Olkowski, Sheila Daar, Helga Olkowski. Taunton Press, 1991. This volume by the founders of the Bio-Integral Resource Center in Berkeley, Calif., is an accessible, non-technical introduction to the principles of least-toxic pest management. Geared to the home-owner and gardener but applicable to museums.

Conservation OnLine has a section on pest management with a large number of articles. See in particular, "Integrated Pest Management: A Selected Bibliography for Collections Care and Managing Pests in Your Collections." http://palimpsest.stanford.edu.

Emergency Preparedness/Safety and Security

Security in Museums, Archives and Libraries: A Practical Guide. The Museums, Libraries and Archives Council, 2003. This comprehensive publication addresses building security, alarms, retail security, personal security, bag searches, key control, operating procedures, contractors, couriers, security staff, and crisis management planning. It includes sample forms for reporting incidents and crimes. (Also available as a PDF from the MLA website: www.mla.gov.uk/documents/security_manual.pdf.)

To Preserve and Protect: The Strategic Stewardship of Cultural Resources. Library of Congress, 2002. Contains essays from the symposium "To Preserve and Protect: The Strategic Stewardship of Cultural Resources," held at the Library of Congress, Oct. 30-31, 2000. Explores the connections between physical security and preservation of museums and libraries. Presents some of the issues involved in the stewardship of our cultural heritage. Includes bibliographical reference and index. While aimed mainly at libraries, it is applicable to museums.

Assessing and Managing Risk

The Canadian Conservation Institute has online resources and tools related to preservation. This includes a database of information on a number of conservation issues and questions. Particularly of note is the Preservation Framework Online, which uses a framework of nine agents of deterioration to assess, avoid, or control potential deterioration of museum objects. www.cci-icc.gc.ca.

The Nonprofit Risk Management Center has an online risk assessment tool; the nine modules focus on an introduction to risk management, employment practices, contracts, special events, harm to clients, transportation, internal controls, technology, and facilities. In addition, it offers an online risk management tutorial. Through a series of exercises, the tutorial demonstrates how the principles of risk management can be integrated into day-to-day operations. The Resource Center offers a number of fact sheets on risk management, liability, and insurance, including one on creating job descriptions for risk managers. The Resource Center also provides free technical assistance to nonprofits. www.nonprofitrisk.org.

Disaster Planning, Preparation, and Implementation

The Northeast Document Conservation Center's website offers a number of technical leaflets to assist in developing a disaster plan, including: Disaster Planning; Emergency Planning Bibliography; Emergency Management Suppliers & Services; Worksheet for Outlining a Disaster Plan. www.nedcc.org.

Resources for Recovery: Post-Disaster Aid for Cultural Institutions. Heritage Preservation, rev. 2005. Prepared by HP in partnership with the Federal Emergency Management Agency (FEMA) and the National Endowment for the Arts (NEA). This originally was developed in 1992 and revised in 2000 as a post-disaster reference guide to financial aid and recovery information. In addition to current information on federal programs providing disaster aid, the publication includes a comprehensive list of essential contacts and online resources. The most recent revision expands the scope of the publication to encompass sources of federal assistance for preparedness, planning, and hazard mitigation, and recovery.

Steal This Handbook! A Template for Creating a Museum's Emergency Preparedness Plan, Allyn Lord, Carolyn Reno, and Marie Demeroukas. Southeastern Registrars Association, 1994. This book walks a museum through the process of creating a disaster/emergency preparedness plan. It outlines components for a plan, emergency procedures, and cleanup procedures. Also includes sample forms and an extensive bibliography.

Insurance

The Nonprofit Risk Management Center offers a guide titled *Insurance Basics for Community-Serving Programs.* Topics include liability of the organization, staff liability, injuries, motor vehicles, boards and executives, special events, financial assets, and buying insurance. The Resource Center offers a number of fact sheets on risk management, liability, and insurance. www.nonprofitrisk.org

Other Sources of Information

General

2003 Museum Financial Information. American Association of Museums, 2003. The latest, most comprehensive financial and operational data from America's museums, the only field-wide survey of museum financial performance. Examines the numbers for a wide range of institutional activities, ranging from attendance, operating and non-operating income and expenses, earned income sources, and costs of collections care to the net profit per square foot of museum stores and food services and the percent of operating expenses devoted to administration and fund raising. This survey of over 800 museums of all types also features a section on demographics—the number, types, and distribution of museums in the United States—and a section on financial trends from fiscal years 2000 to 2002. See also the companion volume *Data by Discipline: 2003 Museum Financial Information,* which presents the information by type of museum.

Facilities Management

Museum Benchmarks 2003, Survey of Facility Management Practices Report, Ian Follett. Facility Management Services Ltd., 2003. The report is the result of a 30-page questionnaire answered by an international group of approximately 80 (mostly large) museums. Includes a four-page executive Summary of Results, a five-page listing of facility-management-related operational definitions and 22 pages of data analysis. Data were gathered and analyzed on the following topics: description of facilities, space utilization, temperature and relative humidity, custodial services, utilities, building maintenance, exterior grounds maintenance, building security, cost of building operations, outsourcing, good/best practices (a seven-page listing) and important issues facing facility managers. Best practices, as listed and briefly described by each institution, also are included. This survey has been administered yearly since 2001. Museums are charged a fee to participate and receive survey results. The report also is available for $1,000 from Facility Management Services, fmsltd@fmsltd.com.

Science and Technology Museums

ASTC Sourcebook of Science Center Statistics 2001. Association of Science-Technology Centers, 2001. Based on the annual survey of the association's museum and science-center membership worldwide, this sourcebook includes data on facilities and programs, attendance, staff, and finances. Exhibitions are also sometimes included and are searchable by topic.

Appendix I: List of Responding Institutions

Here is a list, sorted by discipline, of the 1,162 institutions that answered the survey by the deadline of May 21, 2004, and did not opt out of being credited as a participant. Forty-eight museums asked not to be listed by name.

Our thanks to the several dozen institutions that answered the survey but returned it after the cut-off date (they are not listed here). We regret being unable to include them in the survey analysis.

Institution names were pre-printed on the surveys—if respondents corrected their institution's name, that change is reflected below. If they did not make corrections, their names appear as they are listed in the AAM database.

Aquariums

National Aquarium in Baltimore, MD
North Carolina Aquarium on Roanoke Island, NC
Seattle Aquarium, WA
Virginia Marine Science Museum, VA

Arboretums/Botanic Gardens

Bloedel Reserve, WA
Bowman's Hill Wildflower Preserve, PA
Brookside Gardens, MD
Cutler Gardens, NY
Dubuque Arboretum Association, IA
Frederik Meijer Gardens & Sculpture Park, MI
Highland Botanical Park, NY
Historic Bok Sanctuary, FL
Holden Arboretum, OH
McKee Botanical Garden, FL
Missouri Botanical Garden, MO
Quail Botanic Gardens Foundation, CA
Queens Botanical Garden, NY
Rancho Santa Ana Botanic Garden at Claremont, CA
Rotary Gardens, Inc., WI
Santa Barbara Botanic Garden, CA
Sawtooth Botanical Garden, ID
Texas Discovery Gardens, TX
The New York Botanical Garden, NY
Washington Park Arboretum, WA

Art Museums

Academy Art Museum, MD
Ackland Art Museum, NC
Albany Institute of History and Art, NY
Albright-Knox Art Gallery, NY
Alice C. Sabatini Gallery Topeka & Shawnee Co. Public Library, KS
Allen Memorial Art Museum, OH
Amarillo Museum of Art, TX
Amon Carter Museum, TX
Anderson Museum of Contemporary Art, NM
Arkansas Arts Center, AR
Arkansas State University Fine Arts Center Gallery, AR
Art Association of Jacksonville, IL

Art Complex Museum, MA
Art Gallery, University of New Hampshire, NH
Art Museum at Florida International University, FL
Art Museum of Southeast Texas, TX
ArtPace San Antonio, TX
Arts and Science Center for Southeast Arkansas, AR
Asheville Art Museum, NC
Bakersfield Museum of Art, CA
Ball State University Museum of Art, IN
Baltimore Museum of Art, MD
Bedford Gallery at the Dean Lesher Regional Center for the Arts, CA
Berkeley Art Center, CA
Birger Sandzen Memorial Gallery, KS
Birmingham Museum of Art, AL
Blanden Memorial Art Museum, IA
Booth Western Art Museum, GA
Boston University Art Gallery, MA
Boyden Gallery St. Mary's College, MD
Brattleboro Museum & Art Center, VT
Bronx Museum of the Arts, NY
Burchfield-Penny Art Center, NY
Canajoharie Library and Art Gallery, NY
Cantor Gallery College of the Holy Cross, MA
Center Art Gallery Calvin College, MI
Center for Creative Photography, University of Arizona, AZ
Center for Maine Contemporary Art, ME
Center for the Visual Arts, CO
Chapel Art Center Saint Anselm College, NH
Charles Allis Villa Terrace Art Museum, WI
Charles H. Macnider Museum, IA
Charles Hosmer Morse Museum of American Art, FL
Charles Water House Historic Museum, NJ
Chrysler Museum of Art, VA
Cincinnati Art Museum, OH
Cleveland Museum of Art, OH
Colquitt County Arts Center, GA
Columbia Museum of Art, SC
Columbus Museum, GA
Columbus Museum of Art, OH
Contemporary Art Center, OH
Contemporary Art Museum St. Louis, MO

Corita Art Center, CA
Crocker Art Museum, CA
Currier Museum of Art, NH
Dallas Museum of Art, TX
Danforth Museum of Art, MA
Daum Museum of Contemporary Art, MO
Daura Gallery Lynchburg College, VA
David & Alfred Smart Museum of Art, IL
Dayton Art Institute, OH
De Paul University Art Museum, IL
Decordova Museum and Sculpture Park, MA
Des Moines Art Center Edmundson Art Foundation, IA
Dubuque Museum of Art, IA
Eiteljorg Museum of American Indians and Western Art, IN
El Museo del Barrio, NY
El Paso Museum of Art, TX
Ellen Noel Art Museum, TX
Elvehjem Museum of Art, WI
Eric Carle Museum of Picture Book Art, MA
Fabric Workshop & Museum, PA
Fine Arts Center in Provincetown, MA
Fisher Gallery, CA
Frist Center for the Visual Arts, TN
Gallery of Art & Design, North Carolina State University, NC
Gallery of Contemporary Art, University of Colorado,
    Colorado Springs, CO
Gertrude Herbert Institute of Art, GA
Gibbes Museum of Art, SC
Grants Pass Museum of Art, OR
Greenville Museum of Art, Inc., NC
Grey Art Gallery New York University, NY
Guild Hall Museum, NY
Harn Museum of Art, FL
Heard Museum, AZ
Hearst Art Gallery, CA
Heckscher Museum of Art, NY
Herbert F. Johnson Museum of Art, NY
Hibel Museum of Art, FL
High Museum of Art, GA
Hillwood Art Museum, NY
Hirshorn Museum and Sculpture Garden, DC
Hoyt Institute of Fine Arts, PA
Hunter College Art Gallery, NY
Hyde Collection, NY
International Print Center New York, NY
Isabella Stewart Gardner Museum, MA
Islip Art Museum, NY
J. Paul Getty Museum, CA
Jack S. Blanton Museum of Art, TX
Jacksonville Museum of Modern Art, FL
James A. Michener Art Museum, PA
Japan Society Gallery, NY
Jersey City Museum, NJ
John and Mable Ringling Museum of Art, FL
John D. Barrow Art Gallery, NY

Jonson Gallery, University of New Mexico, NM
Joslyn Art Museum, NE
Juniata College Museum of Art, PA
Kalamazoo Institute of Arts, MI
Katonah Museum of Art, NY
Kimbell Art Museum, TX
Latin American Art Museum, FL
Long Island Museum of American Art, History and Carriages, NY
Los Angeles County Museum of Art, CA
Louise Wells Cameron Art Museum, NC
Lowe Art Museum, FL
Mary & Leigh Block Museum of Art, IL
Maryhill Museum of Art, WA
Mead Art Museum, MA
Memorial Art Gallery, NY
Memphis Brooks Museum of Art, TN
Menil Collection Library, TX
Mennello Museum of American Folk Art, FL
Middlebury College Museum of Art, VT
Midwest Museum of American Art, IN
Mills College Art Gallery, CA
Mint Museum of Art, NC
MIT–List Visual Arts Center, MA
Montclair Art Museum, NJ
Morris Graves Museum of Art, CA
Morris Museum of Art, GA
Mount Holyoke College Art Museum, MA
Museum of Art, FL
Museum of Art Washington State University, WA
Museum of Art, Brigham Young University, UT
Museum of Contemporary Art, CO
Museum of Contemporary Art Los Angeles, CA
Museum of Contemporary Art San Diego, CA
Museum of Craft and Folk Art, CA
Museum of Fine Arts, MA
Museum of Fine Arts, Houston, TX
Museum of Glass International Center for Contemporary Art,
    WA
Museum of International Folk Art Museum of New Mexico, NM
Museum of Miniature Houses and Other Collections, Inc., IN
Museum of Russian Art, MN
Museum of Spanish Colonial Art, NM
Nasher Museum of Art at Duke University, NC
Nasher Sculpture Center, TX
Natalie & James Thompson Art Gallery, School of Art and
    Design, CA
National Academy of Design Museum, NY
National Art Museum of Sport at University Place, IN
National Gallery of Art, DC
National Museum of African Art, Smithsonian Institution, DC
National Museum of Women in the Arts, DC
National Portrait Gallery, Smithsonian Institution, DC
Nevada Museum of Art, NV
New Orleans Museum of Art, LA
Nora Eccles Harrison Museum of Art, UT

Norman Rockwell Museum at Stockbridge, Inc., MA
North Carolina Museum of Art, NC
Old Jail Art Center, TX
Orlando Museum of Art, FL
Pacific Asia Museum, CA
Pensacola Museum of Art, FL
Philbrook Museum of Art, OK
Philip & Muriel Berman Museum of Art, PA
Phillips Collection, DC
Phillips Museum, Franklin and Marshall College, PA
Phoenix Art Museum, AZ
Piedmont Arts Association, VA
Polk Museum of Art, FL
Princeton University Art Museum, NJ
Racine Art Museum Association, WI
Raymer Society for the Arts/Red Barn Studio Museum, KS
Ringling School of Art Selby Gallery, FL
Rockwell Museum, NY
Rose Art Museum, Brandeis University, MA
Saginaw Art Museum, MI
Saint Louis Art Museum, MO
Salina Art Center, KS
San Angelo Museum of Fine Arts, TX
San Antonio Museum of Art, TX
San Diego Museum of Art, CA
San Francisco Museum of Modern Art, CA
Santa Monica Museum of Art, CA
Sarah Moody Gallery of Art University of Alabama, AL
Schein-Joseph International Museum of Ceramic Art, NY
Schmidt Art Center Southwestern Illinois College, IL
Scottsdale Museum of Contemporary Art, AZ
SITE Santa Fe, NM
Smith College Museum of Art, MA
South Texas Institute for the Arts, TX
Southeastern Center for Contemporary Art, NC
Speed Art Museum, KY
Springfield Museum of Art, OH
Sterling & Francine Clark Art Institute, MA
Susquehanna Art Museum, PA
Tacoma Art Museum, WA
Taft Museum of Art, OH
Tampa Gallery of Photographic Arts, FL
Tampa Museum of Art, FL
Tarble Arts Center, Eastern Illinois University, IL
Telfair Museum of Art and Owens-Thomas House, GA
The Butler Institute of American Art, OH
The Jewish Museum, NY
The Light Factory, NC
The Mansfield Art Center, OH
The Nelson-Atkins Museum of Art, MO
The R. W. Norton Art Gallery, LA
The Slater Memorial Museum, Norwich Free Academy, CT
The Studio Museum in Harlem, NY
Toledo Museum of Art, OH
Tucson Museum of Art and Historic Block, AZ

Tufts University Gallery, MA
Tyler Museum of Art, TX
Ulrich Museum of Art, KS
University Museums, Iowa State University, IA
University of Arizona Museum of Art, AZ
University of Iowa Museum of Art, IA
University of Kentucky Art Museum, KY
University of Michigan Museum of Art, MI
University of Northern Iowa Gallery of Art, IA
University of Virginia Art Museum (Bayly Art Museum), VA
University of Wyoming Art Museum, WY
Visual Arts Center of N.W. Florida, FL
Von Liebig Art Center Naples Art Association, FL
Walter Anderson Museum of Art, MS
Walters Art Museum, MD
Washington County Museum of Fine Arts, MD
Weatherspoon Art Museum, NC
Western Gallery, WA
Westmoreland Museum of American Art, PA
Whitehorn House Museum Newport Restoration Foundation, RI
Wichita Art Museum, KS
Williams College Museum of Art, MA
Wiseman & Firehouse Galleries, OR
Woodmere Art Museum, Inc., PA
Worcester Art Museum, MA
Yale University Art Gallery, CT

Children's/Youth Museums
Arizona Museum for Youth, AZ
Austin Children's Museum, TX
Betty Brinn Children's Museum, WI
Children's Hands-On Museum, AL
Children's Museum, MA
Children's Museum of Greater Fall River, MA
Children's Museum of Indianapolis, IN
Children's Museum of La Crosse, WI
Children's Museum of Memphis, TN
Children's Museum of Southeastern Connecticut, CT
Children's Museum of Waxahachie, TX
Coyote Point Museum for Environmental Education, CA
Dupage Children's Museum, IL
Explore & More...A Children's Museum, NY
Fox Cities Children's Museum, WI
Garden State Discovery Museum, NJ
Louisiana Children's Museum, LA
Madison Children's Museum, WI
Miami Children's Museum, FL
Mid-Michigan Childrens Museum, MI
New Britain Youth Museum, CT
Providence Children's Museum, RI
San Antonio Children's Museum, TX
Stepping Stones Museum for Children, CT
The Children's Museum of Denver, CO
The Children's Museum of Houston, TX
The Virginia Discovery Museum, VA

General Museums

Alaska State Museum, AK
Albuquerque Museum, NM
Alfred P. Sloan, Jr. Museum, MI
Allison-Antrim Museum, PA
Anacostia Museum, DC
Anaheim Museum, Inc., CA
Asian Art Museum, CA
Avampato Discovery Museum, WV
Bayonne Community Museum, NJ
Behringer Crawford Museum, KY
Brevard Museum of Art & Science, FL
Brooke County Historical Museum, WV
Bruce Museum of Arts and Science, CT
Buffalo Bill Historical Center, WY
Burritt on the Mountain—A Living Museum, AL
Calusa Nature Center and Planetarium, FL
Camden Archives, SC
Catskill Fly Fishing Center, NY
Cedar Key State Museum, FL
Churchill County Museum and Archives, NV
Cincinnati Museum Center, OH
Colleton Museum, SC
Corpus Christi Museum of Science & History, TX
Cottonlandia Museum, MS
Crater of Diamonds State Park Museum, AR
Crawford City Historical Society, KS
Cripple Creek District Museum, CO
Cullman County Museum, AL
Customs House Museum & Cultural Center, TN
Discovering Stone Mountain Museum, GA
Discovery Museums, Inc., MA
Douglas County Museum of History & Natural History, OR
Dubuque County Historical Society, IA
Elliott Museum, FL
Fenimore Art Museum and Research Library, NY
Ferndale Museum Inc., CA
First Landing State Park, VA
Frank H. McClung Museum, TN
Frick Art and Historical Center, PA
Ft. Payne Depot Museum, AL
Furnas County Museum, NE
Gardner Museum, Inc., MA
Gateway to the Panhandle Museum, OK
Gilcrease Museum, OK
Golden State Museum, CA
High Desert Museum, OR
High Plains Museum, KS
Holland Land Office Museum, NY
Illinois State Museum and Dickson Mounds, IL
Indiana State Museum and Historic Sites, IN
Iron County Museum, MI
Johnson-Humrickhouse Museum, OH
Kenai Visitor & Convention Bureau, Inc., AK

Lacrosse County Historical Society, WI
Lightner Museum, FL
Louisiana Art and Science Museum, LA
Loveland Museum and Gallery, CO
Lowell Area Historical Museum, MI
Maine State Museum, ME
Mandeville Gallery at Union College, NY
Maria Mitchell Association, MA
Maturango Museum of the Indian Wells Valley, CA
McKissick Museum, SC
McPherson Museum, KS
Miracle of America Museum & Pioneer Village, MT
Montgomery Museum & Lewis Miller Regional Art Center, VA
Morris Museum, NJ
Museum of Cultural and Natural History, MI
Museum of Fine Arts, FL
Museum of Idaho, ID
Museum of the Big Bend Sul Ross State University, TX
Museum of the Middle Appalachians Saltville Foundation, VA
Museum of Western Colorado, CO
Muskegon County Museum, MI
Napa Valley Museum, CA
New York State Museum, NY
Northeast Texas Rural Heritage Museum, TX
Northwest Museum of Arts and Culture, WA
Oregon Trail Regional Museum, OR
Otero Museum Association, CO
Overland Trail Museum, CO
Packwood House Museum, PA
Paris-Henry County Heritage Center, TN
Peggy Notebaert Nature Museum, IL
Pierpont Morgan Library, NY
Pine Bluff/Jefferson Historical Museum, AR
Prairie Museum of Art and History, KS
Prairie Trails Museum of Wayne County, IA
Putnam Museum of History and Natural Science, IA
Reading Public Museum and Planetarium, PA
Redwood Library and Athenaeum, RI
Reynolda House, Museum of American Art, NC
Richey Historical Society, MT
San Francisco Airport Museum, CA
Sangre De Cristo Arts and Buell Children's Museum, CO
Siouxland Heritage Museum, SD
Southern Illinois University Museum, IL
Spring Valley Nature Sanctuary & Volkening Heritage Farm, IL
Springfield Library and Museum Association, MA
St. Croix National Riverway, WI
Stauth Memorial Museum, KS
Stengel-True Museum, OH
The Newark Museum, NJ
The Society of the Four Arts, FL
The University Museum, Southern Illinois University, IL
Theodore Roosevelt National Park, ND
Timucan Reserve/Ft. Caroline National Memorial, FL
Valentine Richmond History Center, VA

Virginia Museum of Fine Arts, VA
West Florida Historic Preservation, FL
Whatcom Museum of History and Art, WA
White Pine Public Museum, NV
Winterthur Museum, Garden and Library, DE
Wm. Clark Market House Museum, KY
Yellowstone Gateway Museum of Park County, MT

Historic Houses/Sites

Alden House Museum, MA
Anderson House—The Society of the Cincinnati Museum, DC
Andrew Low House, GA
Ashland—The Henry Clay Estate, KY
Audubon State Historical Site, LA
Awbury Arboretum Association Francis Cope House, PA
Battleship North Carolina, NC
Beaches Area Historical Society, FL
Beaufort Historical Association, NC
Beaumont Heritage Society/John Jay French House, TX
Bennett Place State Historical Site, NC
Billings Farm and Museum, VT
Billings Preservation Society, MT
Bluffton Historical Preservation Society, SC
Bonnet House Museum and Gardens, FL
Burnham Tavern Museum, ME
Burwell-Morgan Mill, VA
Carillon Historical Park, OH
Casa del Herrero, CA
Charnley-Persky House, IL
Chimney Point State Historic Site, VT
Church by the River, MN
Colonial Pennsylvania Plantation, PA
Colonial Williamsburg Foundation, VA
Crawford County Historical Society, PA
Daniel Boone Homestead, PA
David Davis Museum, IL
Dover Historical Society, OH
Dr. Josephus Hall House, NC
Eastern Shore of Virginia Historical Society, VA
Edsel & Eleanor Ford House, MI
Enfield Shaker Museum, NH
Estate Whim Plantation Museum, VI
Exchange Hotel Civil War Museum, VA
Fairfield Heritage Association, OH
Fenton History Center Museum & Library, NY
Florence Ranch Homestead, TX
Fort Davidson State Elephant Rocks State Park, MO
Fort Sumter National Monument, SC
Fresno City & County Historical Society, CA
Furnace Town Living Heritage Museum, MD
Gammel Garden Museum, MN
General Lee Wallace Study and Museum, IN
Genesee Country Village & Museum, NY
George Washington Birthplace National Monument, VA
Georgia Capitol Museum, GA

Glensheen—The Historic Congdon Estate, MN
Glore Psychiatric Museum, MO
Gomez Mill House, NY
Gore Place, MA
Grant-Kohrs Ranch National Historic Site, MT
Hagley Museum and Library, DE
Harry Truman Little White House Museum, FL
Hearst Castle, CA
Hermann-Grima & Gallier Historic House, LA
Hickory Landmarks Society, NC
Hill-Stead Museum, CT
Historic Augusta, Inc., Boyhood Home of
    President Woodrow Wilson, GA
Historic Bethlehem Partnership, Inc., PA
Historic Fallsington, Inc., PA
Historic Fort Steilacoom, WA
Historic Rittenhousetown, PA
Historic Spanish Point, FL
Historical Society of Middletown, NY
Horace Williams House, NC
Independence National Historical Park, PA
James K. Polk Home, TN
John Muir National Historic Site, CA
Kaminski House Museum, SC
Kelly House Museum, CA
Kelton House Museum & Garden, OH
Kenmore Plantation & Gardens, VA
Keyes Foundation Beauregard-Keyes House, LA
Klondike Gold Rush National Historical Park, AK
Koreshan State Historic Site/Koreshan Unity Alliance, FL
Le Vieux Presbytere Town of Church Point, LA
Liberty Hall Historic Site, KY
London Town Foundation Inc, MD
Macculloch Hall Historical Museum & Gardens, NJ
Magnolia Grove, AL
Magnolia Mound Plantation, LA
Marathon County Historical Society, WI
Mathias Ham Museum, IA
McFaddin-Ward House, TX
Middleton Place Foundation, SC
Mifflinburg Buggy Museum, PA
Miners Foundry, CA
Mississippi County Historical Society, MO
Morven Park, VA
Mount Vernon Hotel Museum and Garden, NY
Nichols House Museum, MA
North Wood County Historical Society, WI
Oak Creek Historical Society—Pioneer, WI
Ojai Valley Historical Society & Museum, CA
Old Jail Museum, IN
Paul Revere Memorial Association, MA
Pennsbury Manor, PA
Petersburg Museum, VA
Pieter Claesen Wyckoff House, NY
Ponce DeLeon Inlet Lighthouse, FL

President Benjamin Harrison Foundation, IN
Promont House Museum, OH
Queen Anne's County Historical Sites Consortium, MD
Ramsey House Plantation, TN
Rancho Los Cerritos, CA
Riddick's Folly, VA
Rockwood Mansion Park New Castle County Government, DE
Rocky Mount Museum, TN
Rokeby Museum, VT
Rosemount Museum, CO
Rowan Oak, Home of William Faulkner, MS
Royal Arts Foundation, RI
Saint-Gaudens Memorial, NY
San Buenaventura Mission Museum, CA
Santa Barbara Trust for Historic Preservation, CA
Satterlee Clark House, WI
Seward House, NY
Sierra Historic Sites Association/Fresno Flats Museum, CA
Slater Mill Historic Site, RI
South Coast Railroad Museum, CA
South Park City Museum/South Park Historical Foundation, CO
Statue of Liberty National Monument & Ellis Island Immigration
    Museum, NY
Stephen Phillips Memorial Trust House, MA
Sterne-Hoya House Museum & Library, TX
Steves Homestead, TX
Stranahan House, Inc., FL
Strawbery Banke, Inc., NH
The Mark Twain House and Museum, CT
The Newsome House Museum & Cultural Center, VA
The Shelter House Society, PA
Thomas Edison Birthplace Museum, OH
Tinker Swiss Cottage, IL
Trenton City Museum at Ellarslie, NJ
Tudor Place Foundation, DC
Vizcaya Museum and Gardens, FL
Voelker-Orth Museum, NY
Walt Whitman Birthplace State Historic Site and Interpretive
    Center, NY
Washington County Historical Society, MN
Whalehead Preservation Trust, NC
Wilmington Town Museum Col. Joshua Harnden Tavern, MA
Wilton House Museum, VA
Ybor City Museum Society, FL
Zelienople Historical Society, PA

History Museums/Historical Societies
Adams Museum & House, SD
AIF Engen Ski Museum, UT
Albany Civil Rights Movement Museum
    at Old Mt. Zion Church, GA
Albany Historical Society, Inc., KS
Alger County Historical Museum, MI
American Victory Mariners Memorial and Museum Ship, FL
Anacortes Museum, WA

Anderson County Museum, SC
Arizona EnviroZeum, AZ
Artesia Historical Museum and Art Center, NM
Aspen Historical Society, CO
Association for the Preservation of the Presidential Yacht
    Potomac, CA
Augusta Historical Museum, KS
Aurora History Museum, CO
Avery Research Center for African American History
    & Culture, SC
Aztec Museum and Pioneer Village, NM
Bayside Historical Society, NY
Beaverhead County Museum, MT
Bedford City County Museum, VA
Bedford Historical Society, OH
Beech River Cultural Center, TN
Belding Museum, MI
Bellflower Historical, IL
Benicia Historical Museum, CA
Bethel Historical Society, ME
Big Horn County Historical Museum, MT
Birmingham Civil Rights Institute, AL
Bisbee Mining & Historical Museum, AZ
Blair County Historical Society, PA
Blue Earth County Historical, MN
Bob Bullock Texas State History Museum, TX
Boot Hill Museum, KS
Bosque Memorial Museum, TX
Brick Store Museum, ME
Bridgehampton Historical Society, NY
Brookside Museum/Saratoga County Historical Society, NY
Brown County Pioneer Museum, IN
Buffalo Bill Museum & Grave, CO
Butler County Historical Society, OH
Butler County Historical Society, Home of the Kansas Oil
    Museum, KS
Carroll County Historical Society, OH
Cass County Historical Society/Museum, MN
Cave Creek Museum, AZ
Charles River Museum of Industry, MA
Chattanooga Regional History Museum, TN
Chenango County Historical Society, NY
Chicago Historical Society, IL
Chippewa County Historical Society, MN
City of Greeley Museums, CO
Clark County Historical Museum, WA
Clark County Historical Society, OH
Clarke Historical Museum, CA
Clatsop County Historical Society, OR
Cleveland Bradley Regional Museum Center at Five Points, TN
Clinton County Historical Society, IA
Clinton County Historical Society, OH
Coachella Valley Historical Society, Inc., CA
Cokato Museum, MN
Cold War Museum, VA

College Park Aviation Museum, MD
Collin County Historical Society, Inc., TX
Columbia Gorge Discovery Center, OR
Connecticut River Museum, CT
Constitution Convention Museum State Park, FL
Cook Inlet Historical Society, AK
Cordova Historical Museum, AK
Coryell County Museum Foundation, TX
Cowley County Historical Society, KS
Dacotah Prarie Museum, SD
DEA Museum & Visitors Center, VA
Dearborn County Historical Museum, IN
Dedham Historical Society, MA
Delta County Historical Society, MI
Dennison Railroad Depot Museum, OH
Deschutes County Historical Society, OR
Detroit Historical Museum, MI
Douglas County Historical Society, NV
Downieville Museum, CA
Dufur Historical Society, OR
Dundee Township Historical Society, IL
Dunedin Historical Museum, FL
E. S. Wright Museum, NH
East Hampton Historical Society, NY
Eastside Heritage Center, WA
Escondido Historical Society, CA
Falmouth Historical Society, MA
Falmouth Historical Society, MA
Fifth Marine Regiment Museum, ME
Fitchburg Historical Society, MA
Florida Keys History of Diving Museum, FL
Fort Buford Historic Site, ND
Fort Sam Houston Museum, TX
Fort Walla Walla Museum, WA
Fort Washington Park, MD
Frankenmuth Historical Association Museum, MI
Franklin County Historical Society, WA
Friends of the Ocean City Historical Museum, NJ
Galveston County Historical Museum, TX
Garst Museum, OH
Geauga County Historical Society, OH
Geddes Historic District, SD
Georgia Historical Society, GA
Georgia Old Capital Museum, GA
Goodhue County Historical Society, MN
Grand Army of the Republic Civil War Museum, PA
Grand Lake Area Historical Society, CO
Grant County Museum, WA
Great Smokey Mountain Heritage Center, TN
Greene County Historical Society, PA
Gwinnett History Museum, GA
Harwich Historical Society, MA
Hayward Area Historical Society Museum, CA
Hennepin History Museum, MN
Henry Ford Museum & Greenfield Village, MI

Heritage Society, the Umatilla County Historical Museum, OR
Heritage-Hjemkomst Interpretive Center, MN
Herzstein Memorial Museum/Union County
    Historical Society, NM
Highlands Museum & Discovery Center, Inc., KY
Historic Adobe Museum, KS
Historic Dumfries Virginia, Inc., VA
Historic Museum at Fort Missoula, MT
Historic Pittsford, NY
Historic Sahuaro Ranch, AZ
Historic St. Mary's City, MD
Historical Center for Southeast New Mexico, NM
Historical Museum & Cultural Center Las Cruces, NM
Historical Museum of Southern Florida, FL
Historical Society of Berks County, PA
Historical Society of Delaware, DE
Historical Society of Frederick County, MD
Historical Society of Long Beach, CA
Historical Society of Old Newburyport, MA
Historical Society of Saginaw County, Inc., MI
Historical Society of Saratoga Springs, NY
Historical Society of Schuylkill County, PA
Historical Society of Wells and Ogunquit, ME
Hobart Historical Society Museum, IN
Holocaust Memorial Foundation of Illinois, IL
Hoover Presidential Museum & Library, IA
Houghton County Historical Museum, MI
Howard Steamboat Museum, Inc., IN
Huron City Museum, MI
Illinois & Michigan Canal Museum, IL
Indian Hill Historical Museum, OH
Indiana Historical Society Smith Memorial Library, IN
International Aerospace Hall of Fame, CA
Isabel Miller Museum, AK
Isanti County Historical Society, MN
Itasca County Historical Society, MN
Jackson Hole Historical Society and Museum, WY
James Madison Museum, VA
Jewish Historical Society of Greater Washington, DC
Jewish Museum of Maryland, MD
John Wesley Powell Memorial Museum, Historical
    Archaeological Society, AZ
Joliet Area Historical Museum, IL
Jonesborough/Washington County History Museum, TN
Julia A. Purnell Museum, MD
Kandiyohi County Historical Society, MN
Kankakee County Historical Society, IL
Kentucky Military History Museum, KY
Kerbyville Museum, OR
Kings Mountain Historical Museum, NC
Kitsap County Historical Society Museum, WA
Kona Historical Museum, HI
La Crosse County Historical Society, WI
Lake Forest-Lake Bluff Historical Society, IL
Laurel Museum, MD

Levine Museum of the New South, NC
Lexington History Museum, KY
Lighthouse at Sodus Point, NY
Litchfield Historical Society Museum, CT
Little Compton Historical Society, RI
Littleton Historical Museum, CO
Longyear Museum, MA
Los Angeles Maritime Museum, CA
Luzerne County Historical Society, PA
Lynden Pioneer Museum, WA
Manassas Museum System, VA
Manchester Historical Society, CT
Marietta Museum of History, GA
Marquette County History Museum, MI
Marshall County Historical Museum, GA
Martha's Vineyard Historical Society, MA
Mason County Historical Society, Historic White Pine Village, MI
McKinley Memorial Library, Museum & Birthplace Home, OH
McLean County Museum of History, IL
McLeod County Historical Society, MN
Mendocino County Museum, CA
Merced County Courthouse Museum, CA
Mesa Historical Museum, AZ
Michigan State University Museum, MI
Minnesota Historical Society, MN
Mission Inn, CA
Mommouth County Historical Association, NJ
Mondak Heritage Center, MT
Monroe County Historical Society, IN
Monroe County Local History Room and Library, WI
Montana Historical Society Museum, MT
Monte Vista Historical Society, CO
Montgomery County Historical Society, MD
Moosehead Historical Museum, ME
Morrison County Historical Society, MN
Morton Grove Historical Museum, IL
Mountain Heritage Center Western Carolina University, NC
Museum of American Financial History, NY
Museum of Florida History, FL
Museum of Mobile, AL
Museum of Nebraska History, NE
Museum of North Idaho, ID
Museum of the Albemarle, NC
Museum of Woodcarving, WI
Museum on Main, GA
Mystic Seaport Museum, Inc., CT
Natick Historical Society, MA
National Afro-American Museum & Cultural Center, OH
National Atomic Museum, NM
National Constitution Center, PA
National Czech & Slovak Museum & Library, IA
National Frontier Trails Museum, MO
National Heritage Museum, MA
New Mexico Museum of Space History, NM
New Richmond Preservation Society, Inc., WI

New York City Police Museum, NY
New York Historical Society, NY
Newport Harbor Nautical Museum, CA
Noank Historical Society Inc, CT
Nobles County Historical Society, MN
North Lincoln County Historical Museum, OR
Oakland County Pioneer and Historical Society, MI
Old Aurora Colony Museum and Historical Society, OR
Old Capitol Museum of Mississippi History, MS
Old Colony Historical Society, MA
Old Courthouse Museum, CA
Old Davie School Historical Museum, FL
Old Prison Museums, MT
Old Village Hall Museum, NY
Oldham County Historical Society, KY
Ontario County Historical Society Museum, NY
Opelousas Museum and Interpretive Center, LA
Orange County Historical Museum, NC
Oregon History Center/Oregon Historical Society, OR
Otter Tail County Historical Society, MN
Ox Cart Trails Historical Society, ND
Park City Museum, UT
Parris Island Museum, SC
Pearce Civil War & Western Art Museum Navarro College, TX
Pejepscot Historical Society, ME
Pilgrim Hall Museum, MA
Polk County Historical Museum, FL
Polk County Historical Society, GA
Pope County Historical Society Museum, MN
Port Columbus Civil War Naval Center, GA
Powers Museum Board/City of Carthage, MO
Preble County Historical Museum, OH
Putnam County Historical Society &
    Foundry School Museum, NY
Radnor Historical Society, PA
Reading Historical Society, OH
Red River Historical Museum, TX
Regional Museum of Spartenburg, SC
Reno County Historical Society, KS
Resurrection Bay Historical Society Museum, AK
Roberts County Museum, TX
Rome Historical Society, NY
Rural Life Museum Louisiana State University, LA
Safe Haven, Inc., NY
San Diego Historical Society, CA
San Jacinto Museum of History Herzstein Library, TX
San Joaquin County Historical Museum, CA
San Juan County Historical Society Museum, CO
Sanborn Area Historical Society, NY
Sand Springs Cultural and Historical Museum, OK
Sanguinetti House Museum & Garden/Arizona Historical
    Society, AZ
Saunders County Historical Society, NE
Scantic Academy Museum, CT
Scott County Historical Society, MN

Scurry County Museum, TX
Sedona Historical Society, AZ
Skagit County Historical Museum, WA
Smoky Hill Museum, KS
Somers Historical Society, NY
South Bannock County Historical Center, ID
Southern Oregon Historical Society, OR
Southold Historical Society, NY
Southwest Virginia Museum, VA
St. Charles Heritage Center, IL
St. Simons Island Lighthouse Museum, GA
Stanley-Whitman House, CT
Stearns History Museum, MN
Steele County Museum, ND
Stockholm Historical Society, ME
Stratham Historical Society, Inc., NH
Strong Museum, NY
Studebaker National Museum, IN
Swannanoa Valley History Museum, NC
Tampa Bay History Center, FL
Terwilliger and Memorial Day Museum, NY
Texas City Museum, TX
The Bostonian Society and Old State House Museum, MA
The Cayuga Museum of History and Art, NY
The Farmer's Museum, NY
The History Place, NC
The Lincoln Museum, IN
The Old Guard Museum, VA
Thomas T. Taber Museum of the Lycoming County
    Historical Society, PA
Tintic Mining Museum, UT
Tombstone Courthouse Shp, AZ
Topsfield Historical Society, MA
Tri-Cities Historical Museum, MI
Tularosa Basin Historical Society and Museum, NM
U.S. Army Medical Department Museum, TX
U.S. National Slavery Museum, VA
U.S.S. Constitution Museum, MA
Union County Historical Society Museum, MS
Vallejo Navel & Historical Museum, CA
Virginia Holocaust Museum, VA
Virginia Key Beach Park Trust, FL
Ward W. O'Hara Agricultural Museum, NY
Warren County Historical Society, PA
Washington County Historical Society, IN
Washington County Historical Society, OH
Washington County Historical Society, OR
Washington State Capital Museum, WA
Washington State Historical Society, WA
Washington State History Museum/Washington State Historical
    Society, WA
Watkins Museum of History, KS
Waukesha County Historical Society & Museum, WI
Wellesley Historical Society, MA
Weslaco Museum, TX

West Bat Common School Children's Museum, TX
West Chicago Historical Museum, IL
West County Museum, CA
Wichita-Sedgwick County Historical Museum, KS
Williamsville Historical Society, NY
Willowbrook Museum Village, ME
Wisconsin Veterans Museum, WI
Woodstock Historical Society, VT
Wyandotte County Museum, KS
Yakima Valley Museum, WA

Natural History/Anthropology Museums
Academy of Natural Sciences, PA
Alabama Museum of Natural History/University of Alabama, AL
American Museum of Asmat Art, MN
Anasazi State Park Museum, UT
Anniston Museum of Natural History, AL
Arizona State Museum, AZ
Bernice P. Bishop Museum, HI
Bollinger County Museum of Natural History, MO
Burke Museum of Natural History & Culture, WA
Caddoan Mounds State Historical Site, TX
Carlsbad Caverns National Parks New Mexico, NM
Charlotte County Historical Center, FL
Cleveland Museum of Natural History, OH
College of Eastern Utah Prehistoric Museum, UT
Dallas Museum of Natural History, TX
Denver Museum of Nature & Science, CO
Fernbank Museum of Natural History, GA
Florida Museum of Natural History, FL
Gillespie Museum of Minerals Stetson University, FL
Hastings Museum of Natural and Cultural History, NE
International Museum of Cultures, TX
Lora Robbins Gallery University of Richmond, VA
Monte L. Bean Museum of Life Science, UT
Moses Lake Museum & Art Center, WA
Museum of Anthropology University of Denver, CO
Museum of Anthropology Wake Forest University, NC
Museum of Geology, South Dakota Schools of Mines and
    Technology, SC
Museum of Peoples & Cultures, Brigham Young University, UT
National Museum of Natural History, Smithsonian Institution,
    DC
New Mexico Museum of Natural Science and History, NM
North Carolina Museum of Forestry, NC
Nylander Museum of Natural History, ME
Peabody Museum of Natural History, CT
Phoenix Museum of History Heritage and Science Park, AZ
Pueblo Grande Museum, AZ
Sam Noble Oklahoma Museum of Natural History, OK
San Bernardino County Museum, CA
San Diego Archaeological Center, CA
San Diego Natural History Museum, CA
Utah Museum of Natural History, UT
Utah State University Intermountain Herbarium, UT

Virginia Museum of Natural History, VA
Weinman Mineral Museum, GA

Nature Centers
Brukner Nature Center, OH
Centers for Nature Education Inc, NY
Chippewa Nature Center, MI
Chula Vista Nature Center, CA
Denison Pequotsepos Nature Center, CT
Great Valley Nature Center, PA
Indian Creek Nature Center, IA
Jamestown Audubon Nature Center, NY
Lake View Nature Center, IL
Maymount Nature Center, VA
Norskedalen, WI
Oconaluftee Visitor Center, NC
Riverside Nature Center, TX
Sarett Nature Center, MI
South Short National Science Center, MA
Waterman Conservation Education Center, NY
Wellesley Island State Park, NY

Science/Technology Centers/Museums
Arizona Science Center, AZ
California Oil Museum, CA
California Science Center, CA
Carnegie Science Center, PA
Cernan Earth and Space Center, Triton College, IL
Chippewa Falls Museum of Industry and Technology, WI
Dakota Dinosaur Museum, ND
Discovery Place, Inc., NC
Emerald Coast Science Center, FL
Fernbank Science Center, GA
Franklin Institute, PA
Gheens Science Hall and Rauch Planetarium, KY
Goddard Space Flight Center Visitor Center NASA, MD
Hatfield Marine Science Visitor Center,
    Oregon State University, OR
Hook's Discovery & Learning Center, IN
Impression 5 Science Center, MI
Intel Museum, CA
Invention Factory Science Center, NJ
Kitt Peak National Observatory, AZ
Liberty Science Center, NJ
McWayne Center/Discovery 2000, Inc., AL
Museum of Discovery, AR
Museum of Discovery and Science, FL
Museum of Science, MA
National Great Rivers Museum, IL
Oregon Museum of Science & Industry, OR
Orpheum Children's Science Museum, IL
Rochester Museum & Science Center, NY
Roper Mountain Science Center, SC
Science Central, IN
Science Museum of Minnesota, MN

Science Place, TX
Sciencenter, NY
ScienceWorks Hands-On Museum, OR
SciWorks Science Center & Environmental Parks of Forsyth, NC
Seacoast Science Center, NH
South Florida Science Museum, FL
The Exploratorium, CA
Welder Wildlife Foundation, TX

Specialized Museums
4th Infantry Division Museum, TX
Abbe Museum, ME
Adirondack Museum, NY
Ah Tah Thi Ki Museum Seminole Tribe of Florida, FL
Air Mobility Command Museum, DE
American Clock and Watch Museum, CT
American Museum of Fly Fishing, VT
American Precision Museum, VT
Anderson/Abruzzo Albuquerque Int. Balloon Museum, NM
Apache Cultural Center & Museum, AZ
Auburn Cord Duesenberg Museum, IN
Baldwin Heritage Museum, AL
Barona Cultural Center & Museum, CA
Bead Museum of Washington, D.C., DC
Big Thunder Gold Mine, SD
Caddo Tribal Heritage Museum, OK
Carolina Raptor Center, Inc., NC
Castle Air Museum Foundation, CA
Center for Agricultural Science & Heritage, Inc., IN
Center for Meteorite Studies, AZ
Central Maryland Heritage League, Inc., MD
Chisholm Trail Heritage Center, OK
Cold Spring Harbor Whaling Museum, NY
Connecticut Electric Railway Association, Inc., CT
COPIA: The American Center for Wine, Food and the Arts, CA
Cradle of Aviation, NY
Debence Antique Music World/Oil Region Music Preservation
    Museum, PA
Deke Slayton Museum, WI
Denver Firefighters Museum, CO
Dinosaur Depot Museum, CO
Dr. Francis Medical & Apothecary Museum, AL
Dyersburg Army Air Base Memorial Association, Inc., TN
EAA AirVenture Museum, WI
East Texas Oil Museum at Kilgore College, TX
Fargo Air Museum, ND
Fellowship of Friends/Apollo Museum of Art, CA
Fire Museum of Texas, TX
Florida Gulf Coast Railroad Museum, FL
Florida Holocaust Museum, FL
Fort Polk Military Museum, LA
Freetown Village, Inc., IN
Gemological Institute of America, Museum Department, CA
Georgia Music Hall of Fame, GA
Gilmore Car Museum, MI

Harness Racing Museum & Hall of Fame, NY
Hill Aerospace Museum, UT
Historic Aviation Memorial Museum, TX
Historic Costume & Textiles Collection,
    Ohio State University, OH
Historical Electronics Museum, MD
Historical Society & Museum for the California Dept.
    of Forestry & Fir, CA
Hollywood Bowl Museum, CA
Hugh Moore Historical Park and Museums, Inc., PA
Indian Center Museum, KS
Indian Pueblo Cultural Center Museum, NM
Indiana Railway Museum, IN
Italian American Museum, NY
Jacques Marchais Museum of Tibetan Art, NY
Japanese American National Museum, CA
Jim Crow Museum, Ferris State University, MI
Kansas Cosmosphere & Space Center, KS
Laupahoehoe Train Museum, HI
Macaulay Museum of Dental History, SC
Marietta Gone with the Wind Museum, GA
Martin & Osa Johnson Safari Museum, KS
Mashantucket Pequot Museum & Research Center, CT
Mel Fisher Maritime Museum, FL
Minnesota Air & Space Museum, MN
Mitchell Gallery of Flight Museum, WI
Mitchell Museum of the American Indian, IL
Morikami Museum and Japanese Garden, FL
Motorcycle Hall of Fame Museum, OH
Museum of Carousel Art and History, OH
Museum of the American Hungarian Foundation, NJ
Museum of the Red River, OK
Museum of the Soldier, Inc., IN
National Air and Space Museum, Smithsonian Institution, DC
National Automotive and Truck Museum, IN
National Automotive Museum, The Harrah Collection, NV
National Building Museum, DC
National Corvette Museum, KY
National Military Heritage Museum, MO
National Museum of American Jewish History, PA
National Museum of Racing, Inc., NY
National Museum of the Morgan Horse, VT
National Music Museum, SD
Naval Undersea Museum, WA
New England Air Museum, CT
New England Maple Museum, VT
New England Ski Museum, NH
New Hampshire Antique and Classic Boat Museum, NH
New Mexico Farm and Ranch Heritage Museum, NM
New York Museum of Transportation, NY
Northwest Railway Museum, WA
Old Colony & Fall River Railroad Museum, Inc., MA
Orange County Firefighters Museum, NY
Pacific Aviation Museum—Pearl Harbor, HI
Palmer Foundation Chiropractic History, IA

Patriots Point Naval/Maritime Museum, SC
Piper Memorial Medical Museum, MO
Portland Harbor Museum, ME
Presidential Pet Museum, MD
Railroad Museum of Pennsylvania, PA
Reading Company Technical & Historical Society Inc, PA
Salamanca Rail Museum, NY
San Diego Automotive Museum, CA
San Diego Model Railroad Museum, CA
Santa Barbara Maritime Museum, CA
Santa Maria Museum of Flight, CA
Sheldon Jackson Museum, AK
Ships of the Sea Maritime Museum, GA
Skirball Museum Cincinnati, OH
Sloss Furnaces National Historic Landmark, AL
Smokey Bear Historical Park, NM
Soldiers & Sailors National Military Museum & Memorial, PA
Southeast Museum of Photography, FL
Southeastern Railway Museum, GA
Southern Michigan Railroad Society, Inc., MI
Spellman Museum of Stamps and Postal History, MA
Spertus Museum, IL
S.S. William G. Mather Museum, OH
St. Augustine Lighthouse & Museum, FL
Stanley Museum, Inc., ME
Stars and Stripes Museum/Library, MO
Stetten Museum of Medical Research NIH, MD
Swedish American Museum Association of Chicago, IL
Texas Maritime Museum, TX
Texas Prison Museum, TX
Texas Ranger Hall of Fame, TX
Texas Sports Hall of Fame, TX
The Enchanted Mansion, LA
The Humphrey Forum, MN
The James S. Copley Library, CA
The Judaica Museum of the Hebrew Home for the Aged at
    Riverdale, NY
The Women's Memorial Foundation, VA
U.S. Army Quartermaster Museum, VA
U.S. Army Transportation Museum, VA
U.S. Coast Guard Museum, CT
U.S. Golf Association Museum & Archives, NJ
United States Holocaust Memorial Museum, DC
University of Wisconsin Insect Research Collection, WI
Vesterheim, the Norwegian-American Museum, IA
Virginia Aviation Museum, VA
Virginia Living Museum, VA
W. M. Keck Museum, NV
Warther Museum, Inc., OH
White Sands Missile Range Museum, NM
World Kite Museum & Hall of Fame, WA

Zoos

Arizona Zoological Society, AZ
Audubon Zoological Garden, LA

Bramble Park Zoo, SD
Chaffee Zoological Gardens, CA
Cheyenne Mountain Zoo, CO
Cincinnati Zoo and Botanical Garden, OH
Columbus Zoo, OH
Dakota Zoo, ND
Honolulu Zoo, HI
Jacksonville Zoo and Gardens, FL
Lee Richardson Zoo, KS
Los Angeles Zoo and Botanical Gardens, CA
Lowry Park Zoo, FL
Miami Metrozoo, FL
Minnesota Zoo, MN
Pueblo Zoo, CO
Sacramento Zoo, CA
San Antonio Zoological Society, TX
Santa Barbara Zoological Gardens, CA
The Oregon Zoo, OR
The Toledo Zoo, OH
Washington Park Zoo, IN
Woodland Park Zoo, WA

Other
Bloomington Art Center, MN
Center for Photography Woodstock, NY
Higginbotham Museum, MD
Silvermine Guild Art Center, CT
The Studio, an Alternative Space for Contemporary Art, NY

Appendix II: Copy of the Survey Instrument

AMERICAN **ASSOCIATION OF MUSEUMS**

Dear Colleague,

In these difficult financial times, it is critical that museums make sound strategic decisions about their operations. Enclosed is the *2004 AAM Facilities and Risk Management Survey*, the first in a series of "Museum Practice" surveys designed to aid you in that effort.

By answering this survey, you'll ensure that the results accurately reflect museums similar to yours, enabling you to make comparisons to other institutions for the purpose of setting goals, evaluating performance, and making decisions about whether and how to change. The survey results also will give you the information you need to make decisions about:

- Insurance
- Facility rentals
- Catering
- Parking and associated income

- Building space usage
- Emergency preparedness
- Facilities use and maintenance policies

Please ask the staff member best able to provide information about these areas to complete the survey.

This survey has been developed by a committee of your peers, comprised of representatives from the relevant AAM Standing Professional Committees. All of its questions are equally important. Committee members are confident that most museums have this information available in existing documents and that all institutions will benefit from reviewing these areas of their operations. **However, if you cannot answer some of the questions, send us what you can.** We'd prefer to receive 90 percent of your data rather than exclude your museum from the survey.

Each museum's response is confidential and will be reported only in a combined and anonymous format. However, we plan to publicly recognize those museums that participate in this survey. If you do not want your institution listed as a survey participant, please note that when you answer question 2.

In thanks for your cooperation, we have enclosed a 10-percent discount coupon for the AAM Bookstore, good for any purchase of $50 or more between now and July 31, 2004. Please submit this coupon with your next bookstore order.

Please return this survey by **May 21, 2004** in the envelope provided. If you have any questions, contact Elizabeth Merritt at bmerritt@aam-us.org.

Thank you for working with AAM to ensure that museums continue to have the resources they need to serve the public interest.

Yours sincerely,

Edward H. Able, Jr.
President & CEO

Louis B. Casagrande
Chair

1575 EYE STREET NW, SUITE 400
WASHINGTON, DC 20005
202.289.1818
FAX 202.289.6578

2004 Museum Facilities and Risk Management Survey

I. Contact Information

1. Please complete or update your mailing information below:

   Contact:_____

   Institution:_____

   Address:_____

   City:_____ St:_____ Zip:_____

   (P)

2. AAM would like to credit your museum as having participated in the *2004 Museum Facilities and Risk Management Survey*. Check here [❑] if you do **NOT** want your institution to be listed as a participant. **NOTE**: only aggregate data will be published. All individual responses are confidential.

NOTE: Definitions of terms that are in *bold italics* are provided in the attached glossary. To ensure accurate reporting, please refer to the glossary when completing this form.

II. Your Institution

3. Please check which **ONE** of the following **BEST** describes your institution: (please select only **ONE**):

   ❑ a. Aquarium
   ❑ b. Arboretum/botanic garden
   ❑ c. Art museum
   ❑ d. Children's/youth museum
   ❑ e. *General museum*
   ❑ f. Historic house/site
   ❑ g. History museum/historical society
   ❑ h. Natural history/anthropology museum
   ❑ i. Nature center
   ❑ j. Science/technology center/museum
   ❑ k. *Specialized museum*
   ❑ l. Zoo
   ❑ m.Other:_____

4. Does your institution have a *parent organization*?   ❑ a. Yes
                                                          ❑ b. No

   IF YES: Which **ONE** of the following **BEST** describes your institution's parent organization?

   ❑ a. College/university
   ❑ b. Museum or *museum system* (e.g., state, local, private nonprofit, etc.)
   ❑ c. Other: _____

5. Which **ONE** of the following **BEST** describes your institution's *governing authority*? (please select only **ONE**). **NOTE**: If your institution has a parent organization, please indicate the nature of your **PARENT'S** governing authority.

   ❑ a. Municipal   ❑ e. Tribal
   ❑ b. County   ❑ f. Private nonprofit
   ❑ c. State   ❑ g. For-profit
   ❑ d. Federal   ❑ h. *Dual governance* (please indicate governing entities: letter ____ and letter ____)

6. In what year was your institution first opened regularly to the public? _____ OR ❑ Not yet open

7. Please indicate the number of paid staff positions as of January 1, 2004. **If none, please write in a zero:**

   A. Full-time paid positions: _____ staff   B. Part-time paid positions:_____ staff

8. What is the month and year of your most recently **completed** fiscal year?   Month:_____ Year: _____

Page 1 of 6

American Association of Museums

9. Please fill in the following using data from your institution's most recently completed fiscal year:

A. Total *operating income*: $_____

B. Total *operating expenses*: $_____

C. Total attendance: _____

III. Insurance

10. If your institution does **NOT** have a parent organization, **PLEASE SKIP TO QUESTION 11**.

A. In what ways is your parent organization involved in your insurance coverage?

❑ a. Institution is fully covered under parent's insurance
❑ b. Institution is covered under parent's insurance, but maintains separate rider(s) for:_____
❑ c. Institution is **NOT** covered under parent's insurance

B. Does your parent organization: ❑ a. Pay all costs for insurance coverage for your institution
❑ b. Pay some costs for insurance coverage for your institution
❑ c. Not pay for any insurance coverage for your institution

C. Does your parent organization have insurance
regulations/guidelines to which your institution must adhere? ❑ a. Yes ❑ b. No

11. Please indicate the status of the following types of insurance coverage for your institution:

	Presently carry	Presently carry, but considering dropping by 2005	Investigating/planning to carry by 2005
a. *Commercial/general liability*	❑	❑	❑
b. Automobile	❑	❑	❑
c. Collections/fine arts	❑	❑	❑
d. Directors & Officers liability	❑	❑	❑
e. Event cancellation	❑	❑	❑
f. Exhibitions/loans	❑	❑	❑
g. Transit (if separate policy from exhibitions/loans)	❑	❑	❑
h. Terrorism	❑	❑	❑
i. Other (describe below)	❑	❑	❑

_____

12. What were your institution's total insurance costs for your most recently completed fiscal year?

Paid by your institution: $_____   Paid by your parent organization: $_____

13. Does your institution maintain a fund to offset small claims/deductibles? ❑ a. Yes (fund size: $_____)
❑ b. No

14. Is your institution or its parent "self-insured"? ❑ a. Yes ❑ b. No

IF YES: A. Does this mean (check all that apply):

❑ a. We set aside and manage a designated fund with internal loss assessment and claim payment
❑ b. Institution replaces/repairs damage out of the general fund budget
❑ c. Institution does not actually replace the value of losses
❑ d. Other:_____

B. What is your institution's threshold for self-insured claims? $_____ or ❑ None

Page 2 of 6

IV. Facilities Management/Use Policies and Maintenance

15. Please indicate which, if any, of the following are allowed by policy in your buildings:

Check if item is ALLOWED	Collection areas	Exhibit areas	Staff offices	Public spaces	Grounds
a. Open flames	❏	❏	❏	❏	❏
b. Food	❏	❏	❏	❏	❏
c. Beverages (other than water)	❏	❏	❏	❏	❏
d. Live plants	❏	❏	❏	❏	❏
e. Fresh flowers	❏	❏	❏	❏	❏
f. Dried plant material	❏	❏	❏	❏	❏
g. Personal artwork	❏	❏	❏	❏	❏
h. Filming	❏	❏	❏	❏	❏
i. Photography	❏	❏	❏	❏	❏

16. Does your institution rent space to outside groups?   ❏ a. Yes   ❏ b. No

IF YES: A. Please indicate which of the following groups you would or have rented to:

	WOULD rent to	HAVE rented to in past 5 years
a. Religious groups	❏	❏
b. Political groups	❏	❏
c. Private groups (weddings, parties, graduations, etc.)	❏	❏
d. Corporate groups	❏	❏
e. Non-religious, nonprofit groups	❏	❏
f. Other (specify below)	❏	❏

_____

B. Rental revenue goes to: ❏ a. The institution's budget
(check all that apply)   ❏ b. The general fund of the parent organization
❏ c. Other:_____

17. Does your institution have an exclusive agreement with caterers?   ❏ a. Yes, one caterer
❏ b. Yes, maintain a list of accepted caterers
❏ c. No

IF YES: What is the typical percent commission your institution takes on this arrangement? _____ %

18. How many staff at your institution or parent organization have maintenance (e.g., care and repair) of the museum facilities as their **PRIMARY** job function?

A. Number of full-time maintenance staff:_____   B. Number of part-time maintenance staff:_____

V. Space Usage

19. Does your institution have or use *off-site facilities* for any purpose? ❏ a. Yes
❏ b. No

20. What is the total interior square footage of **ALL** your institution's buildings? _____ sq. ft.

Page 3 of 6

21. Please indicate the following for your institution's structure(s):

	Building date (Year)	Approximate total interior square footage	Number of staff based primarily in this building
a. Building #1	_____	_____ sq. ft.	_____ staff
b. Building #2	_____	_____ sq. ft.	_____ staff
c. Building #3	_____	_____ sq. ft.	_____ staff
d. Building #4	_____	_____ sq. ft.	_____ staff
e. Building #5	_____	_____ sq. ft.	_____ staff
f. Building #6	_____	_____ sq. ft.	_____ staff

NOTE: If your institution has more than six buildings, please photocopy this page and append the extra sheet to your survey.

22. Have you done a building expansion or renovation in the past three years? ❑ a. Yes ❑ b. No

23. Thinking about **ALL** of your institution's buildings, please provide the following information regarding space allocation:

	Present in your institution?	Approximate sq. ft. presently allocated	Over the last five years, has the size of this area changed as a percentage of total institution space?		
			Increased	Decreased	Remained the same
a. Exhibitions	❑ a. Yes ❑ b. No	_____ sq. ft.	❑	❑	❑
b. Collections storage	❑ a. Yes ❑ b. No	_____ sq. ft.	❑	❑	❑
c. Non-collections storage	❑ a. Yes ❑ b. No	_____ sq. ft.	❑	❑	❑
d. Offices	❑ a. Yes ❑ b. No	_____ sq. ft.	❑	❑	❑
e. Education (classrooms)	❑ a. Yes ❑ b. No	_____ sq. ft.	❑	❑	❑
f. Library/research	❑ a. Yes ❑ b. No	_____ sq. ft.	❑	❑	❑
g. Museum store	❑ a. Yes ❑ b. No	_____ sq. ft.	❑	❑	❑
h. Public space/public functions	❑ a. Yes ❑ b. No	_____ sq. ft.	❑	❑	❑
i. Food service	❑ a. Yes ❑ b. No	_____ sq. ft.	❑	❑	❑
j. Auditoriums/theaters	❑ a. Yes ❑ b. No	_____ sq. ft.	❑	❑	❑
k. Maintenance	❑ a. Yes ❑ b. No	_____ sq. ft.	❑	❑	❑
l. Conservation/collections prep	❑ a. Yes ❑ b. No	_____ sq. ft.	❑	❑	❑

24. Does your institution offer: ❑ a. On-site parking (number of spaces:_____)
    ❑ b. Off-site parking (number of spaces:_____)
    ❑ c. No institution-controlled parking **[SKIP TO QUESTION 26]**

25. Is there a fee for this parking? ❑ a. Yes   ❑ b. No

   IF YES: A. What are the per vehicle parking rates for: a) automobiles: $_____
   b) buses: $_____
   c) RVs: $_____

   B. What was your institution's total **NET** revenue from parking for your most recently completed fiscal year? $_____

Page 4 of 6

VI. Emergency Preparedness, Safety/Security, Risk Management

26. Does your institution have an emergency preparedness/disaster plan?   ❏ a. Yes

        ❏ b. No **[SKIP TO QUESTION 30]**

27. When was your most recent practice/drill of your emergency preparedness/disaster plan?

     ❏ a. Practiced in the year: _____   ❏ b. Never practiced   ❏ c. Not sure

28. Which of the following does your emergency preparedness/disaster plan cover? (check all that apply)

     ❏ a. Fire   ❏ d. Earthquake   ❏ g. Terrorism   ❏ j. Toxic chemical/gas spill
     ❏ b. Flood   ❏ e. Bomb threat   ❏ h. Theft
     ❏ c. Severe weather   ❏ f. Civil unrest   ❏ i. Other:_____

29. Has this plan ever been implemented for an emergency/disaster?

     ❏ a. Yes   ❏ b. No

     IF YES: A. In what year(s) ? _____

               B. For what event(s)? (Write in the appropriate letter code(s) from question 28:) _____

30. Please indicate which of the following kinds of training are provided to staff:

	Is this training provided?		Is this training:		
			Mandatory for ALL staff	Mandatory for SOME staff	Optional
a. *Emergency response*	❏ a. Yes	❏ b. No	❏	❏	❏
b. First Aid/CPR	❏ a. Yes	❏ b. No	❏	❏	❏
c. *General health and safety*	❏ a. Yes	❏ b. No	❏	❏	❏
d. *Hazardous material handling*	❏ a. Yes	❏ b. No	❏	❏	❏

31. Which staff member, by job category, has primary responsibility for *risk management*? (check **ONE**)

     ❏ a. Director/CEO/Head of museum   ❏ g. Security
     ❏ b. Collections staff: curator/registrar/collection manager   ❏ h. Facilities management
     ❏ c. Development/Marketing/PR/Membership   ❏ i. Visitor services
     ❏ d. Educator   ❏ j. Exhibition
     ❏ e. Manager/administrator   ❏ k. Other:_____
     ❏ f. Conservator

32. Is risk management responsibility identified in the person's job description?   ❏ a. Yes

                 ❏ b. No

33. Has your institution completed the AAM Registrars Committee's Standard Facility Report?   ❏ a. Yes

                 ❏ b. No

     IF YES: Would your institution be willing to provide a copy to AAM   ❏ a. Yes
                in the future for use in compiled, statistical data?   ❏ b. No
                                                     ❏ c. Not sure

34. Does your institution practice *integrated pest management*?   ❏ a. Yes

                 ❏ b. No

35. Please indicate which of the following written, formally approved policies, plans, or agreements are held by your institution.
NOTE: These can exist as separate documents or as part of a larger policy/plan/agreement document.

CODES:
M = Monthly
Q = Quarterly
A = Annually
O = Other regular interval
X = As needed

CODES:
A = Director/CEO/Head
B = Collections staff
C = Development/Marketing/PR
D = Educator
E = Manager/admin.
F = Conservation
G = Security
H = Facilities mgmt.
I = Visitor services
J = Exhibition
K = Govern. authority
L = Other

	Does institution have?	Year first approved	How frequently is it updated?	Year last updated	Who is primarily responsible for policy development?	Who is primarily responsible for policy implementation?
a. Facilities use policy	❑ a. Yes ❑ b. No ❑ c. In development	_____	Code: ____	_____	Code: ____	Code: ____
b. Building rental policy	❑ a. Yes ❑ b. No ❑ c. In development	_____	Code: ____	_____	Code: ____	Code: ____
c. Special events policy for outside groups	❑ a. Yes ❑ b. No ❑ c. In development	_____	Code: ____	_____	Code: ____	Code: ____
d. Special events policy for museum-sponsored events	❑ a. Yes ❑ b. No ❑ c. In development	_____	Code: ____	_____	Code: ____	Code: ____
e. Filming policy	❑ a. Yes ❑ b. No ❑ c. In development	_____	Code: ____	_____	Code: ____	Code: ____
f. Filming agreement	❑ a. Yes ❑ b. No ❑ c. In development	N/A	Code: ____	_____	Code: ____	Code: ____
g. Policy on use of funds resulting from insurance claims on losses to collections	❑ a. Yes ❑ b. No ❑ c. In development	_____	Code: ____	_____	Code: ____	Code: ____
h. *Cyclical maintenance plan*	❑ a. Yes ❑ b. No ❑ c. In development	_____	Code: ____	_____	Code: ____	Code: ____
i. Emergency preparedness/disaster plan	❑ a. Yes ❑ b. No ❑ c. In development	_____	Code: ____	_____	Code: ____	Code: ____
j. *Historic structure master plan*	❑ a. Yes ❑ b. No ❑ c. In development	_____	Code: ____	_____	Code: ____	Code: ____
k. *Integrated pest management plan*	❑ a. Yes ❑ b. No ❑ c. In development	_____	Code: ____	_____	Code: ____	Code: ____

THANK YOU! Please return your completed survey by MAY 21, 2004 to:
AWP Research • 898 Broad Oaks • Herndon, VA 20170

Page 6 of 6

If you have questions about this survey, please contact: Elizabeth Merritt, Director, Museum Advancement & Excellence, at 202-218-7661 or via e-mail at bmerritt@aam-us.org.

Appendix III: List of Figures

All figures are tables unless otherwise noted.

1.1 Discipline Type

1.2 Estimated Number of Museums by Discipline

2.1 Operating Expenses Categories (FY2003)

2.2 Operating Expenses

2.3 Operating Expenses Bar Chart

3.1 Physical Size Categories

3.2 Total Interior Square Footage

3.3 Total Interior Square Footage Bar Chart

4.1 Have a Parent Organization

4.2 Type of Parent Organization

5.1 Governing Authority

6.1 Paid Full-time Staff

6.2 Paid Part-time Staff

7.1 Number of Buildings

7.2 Interior Space

7.3 Space

7.4 Space Allocation (as a percentage of total interior square feet)

7.5 Space Allocation (in square feet)

7.6 Space Increase/Decrease

8.1 What Is Allowed in Building by Policy

8.2 What Is Allowed in Exhibit Areas

9.1 Practice Integrated Pest Management

10.1 Does Institution Rent Space to Outside Groups

10.2 Groups Space Is/Would Be Rented to

10.3 Rental Revenue Goes to

10.4 Catering

11.1 Number of Full-time/Part-time Maintenance Staff

12.1 Is Risk Management Identified in the Job Description

12.2 Risk Management in Job Description by Position Title

12.3 Primary Responsibility for Risk Management

13.1 Emergency/Disaster Plan

13.2 Implementation of Emergency/Disaster Plan

13.3 For What Events Was Plan Implemented

13.4 What Does the Emergency Plan Cover

14.1 Types of Training Provided to Staff

15.1 Insurance Coverage Held by Respondents

15.2 Insurance Coverage by Governance and Operating Expenses

15.3 Collections Insurance by Discipline

15.4 Parental Involvement in Insurance

15.5 Does the Parent Organization Pay for Insurance

15.6 Meaning of Self-Insurance

15.7 Does the Museum Maintain a Small Claims/Deductibles Fund

15.8 Insurance Costs—Overall

16.1 Policies/Plans

16.2 Policy Update Schedule

16.3 Responsibility for Policy/Plan Development

16.4 Responsibility for Policy/Plan Implementation

16.5 Presence of Policies/Plans by Governance, Size

Index

anthropology museums, 113–118
  caterers, 116
  emergency plans, 116
  insurance, 117–118
  policy, 115, 118
  space, 114–115
  space rental, 116
  staff, 117
aquariums, 71–76
  caterers, 74
  emergency plans, 74
  insurance, 75–76
  policy, 73, 76
  space, 72–73
  space rental, 74
  staff, 75
arboretums, 77–82
  caterers, 80
  emergency plans, 80
  insurance, 81–82
  policy, 79, 82
  space, 78–77
  space rental, 80
  staff, 81
art museums, 83–88
  caterers, 86
  emergency plans, 86
  insurance, 87–88
  policy, 85, 88
  space, 84–85
  space rental, 86
  staff, 87

benchmarking, 10
botanic gardens, 77–82
  caterers, 80
  emergency plans, 80
  insurance, 81–82
  policy, 79, 82
  space, 78–77
  space rental, 80
  staff, 81

caterers and catering, 39
  aquariums and zoos, 74
  arboretums and botanic gardens, 80
  art museums, 86

children's museums, 92
  general museums, 98
  historic houses/sites, 104
  history museums/historical societies, 110
  municipal or county museums, 140
  natural history/anthropology museums, 116
  nature centers, 122
  operating expenses over $6 million, museums with, 173
  parent organization, museums with, 153
  parent organization, other nongovernmental, museums with, 166
  specialized museums, 134
  state museums, 146
  university parent, museum with, 159
children's museums, 89–94
  caterers, 92
  emergency plans, 92
  insurance, 93–94
  policy, 91, 94
  space, 90–91
  space rental, 92
  staff, 93
Commercial General Liability insurance, 53

demographics, 12
Directors and Officers insurance, 53
disasters. *See* emergency plans
discipline type, 13–15

emergency plans, 48–52
  aquariums and zoos, 74
  arboretums and botanic gardens, 80
  art museums, 86
  children's museums, 92
  general museums, 98
  historic houses/sites, 104
  history museums/historical societies, 110
  municipal or county museums, 140
  natural history/anthropology museums, 116
  nature centers, 122
  operating expenses over $6 million, museums with, 173
  parent organization, museums with, 153
  parent organizations, other

nongovernmental, museums with, 166
  specialized museums, 134
  state museums, 146
  university parent, museum with, 159
Event/Exhibition Cancellation insurance, 53

facilities and risk management, 11, 24–70
facilities management, 29–32
figures, listed, 200
financial planning, 44–45
Fine Art and Collections insurance, 53
fires and flames, 32–33

general museums, 95–100
  caterers, 98
  emergency plans, 98
  insurance, 99–100
  policy, 97, 100
  space, 96–97
  space rental, 98
  staff, 99
glossary, 176
governance, 19–22

health insurance, 61–67
  see also insurance
historic houses/sites, 101–106
  caterers, 104
  emergency plans, 104
  insurance, 105–106
  policy, 103, 106
  space, 102–103
  space rental, 104
  staff, 105
history museums/historical societies, 107–112
  caterers, 110
  emergency plans, 110
  insurance, 111–112
  policy, 109, 112
  space, 108–109
  space rental, 110
  staff, 111

insurance, 52–60
  aquariums and zoos, 75–76
  arboretums and botanic gardens, 81–82

art museums, 87–88
children's museums, 93–94
costs, 44–46, 60
coverage, 57
general museums, 99–100
historic houses/sites, 105–106
history museums/historical societies, 111–112
municipal or county museums, 141–142
natural history/anthropology museums, 117–118
nature centers, 123–124
operating expenses over $6 million, museums with, 174–175
parent organization, museums with, 154–155
parent organizations, other nongovernmental, museums with, 167–168
specialized museums, 135–136
state museums, 147–148
university parent, museum with, 160–161
value determination, 57–58
   see also health insurance

municipal or county museums, 137–142
   caterers, 140
   discipline, 137
   emergency plans, 140
   insurance, 141–142
   policy, 139, 142
   space, 138–139
   space rental, 140
   staff, 141
museums, number in U.S., 7–8
   see also particular type
museum system, 149–155, 176–177
   see also parent organization

natural history museums, 113–118
   caterers, 116
   emergency plans, 116
   insurance, 117–118
   policy, 115, 118
   space, 114–115
   space rental, 116
   staff, 117
nature centers, 119–124
   caterers, 122
   emergency plans, 122
   insurance, 123–124

policy, 119, 124
space, 119–120
space rental, 122
staff, 123

operating expenses, 15–17
operating expenses over $6 million, museums with, 169–175
   caterers, 173
   discipline, 169
   emergency plans, 173
   insurance, 174–175
   policy, 172, 175
   space, 171–172
   space rental, 173
   staff, 174

parent organization, museums with, 20–21, 149–155
   caterers, 153
   discipline, 149
   emergency plans, 153
   insurance, 154–155
   policy, 152, 155
   space, 151–152
   space rental, 153
   staff, 154
parent organizations, other nongovernmental, museums with, 162–168
   caterers, 166
   discipline, 162
   emergency plans, 166
   insurance, 167–168
   policy, 165, 168
   space, 164–165
   space rental, 166
   staff, 167
pest management, 33–35, 36
policy, 68–70
   aquariums and zoos, 73, 76
   arboretums and botanic gardens, 79, 82
   art museums, 85, 88
   children's museums, 91, 94
   general museums, 97, 100
   historic houses/sites, 103, 106
   history museums/historical societies, 109, 112
   municipal or county museums, 139, 142
   natural history/anthropology museums, 115, 118

nature centers, 119, 124
operating expenses over $6 million, museums with, 172, 175
parent organization, museums with, 152, 155
parent organizations, other nongovernmental, museums with, 165, 168
specialized museums, 133, 136
state museums, 145, 148
university parent, museum with, 158, 161
property insurance, 52–53

respondents, 8
   profile, 13-23
responding institutions
   listed, 181–192
   snapshot, 12
risk assessment, 46–48
risk management, responsibility, 42–44

science/technology center/museum, 125–130
   caterers, 128
   emergency plans, 128
   insurance, 129–130
   policy, 127, 130
   space, 126–127
   space rental, 128
   staff, 129
self-insurance, 59–60
silent tax, 61–62
size categories, 17–19
space and space allocation, 25–28
   aquariums and zoos, 72–73
   arboretums and botanic gardens, 78–77
   art museums, 84–85
   children's museums, 90–91
   general museums, 96–97
   historic houses/sites, 102–103
   history museums/historical societies, 108–109
   municipal or county museums, 138–139
   natural history/anthropology museums, 114–115
   nature centers, 119–120
   operating expenses over $6 million, museums with, 171–172
   parent organization, museums with, 151–152
   parent organizations, other

nongovernmental, museums with, 164–165

specialized museums, 132–133

state museums, 144–145

university parent, museum with, 157–158

space rental, 35, 37–41

arboretums and botanic gardens, 80

aquariums and zoos, 74

art museums, 86

children's museums, 92

general museums, 98

historic houses/sites, 104

history museums/historical societies, 110

municipal or county museums, 140

natural history/anthropology museums, 116

nature centers, 122

operating expenses over $6 million, museums with, 173

parent organization, museums with, 153

parent organizations, other nongovernmental, museums with, 166

specialized museums, 134

state museums, 146

university parent, museum with, 159

specialized museums, 131–136

caterers, 134

emergency plans, 134

insurance, 135–136

policy, 133, 136

space, 132–133

space rental, 134

staff, 135

staff, 22–23, 41

aquariums and zoos, 75

arboretums and botanic gardens, 81

art museums, 87

children's museums, 93

general museums, 99

historic houses/sites, 105

history museums/historical societies, 111

municipal or county museums, 141

natural history/anthropology museums, 117

nature centers, 123

operating expenses over $6 million, museums with, 174

parent organization, museums with, 154

parent organizations, other nongovernmental, museums with, 167

specialized museums, 135

state museums, 147

university parent, museum with, 160

state museums, 143–148

caterers, 146

discipline, 143

emergency plans, 146

insurance, 147–148

policy, 145, 148

space, 144–145

space rental, 146

staff, 147

survey

changes from the last survey, 11–12

data interpretation, 8–10

data use, 10–12

instrument, 193–199

method, 7

training, emergency preparedness, 51–52

Umbrella Liability insurance, 53

university parent, museum with, 156–161

caterers, 159

discipline, 156

emergency plans, 159

insurance, 160–161

policy, 158, 161

space, 157–158

space rental, 159

staff, 160

validation, 10

Workers' Compensation insurance, 53

zoos, 71–76

caterers, 74

emergency plans, 74

insurance, 75–76

policy, 73, 76

space, 72–72

space rental, 74

staff, 75